The Foundations of
Economic Method

The Foundations of Economic Method

LAWRENCE A. BOLAND
Professor of Economics Simon Fraser University

London
GEORGE ALLEN & UNWIN
Boston   Sydney

George Allen & Unwin (Publishers) Ltd,
40 Museum Street, London WC1A 1LU, UK

George Allen & Unwin (Publishers) Ltd,
Park Lane, Hemel Hempstead, Herts HP2 4TE, UK

Allen & Unwin Inc.,
9 Winchester Terrace, Winchester, Mass 01890, USA

George Allen & Unwin Australia Pty Ltd,
8 Napier Street, North Sydney, NSW 2060, Australia

First published in 1982
Reprinted in 1984

British Library Cataloguing in Publication Data

Boland, Lawrence A.
   The foundations of economic method.
1.Economics–Methodology
I.Title
330'.01'8   hb131
ISBN 0-04-330328-5
ISBN 0-04-330329-3   pbk

Library of Congress Cataloging in Publication Data

Boland, Lawrence A.
The foundations of economic methods.
Bibliography: p.
Includes index.
   1. Economics–Methodology.   I.Title.
HB131.B64   330'.072   82-4100
ISBN 0-04-330328-5   AACR2
ISBN 0-04-330329-3 (pbk.)

Set in 10 on 11 point Times
and printed in Great Britain
by Biddles Ltd, Guildford, Surrey

TO MY FAMILY
   Brenna, Alana and Irene

Contents

Acknowledgements

I wish to thank the editors of the following journals for giving me permission for the use of copyright material: *The Canadian Journal of Economics, The Quarterly Journal of Economics, The Journal of Economic Literature,* and *The South African Journal of Economics.* In addition I wish to thank the American Enterprise Institute for permission to quote from their special issue of *The Journal of Money, Credit and Banking.*

As well, I wish to take this opportunity to thank Shyam Kamath, Irene Gordon, Malcolm Rutherford, Chris Jensen, David Hammes and Donna Wilson for reading and criticizing the original manuscript, and Elizabeth Bland for editing the final version. Also, I wish to thank my friends and colleagues, especially Clyde Reed, John Richards and John Chant, for their helpful suggestions and criticisms - and Stan Wong for his ever-valuable advice.

Preface

Given that most textbooks on neoclassical economic theory begin with a chapter about methodology, one might easily conclude that most economists think that the methodology of economics is absolutely fundamental. This is an illusion. The view that the appropriate methodology must be in hand *before* we begin our analysis of the facts is an artifact of an old-fashioned philosophy of science (viz., Inductivism) that was long ago discarded. According to the currently accepted philosophy of science (viz., Conventionalism), the nature of neoclassical theory is supposed to be quite independent of any individual economist's opinion of the appropriate methodology of economics. Today, we are supposed to believe that there is no need to discuss methodology simply because it does not matter. I shall endeavor to show that it does matter - and that, furthermore, methodology cannot be easily detached so as to be simply dispatched in an introductory chapter. The pressing theoretical problems that continue to challenge neoclassical theorists today are direct consequences of implicitly accepted views of the appropriate methodology for neoclassical economics.

Although I have written this book for economists - it has not been tailored to the tastes of philosophers - it is presumed that the reader is aware of the more elementary views of methodology found in standard textbooks and books on the history of economic thought. Since I cannot see how one can understand economic methodology without understanding economic theory, I shall presume that the reader has successfully negotiated a course through intermediate micro- and macroeconomic theory.

My argument in this book is rather straightforward. I shall argue that every neoclassical research program is designed (1) to be consistent with acceptable ways of dealing with the Problem of Induction, and (2) to provide a methodological individualist explanation of economic behavior of the economy, that is, one which is based on the methodological prescription that allows only individuals to be posited as the locus of decision-making. With this in mind, I shall argue that neoclassical economists have thereby made their research program an impossible task because the Problem of Induction cannot, and need not, be solved. They compound this difficulty with psychologism, that is, by erroneously identifying individuals with psychological states. I will not press the additional point that the Conventionalist view of methodology (viz., that an individual's view of methodology does not matter) is inconsistent with a neoclassical theory which is supposed to see the individual as the center of everything - but this point does show that usual reluctance to discuss methodology might lead to certain inconsistencies.

If my argument concerning the design of neoclassical economics and its reliance on psychologism is correct, then it will be seen that most of the leading *theoretical* problems are impossible to solve. However, I shall also attempt to show that the essential individualist spirit of neoclassical economics can be preserved if the Problem of Induction is rejected and the concept of individualism is freed of its usual psychologism. All of this is a matter of fundamental methodology and thus for theoretical reasons we need to examine the foundations of economic method.

L.A.B.
Burnaby, British Columbia
8 October 1981

Introduction

UNDERSTANDING THE METHODOLOGY OF ECONOMICS

> It has often been said, and certainly not without justification, that the man of science is a poor philosopher. Why then should it not be the right thing for the physicist to let the philosopher do the philosophizing? Such might indeed be the right thing at a time when the physicist believes he has at his disposal a rigid system of fundamental concepts and fundamental laws which are so well established that waves of doubt cannot reach them; but, it cannot be right at a time when the very foundations of physics itself have become problematic as they are now. At a time like the present, when experience forces us to seek a newer and more solid foundation, the physicist cannot simply surrender to the philosopher the critical contemplation of the theoretical foundations; for, he himself knows best, and feels more surely where the shoe pinches....
>
> Albert Einstein [1936]

How to Study the Methodology of Economics

In this book we shall examine the neoclassical economists' methodology. By the term 'methodology' we mean their view of the relationship between their theories and their methods of reaching conclusions about the nature of the real world. To many this endeavor may seem to be an easy task. But we shall argue that the methodology of economics is not as obvious as it might first appear because the actual practice of methodology is taken for granted. We shall argue that what is usually discussed under the topic of 'economic methodology' is more concerned with the interests of philosophers of science than with the interests of economic theorists and therefore that a proper study of methodology should be concerned with the actual role of methodology as manifested in the nature of neoclassical theories.

Few economists find it necessary to question what they call their 'methodology'; most are quite convinced that they can survive without ever examining their methods of analysis. As fads go, methodology is not considered to be a 'mainstream' research topic. Where actually offered in a economics curriculum methodology is more an intellectual 'luxury' item for which there is little demand. Why, then, would anyone want to increase the supply of such studies?

The absence of a demand for new methodology does not preclude there being an old methodology that is still being used like a set of old tools. The prevailing views of methodology in neoclassical economics are, in effect, part of our intellectual capital. The reason why there is no market for new methodology is that the potential demanders are quite satisfied with the productivity of their methodology and they cannot see any potential for improvement. However, it is still necessary to examine the tools occasionally to see if they are doing their job. Our central concern here will be that what is often taken for granted in methodology is what is most important to examine.

Before we assess the productivity of the prevailing views of methodology, we shall examine the role of methodology in neoclassical theory. We shall argue that although our methodological capital is often taken for granted, the prevailing methodology of neoclassical economics plays an essential role in *theoretical* questions considered quite topical today. Neoclassical methodology plays a role both by affecting the nature of the theoretical questions which have the highest priority and then by affecting the viability of the solutions to those problems.

Since neoclassical economics is a discipline which is primarily concerned with the consequences of 'rational' decision-making, methodology - as a study of methods of assessing information and of changing knowledge - cannot be considered irrelevant. Any decision-maker must have some knowledge from which to determine, and by which to assess, the options available. What do we presume about the individual decision-maker's knowledge? Or, better still, what do we presume about the individual decision-maker's methodology that allows for 'rational' choices? If neoclassical economics is supposed to explain, or even just to describe, the process of making decisions, surely the methods utilized by the decision-maker must play a central role in the *process* and thereby in the outcome of the process.

If it is granted for the moment that decision-makers do depend on some sort of methodology in their decision-making process, is there any relationship between the neoclassical economist's conception of that practical methodology and the methodology utilitized in forming explanations of that process? We shall argue that there is. And moreover, we shall argue that this unexplored relationship is the major obstacle in the further development of a successful neoclassical theory of an economy as envisaged by Adam Smith, Alfred Marshall or Leon Walras - that is, one which consists only of individual decision-makers.

But if methodology is so important, why is it not a high-priority research topic? The answer to this question is that most economists think there is only one possible methodology or that all other approaches are irrational.

Our study of the methodology of neoclassical economics involves the recognition of an uncommon distinction. Specifically, we shall distinguish between two different perspectives on the role of methodology in neoclassical economics. First, we shall examine the methodology embodied in every neoclassical theory or analysis. That is, we shall be concerned with the views of how neoclassical economists explain the behavior of the decision-makers in the economy. Although we shall examine the alternative views, we nevertheless argue that one view dominates the economists' explanation of their own behavior with respect to methodology. Second, we shall study the consequence of this dominance on the economic theorist's conception of the methodology of the individual decision-maker who is the object of economic studies.

What is important about this distinction is that there is always the possibility that the methodology practiced by neoclassical economists is inconsistent with the methodology assumed to be the basis of the individual decision-making process. What is interesting is that even without explicit discussion of methodology there is, nevertheless, a remarkable consistency between these two perspectives. However, we shall also argue that this is one of the major shortcomings of neoclassical economics. The view which dominates neoclassical theory, both in practice and in its conception of rational decision-making, is based on an inadequate theory of knowledge. Although at first this may seem to be a criticism of neoclassical theory, we shall also argue that the dominant view is not necessary to the neoclassical conception of rational decision-making and hence neoclassical theory can be easily improved by a broader view of methodology.

The second perspective, the neoclassical conception of the rational decision-maker's methodology, will be the primary topic of this book because it is here that the study of methodology can have a profound impact on the nature of specific neoclassical theories. Before we can examine the theoretical issues of the appropriate conception of the decision-maker's methodology, we need to develop a clear idea about the mainstream methodology embodied in neoclassical economics. But first, we have to do a little detective work because the embodied methodology is not very visible. On the one hand, few economists discuss methodology while they are using it because they take it for granted; and on the other hand, when it is discussed, few neoclassical economists practice what they preach.

Textbook rituals and relics

The explicit discussions of methodology which appear at the beginning of many undergraduate economics textbooks are poor reflections of the actual methods embodied in the economics theories presented later in those textbooks. The textbook discussions are nothing more than ritual exercises. They serve no other purpose and they have virtually no bearing on the nature of the theories which are presented.

In principle, the textbook methodology chapters should be a good guide to an understanding of the methodology actually used in economics. The ritual they serve would have us believe that by following the correct methodology we are guaranteed the avoidance of virtually all mistakes. We are told that economic theory is based on some principles of methodology, such as the recognition of the importance of distinguishing between 'normative' and 'positive' statements. The latter are supposedly scientifically superior to the former and are sometimes distinguished from 'tautologies'. Again, positive statements are to be preferred. We are sometimes told that economists agree that only 'testable' statements are scientifically important. Recent textbooks also urge us to recognize that all 'facts' are 'theory-laden' and thus that economic theory can never 'prove' anything.

Any textbook chapter on methodology that consists of such a collection of observations is useless because it is an *ad hoc* hodgepodge of relics from ancient methodological disputes. The difficulty with historical relics living in current practice is not that they are old but that they are taken for granted. Methodological problems can be fundamental. And to that extent it is rather dangerous to take them for granted. But worse than this, the items in the collection very often are contradictory. Not only are the textbook principles of methodology relics from old debates over the appropriate methodology to use in economics, but also often both sides of the debates are advocated.

Methodology vs. techniques

Anyone interested in studying the methodology of economics will have to look somewhere other than textbooks. The only other apparent sources are the explicit discussions of methodology which appear in econometrics articles. For our purposes these simply misuse the term 'methodology'. Presentations of methodology in typical econometrics articles are really nothing more than reports about the mechanical procedures used, without any hint of the more philosophical questions one would expect to find in a book on methodology. So-called 'methodological critiques' turn out, upon examination, to be critiques of the statistical definitions or statistical tests used in the study in question. Similarly, 'methodological issues' turn out to be questions of whether to use 'comparative statics' or whether to use a 'moving average' or discrete observations, etc.

Of course, everyone is free to use the word 'methodology' in any way he or she wishes. All that is important here is to recognize that questions about appropriate research techniques are of little interest to those interested in the more traditional philosophical questions of epistemology or methodology; that is, questions about the relationship between our theoretical knowledge and our conceptions of the world around us. Specifically, studies of research techniques will yield virtually no clues about the objectives of a particular line of research or theoretical investigation. And above all, there is nothing involved in the questions of research techniques which could be identified as being 'neoclassical'.

Methods of understanding methodology

If we cannot be guided either by textbook methodology chapters or by econometrics 'methodology', how can we hope to understand economic methodology? Perhaps the answer can be found in the practice of the economics profession. But how can we bring to light the actual methodology practiced by neoclassical economists?

Traditionally, there has been only one approach to the understanding of economics methodology - one studies methodology by reviewing all of the famous past debates about methodology [Albert, 1979; Blaug, 1980]. This popular approach has its shortcomings primarily in that it contributes new life to old relics and skeletons which would better be left to rest in peace. The major shortcoming is that historians tend to focus on high-profile exceptions to the rule rather than on the more mundane, everyday methods that are tacitly employed by practicing economists.

At first blush one might consider the history of economic methodology as a special case of the history of scientific methodology. This approach begs the methodological question of whether there really is a unity of method in all sciences [Agassi, 1969b]. Those economists who do not ascribe to the unity-of-method philosophy are lost in the shuffle. And probably worst of all, few of the economics writers who ascribe to the unity-of-method approach are likely to be sufficiently competent in matters of physics or chemistry to draw meaningful parallels with economics and to avoid giving life to relics from the history of the physical sciences.

Note that the traditional approach is serial in nature, as is evident in the usual classification of methodology as a branch of the study of the history of economic thought (see, for example, the *Journal of Economic Literature* classifications). If we think of the history of thought approach to economic methodology as a 'time-series' explanation of current practice, the obvious alternative would be a 'cross-sectional' explanation.

The major disadvantange of the time-series approach is that it presumes a certain continuity of the nature of economics and the concept of continuity begs certain questions that need to be examined. For example, why do economists continue to use one particular methodology or take one particular perspective when there are alternatives available? Such a continuity perspective does not always explain *why* economists adhere to their practiced methodology. One of the advantages of a cross-sectional study of current methodology is that it immediately requires consideration of the reason for consciously perpetuating a particular methodology or consideration of why it is taken for granted. This is important, as we wish to examine those problems which are 'hidden' because they are taken for granted and which are the foundation of most methodological strategies pursued by economic theorists and model-builders.

Obviously, even if one looked only at the current practice of economists, it would be impossible to avoid making references to philosophical relics, since much of everyday thought can be traced back to antiquity. One difficulty with the historical, or time-series, approach to methodology is that it gives life to all relics regardless of their relevance to current practice. There is no doubt that some relics do still live in the body of economic analysis today; but if they are still alive, their reason for existence must be found in current practice and not just in the fact that they existed many years ago.

The cross-sectional approach used in this book will be very different from the usual discussions of economics methodology. Rather than attempting to explain which philosophical problems troubled Sir Isaac Newton, we will be more concerned with the philosophical problems that directly or indirectly impinge on the theoretical and practical concerns of today's economists.

Methodology as Agenda

The study of neoclassical methodology presented here will focus on the *research agenda* of every neoclassical theory, analysis, article, etc. The idea of an 'agenda' is not novel. It is rather standard in theories of organizations [e.g., Arrow, 1974]. The idea of an agenda is also appreciated by anyone familiar with parliamentary procedures. The chairman of a committee, for example, runs a meeting according to an agenda. The agenda of a meeting is a list of items to be handled and their relative position on the list indicates their priority, in the sense that they are handled in the order of their appearance on the list.

We will employ the idea of an agenda as an ordered list of items to be handled in any research program. Specifically, a research agenda is an ordered list of theoretical or philosophical problems that either are to be solved by the research conducted or are problems whose solutions play a necessary role in the solutions of the other problems to be considered.

Paradigms and research programs

Every essay, research report, article, book, etc., is written according to a specific 'agenda'. The agenda may be different for each, although many will have common items. The objective of a cross-sectional study of current practice in neoclassical economics is to identify those items which appear on every agenda.

Those readers familiar with the view of science advocated by Thomas Kuhn or Imre Lakatos will likely consider the common agenda items to be the 'paradigm' or 'research program'. Although such a consideration is quite compatible with what will be presented here, it can be a bit misleading, since their view of science is based on an historical or continuity view of natural science. Most applications of their view of science tend to identify the explicit assumptions traditionally used by neoclassical economists as the essence of the neoclassical paradigm. The most common example of a paradigm is the use of the maximization hypothesis in neoclassical analysis. We will argue that such *explicit* assumptions are not enough to specify the agenda.

The cross-sectional approach utilized here will go beyond the Kuhn-Lakatos view by considering any particular neoclassical research program or paradigm to be only one specific *implementation* of the neoclassical agenda. That is, we are concerned with the agenda which is the common foundation of many diverse research programs varying from that of Stigler and Becker [1976] to those of Alchian [1950], Clower and Leijonhufvud [1973], Solow [1979] or, perhaps more surprising, of Simon [1979] or Leibenstein [1979]. It will be apparent that what the followers of Kuhn or Lakatos commonly consider the 'paradigm' of neoclassical economic theory represents only a small subset of the items on any particular research agenda - usually they identify only the maximization hypothesis. For the purposes of this study of methodology, the concept of a research program will have to be expanded to require a complete specification of the research agenda by identifying the implicit as well as the explicit agenda items. The cross-sectional approach presented here will be distinguished primarily because the items on the agenda are considered as specific problems to be dealt with in any given article or research project.

An example of a neoclassical methodology agenda

Before this introduction becomes any more abstract, let us consider a typical neoclassical agenda. Over the last thirty years the Ordinal Demand Theory of Hicks and Allen [1934] has been the subject of extensive analysis [e.g., Chipman *et al.*, 1971]. The purpose of the analysis is to identify a specific set of assumptions which together will be just sufficient to yield a traditional set of results. Stating the purpose this way immediately begs two questions. What is the traditional set of results? And, what assumptions are admissible into the set?

To keep this example straightforward let us follow Samuelson's lead and require that any given theory of demand at least be able to yield his 'Fundamental Theorem of Consumption Theory', namely the proposition that the slope of the demand curve for any normal good be negative [1953, p. 2]. The only limitations on admissible assumptions are that they must include (a) an assumption that an individual's utility function exists, and (b) an assumption that utility is being maximized subject only to the constraints of given prices and a given income. Beyond these simple requirements, virtually anything goes [cf. Boland, 1974].

The problem which any particular neoclassical analysis of demand must solve is: how can the utility function be specified so as to yield the 'Fundamental Theorem'? For example, should we assume cardinal or ordinal utility or is it enough to assume diminishing marginal rates of substitution? These problems form the visible agenda of neoclassical demand theory; and its specification is the task of a broader methodological agenda, which is usually hidden because it is taken for granted.

The broader methodological hidden agenda is concerned with questions about why one would ever bother with individual utility functions, maximization hypotheses, etc. To discover the nature of a given methodological agenda, we need to ask questions such as 'What problem is solved by treating the individual as the sole possessor of a specific utility function?', 'What problem is solved by assuming the demander is a maximizer rather than, say, a "satisficer"?', 'What problem is solved by establishing that demand curves are usually downward sloping?', and so on.

Foundations as Problems on the 'Hidden Agenda'

It will be argued here that the foundations of neoclassical economic methodology, the hidden agenda, consist of two related but autonomous methodological problems. The first is the much discussed 'Problem of Induction'. The other is the less discussed but more pervasive 'Explanatory Problem of Individualism'. The nature and significance of these two methodological problems will be explained in Chapters 1 and 2. How the foundations influence the research programs in neoclassical economics will be examined in Chapters 3 through 6. How they are reflected in the actual practice of methodology in mainstream neoclassical economics will be presented in Chapters 7 through 9. More general questions about the market for new alternatives to the foundations will be examined in Chapters 10 through 12.

The strategy employed throughout this book is the following. Every essay, article, research report, etc., will be considered to be an offered solution to a specific problem or set of problems. To understand an essay (or article, etc.) is to understand the problem-situation [Popper, 1945/66; Latsis, 1972]. The problem-situation or 'situational logic' approach to understanding is easy for trained economists to appreciate, since it is also the basis for most neoclassical economics analyses. Again, for example, we can see that Ordinal Demand Theory is based on an analysis of a specific problem-situation. Namely, maximizing utility is claimed to be the demander's objective and constraints are formed by the givenness of the prices and income.

Our approach then is to presume that every problem-situation consists of a set of one or more objectives and a set of one or more constraints which impede the attainment of the objectives. However, we must be careful here to distinguish between two different problem-situations. One is the situation facing the individual demander or supplier as hypothesized by the theorist; the other is the situation facing the theorist as hypothesized by the methodologist. The latter methodological problem-situation will be the primary focus of our analysis.

PART I

THE 'HIDDEN AGENDA' OF NEOCLASSICAL ECONOMICS

1

The Problem *of* Induction vs. the Problem *with* Induction

> Scientists never 'explain' any behavior, by theory or by any other hook. Every description that is superseded by a 'deeper explanation' turns out upon careful examination to have been replaced by still another description, albeit possibly a more useful description that covers and illuminates a wider area. I can illustrate by what everyone will agree is the single most successful 'theory' of all time. I refer to Newton's theory of universal gravitation.
>
> Paul Samuelson [1964]

> All theory depends on assumptions which are not quite true. That is what makes it theory.
>
> Robert Solow [1956]

Some Background

The Problem of Induction
Since the time when Adam Smith's friend David Hume observed that there was no logical justification for the common belief that much of our empirical knowledge was based on inductive proofs [Hume, 1739; Russell, 1945], methodologists and philosophers have been plagued with what they call the 'Problem of Induction'. The paradigmatic instance of the Problem of Induction is the realization that we cannot provide an inductive proof that 'the sun will rise tomorrow'. This leads many of us to ask, 'So *how* do we know that the sun will rise tomorrow?' If it is impossible to provide a proof, then presumably we would have to admit that we do not know! Several writers have recently claimed to have solved this famous problem [Popper, 1972; Hollis and Nell, 1975] - which is quite surprising, since it is impossible to solve. Nevertheless, what it is and how it is either 'solved' or circumvented is fundamental to understanding all contemporary methodological discussions.

Since the Problem of Induction is fundamental, we will need a clear statement of it. Before attempting this, let us clarify some of its elementary parts. First, there is the implicit presumption that empirical knowledge requires logical justification. We will call this 'Justificationism'. Justificationism probably needs little explanation at this stage, since it is widely accepted, but for future reference, let us be specific.

> *Justificationism* is the methodological doctrine that asserts that nobody can claim to possess knowledge unless he or she can also demonstrate (with a proof) that his or her knowledge is true; that is, everyone must justify his or her knowledge claims.

Crudely stated, this requirement says, 'knowledge' is not Knowledge unless it is *true* knowledge. Second, there is the further requirement that the justification of empirical (true) knowledge requires an inductive, as opposed to a deductive, proof. We will call this 'Inductivism'. Although Inductivism has been around for several hundred years, our view of it will be the following:

> *Inductivism* is the methodological doctrine that asserts that any justification of one's knowledge must be logically based *only* on experiential evidence consisting of particular or singular observation statements; that is, one must justify his or her knowledge using only verifiable observations that have been verified by experience.

Given Inductivism, any straightforward solution to the Problem of Induction requires an 'Inductive logic', that is, there must be a form of logic which permits arguments consisting of only 'singular statements' (e.g., 'The sun rose in Vancouver at 5:28am on the May 16, 1981'), while the conclusions that validly follow may be 'general statements' (e.g., 'The sun will rise every day'). Now we can state the famous problem:

> The *Problem of Induction* is that of finding a general *method* of providing an inductive proof for anyone's claim to empirical knowledge.

In other words, this is the problem of finding a form of logical argument in which (a) the conclusion is a *general* statement, such as one of the true 'laws' of economics, or the conclusion is the choice of the true theory or model from among various competitors; and (b) the assumptions include *only* singular statements of *particulars* (such as simple observation reports). With an argument of this form one is said to be arguing inductively from the truth of particulars to the truth of generals. (On the other hand, a deductive form of argument proceeds from the truth of generals to the truth of particulars.) If one could solve the Problem of Induction, the true 'laws' or general theories of economics (i.e., economic knowledge) could then be said to be induced logically from particular observations.

For very many years virtually everyone believed that science and its 'scientific method' represented a solution to the Problem of Induction [Agassi, 1963]. Their belief was based on the commonly accepted view that Newtonian physics represented *true* knowledge, since there were many reports of the existence of inductive proofs of that knowledge. Late in the nineteenth century, when doubts were raised concerning the absolute truth of Newtonian physics, a more moderate claim for science was developed [e.g., Poincare, 1905/52; Duhem, 1906/62; Eddington, 1928].

The Problem of Induction in economics
It is interesting to note that except for some recent books explicitly about methodology [Hollis and Nell, 1975; Stewart, 1979; Blaug, 1980; etc.], economics writers have rarely been concerned with this allegedly fundamental problem. There is a very simple reason for this. For most of the nineteenth century, economists simply believed that the Problem of Induction had been solved; thus it did not need any further consideration. After all, Newton seems to claim to have arrived at the laws of physics from scientific observation using inductive methods [e.g., Newton, 1704/1952]. In Adam Smith's time, inductive generalization was the paradigm of rational thinking; Newton's physics was the paradigm of inductive generalization.

Unfortunately, Hume's critical examinations of logical justifications for the acceptance of inductive proofs were largely ignored [Russell, 1945, pp. 659ff.]. Consequently, most thinkers continued to believe that there was an inductive logic. Thus there was no apparent reason to doubt the claims made for the scientific basis of Newton's physics. And there was no reason to doubt the possibility of rational (i.e., inductive) decision-making. Supposedly, whenever one had all the facts, one only needed to be inductively rational to arrive without doubt at correct decisions. Moreover, whenever one made an error in judgement, it would have had to be due to either an irrational moment or a failure to gather all the facts.

Although economic theory has been deeply affected by the eighteenth-century beliefs about rational decision-making, the rationalism of economic theory is not obviously inductivist - with the possible exception of the distinction between 'positive' and 'normative' economics. At least, very little of the faith in rationalism *appears* to have survived as explicit inductivism. The reason for the absence of explicit inductivism in mainstream economics today is that neoclassical economics reflects the concerns of late nineteenth-century and early twentieth-century philosophers, who were becoming aware of the possibility that Newton's physics might not actually be true and, more important, that inductivism might not be able to live up to its promises.

It can be argued that anyone who believed that Newton's physical laws were true because they had been inductively proven must have been in some way mistaken. Such an argument would lead to two questions: (1) Did Newton fail to prove his theory true because he was mistaken about the objective *quality* of his 'facts'? (2) Was Hume correct about the absence of an adequate inductive logic, so no *quantity* of 'facts' could ever prove Newton's theory true? In response to such questions modern economic methodology falls generally into one of two opposing methodological camps depending on the answers given. On the one hand (for want of a better name), there are the 'conservative' methodologists who would give an affirmative answer to (1) and a negative one to (2) and would promote the importance of the distinction between 'positive' and 'normative' economics. On the other hand, there are the 'liberal' methodologists who would give a negative answer to (1) and an affirmative one to (2) and would find the views of Solow and Samuelson, quoted above, more to their liking.

The problem with induction
The major point to be stressed here is that both methodological positions are based on Justificationism as well as on some form of Inductivism. And thus, both methodological positions accept the Problem of Induction. They differ only in regard to how the problem *with* induction is recognized.

The 'conservative' methodologists in economics say that there is nothing fundamentally wrong with inductive arguments, with the one possible exception that we must be very careful in the collection of 'facts'. For the 'conservative' methodologists, if there should be a problem with the application of induction in economics or other social sciences, then it is that there are not enough 'hard facts' [e.g., Leontief, 1971]. Specifically, before beginning an inductive proof one must be careful to eliminate subjective or 'normative' opinions about what are the 'facts'. The 'conservative' methodologists thus stress that for economics to be scientific it must be based on 'positive' rather than 'normative' statements.

The 'liberal' methodologists in economics take a position which is less optimistic but more devious. Rather than simply admitting that some theories which were once thought to be true are actually false, the 'liberals' obfuscate the methodological questions by denying that (non-tautological) theories could ever be true. For example, they might argue that only a tautology can be true and a self-contradiction can be false [see further, Quine, 1965].

Theories, according to the 'liberal' methodologists, are to be considered 'better' or 'worse', rather than true or false. The reason for this switch is that the 'liberal' methodologists still think that the Problem of Induction must be solved before one can discuss 'truth' but, to their credit, they recognize that there is a problem with inductive logic. Specifically, they realize that no *finite* quantity of true singular statements could ever prove that any given general statement is true. In short, they admit that there is no inductive logic, and *that* is the problem *with* induction.

The retreat to Conventionalism

Despite the generous nods given to the positive/normative distinction in many economics textbooks, this popular distinction is nothing but a relic left over from late nineteenth-century attempts to save Inductivism. Since almost all economists have by now accepted that there is a problem with induction, one has to wonder why economics textbooks continue to promote the positive/normative distinction. The reason appears to be quite simple: For methodologists in economics, the Problem of Induction is still not dead!

The most commonly adopted methodological position, in effect, puts Inductivism on a 'back-burner' for the present and temporarily puts a different requirement, 'Conventionalism', in its place along with Justificationism. It will be argued here that, despite the attendant smoke, noise and celebration, the methodological controversies of the early 1960s were merely family squabbles. That is to say, virtually all economic methodologists bow to the Problem of Induction [possible recent exceptions are Latsis, 1972; Wong, 1973; Newman, 1976; Coddington, 1979]. Since this problem is insolvable without an inductive logic, most methodological arguments in economics today are about the appropriate way to circumvent the Problem of Induction.

Given Conventionalism, it would appear that economists as methodologists do not attempt to solve the Problem of Induction itself but instead try to solve a weaker form of the Problem of Induction. For the purpose of discussing methodology the problem-shift is unfortunate because the modified form of the Problem of Induction, which will be called the 'Problem of Conventions', is a bit more complicated than the original problem. The aim of the original Problem of Induction was a straightforward, objective, inductive proof of the (absolute) truth of any true theory. Contrarily, as we shall see, the aim of the Problem of Conventions is a choice of the 'best' theory according to conventional measures of acceptable 'truth'. Without an inductive logic, the solution to the Problem of Conventions can get rather complicated (in exactly the same way welfare economics has difficulties with social choices [Boland, 1971a]). To add to the complications, there are many different measures to choose from [Boland, 1971a], and the measure used may or may not involve 'inductive' evidence.

The Problem of Conventions
Let us now state the problem which dominates economic methodology today.

The *Problem of Conventions* is the problem of finding generally acceptable criteria upon which to base any contingent, *deductive* proof of any claim to empirical 'knowledge'.

Note that although the problems of Induction and of Conventions differ regarding the nature of the proof required for justification, they are the same in regard to the requirement of Justificationism. The word 'knowledge' has been specifically enclosed in quotation marks because one of the consequences of the presumed Justificationism is that 'knowledge' is not (true) Knowledge unless it has been absolutely proven true, and deductive proofs always depend on given assumptions.

Where pure Inductivism requires a final (absolute) inductive proof for any true theory, Conventionalism requires only a *conditional* deductive argument for why the chosen theory is the 'best' available. This poses a new problem. Since we assume because we do not know, deductive arguments always have assumptions. Therefore, the choice of any theory is always open to question. That is, one can always question the criteria used to define 'best' or 'better'. Thus, there is always the danger of an infinite regress - for example, by what meta-criteria would we choose the criteria of 'best'? There is also the danger of circular arguments - for example, the operative criteria are appropriate because they are sufficient to justify our choice. Ultimately, the Problem of Conventions becomes one of providing a justification while at the same time avoiding an infinite regress and a circular justification - and all this is to be done without an inductive logic!

Conventionalism vs. Inductivism
The 'conservative' methodologists (those who still do not wish to abandon Inductivism completely) might say that the Problem of Conventions is too precarious and tentative and that we would be better off trying to solve the original Problem of Induction - for example, by finding a way to establish objective facts [Rotwein, 1980]. The 'liberal'

methodologists (who deny the possibility of inductive logic) can counter by arguing that any claimed solution to the Problem of Induction is an illusion and that the 'solution' is but another instance of the Problem of Conventions. Their reasoning is simple. There are no 'objective facts' because all 'facts' are 'theory-laden' [e.g., Hanson, 1965; Popper, 1972; Samuelson and Scott, 1975; etc.] - that is, any claimed 'facts' must have been based on the acceptance of one or more theories. Thus, according to the 'liberal' view, any inductive 'proof' cannot be complete because every reported 'fact' will require a proof too. Hence, we will begin an infinite regress unless we have already accepted 'conventions' concerning the 'truth' of the 'facts'. In other words, the most we could ever expect to achieve is a logically consistent, deductive proof based on the prior acceptance of a set of 'conventions'. In this manner, the 'liberal' methodologists can claim that our concern is not whether a theory is *true*, but only whether our argument in its favor is logically *valid*.

The 'conservative' methodologists still need not concede defeat. If all facts are theory-laden, our being concerned only with logical validity might mean that our ultimate goal can only be the creation of tautologies. The 'liberal' methodologists have handled this possiblity with the *ad hoc* prescription that all economic theories and models must at the very least be 'falsifiable' or 'testable'. This prescription does avoid tautologies - but it does so only at the expense of leaving room for the 'conservative' methodologists to argue that empirical (i.e., inductive) evidence must play a role. Even though empirical evidence cannot provide a final proof, incomplete induction may be employed in the creation of competing theories or models, leaving deductive arguments for the justification of the choice between them. This view also allows inductive evidence to be involved in the choice criteria used.

We can easily see that this is indeed a family dispute between 'liberal' and 'conservative' methodologists and that it could probably go on forever, since there never will be the decisive arbiter of final (inductive) proofs. Both positions advocate a form of Conventionalism. Where the 'liberals' argue for a pure Conventionalism without any necessary role for inductive evidence (the so-called Hypothetical-Deductive model), the 'conservatives' advocate a more modest form of Conventionalism which does not completely abandon Inductivism or the need for some inductive evidence. As long as we continue to presume the necessity of logical justification (i.e., Justificationism) while admitting the impossibility of inductive proofs of general statements, some form of Conventionalism will always be seen to be a 'better' methodological position than pure Inductivism (that is, the strict requirement of final inductive proof). But perversely and more significantly, we must observe that it is seen to be 'better' only if dealing with the Problem of Induction is still considered an important objective.

In some sense the only difference between the 'liberal' and 'conservative' positions is that only the latter holds out for a long-run solution to the Problem of Induction. In the short run - that is, for day-to-day methodological concerns - the positions are identical. Both positions require that the Problem of Conventions be solved in the short run. The 'conservative' methodologists thus have two viewpoints. They adopt Conventionalism in the short run and hold out for Inductivism in the long run. Given their schizophrenia, discussing methodology in economics is often rather difficult because it is not always clear which viewpoint is operative. For the remainder of the book, except where specifically noted, we will identify Conventionalism with the short-run viewpoint so that we do not have to distinguish between the 'conservative' and 'liberal' positions.

Conventionalism in Economics

The effects of Conventionalism

For our purposes it is unfortunate that the term 'Conventionalism' has been promoted as a pejorative one by the philosopher Karl Popper and his followers. Many can rightfully object to the apparent name-calling that is implied by the use of such terms as 'Conventionalist', 'Inductivist', 'Instrumentalist', and the like. Few philosophers today would promote themselves as Conventionalists. But more important, in economics it is very difficult to find anyone who exactly fits one of the molds delineated by Popper. Nevertheless, Popper's methodological categorization does serve an heuristic purpose. Despite the possible entertainment value, we do not wish to label individuals with peculiar philosophical tastes. Our only concern here will be the identification of impersonal items on the impersonal hidden agenda of neoclassical economics.

Our argument here is that the first item on the hidden agenda of any neoclassical article is the Problem of Induction. The agenda item usually appears, however, in its weaker, modified form, as the Problem of Conventions.

When we say that any particular problem is on the hidden agenda of a given article we are saying either that one of the objectives of the article is to solve that problem or that it is presumed to have been solved already and that what appears in any given neoclassical article will be consistent with the presumed solution. Since the solution of the Problem of Conventions (and, hence, a circumvention of the Problem of Induction) is taken for granted, it might be difficult to find direct evidence of its presence. However, two clues to its presence can be identified.

First and foremost is the absence of references to any theory being either true or false. The reason for this lacuna is that, *given Conventionalism*, if one were to refer to a theory being true, then it would imply that one has solved the Problem of Induction and thus has the ability to prove the theory's truth. But this would be inconsistent, as Conventionalism is predicated on a denial of the possibility of solving the Problem of Induction. So, strictly speaking, Conventionalism precludes any references to truth or falsity.

The conventionalist ban on the use of the terms 'true' and 'false' would present obvious difficulties even for simple discussions. It would also complicate the use of other terms such as 'knowing' and 'knowledge', as well as 'explaining' and 'explanation'. The reason for the ban on the use of the words 'knowledge' and 'explanation' is somewhat elusive. It seems to be due to a variation of the presumption of Justificationism, that to know is to have obtained 'true knowledge' and, similarly, 'to explain' is to give a 'true explanation'.

Although the ban on using the terms 'true' and 'false' in their literal sense is rather complete, the terms 'knowledge' and 'explanation' do appear often in the literature. What needs to be understood, however, is that there is a presumption that whenever the term 'explanation' is used one never means literally true explanation. Instead, an 'explanation' only means a 'true' explanation *relative* to some accepted conventional measures of 'approximation' [Samuelson, 1952; 1964; Simon, 1979].

Consider, for example, the old debates over the theory of imperfect competition [Archibald, 1961; Stigler, 1963]. Some argue that the concept of imperfect competition is empty or arbitrary and unduly complex. Simplicity would be served by merely applying perfect competition or monopoly where appropriate [Friedman, 1953]. The dispute thus becomes one of 'which is a better approximation' - a simplifying approximation which gives more positive results, or a generalizing approximation which allows for a better description of what firms actually do? This dispute will not be resolved without an accepted criterion of approximation [Boland, 1970b; 1971a].

The second clue to the presence of Conventionalism is the apparent concern for making a choice among competing theories or models [e.g., Tarascio and Caldwell, 1979; cf. Boland, 1971a]. As mentioned above, most methodological articles and debates have been about the criteria to be used in any 'theory choice'. There is virtually no discussion of *why* one should ever be required to choose *one* theory! The reason for the lack of discussion of the motivation for 'theory choice' is that the Problem of Conventions is simply taken for granted. A direct consequence of accepting the need to solve the Problem of Conventions is the presumption that any article or essay must represent a revealed choice of a theory and that any such choice *can* be justified. The only question of methodological interest in this case concerns how to reveal the criteria used to justify the theory choice.

Conventionalism and 'theory choice' criteria

Given the Problem of Conventions, most questions of methodology reduce to what amount to exercises in economic analysis. Specifically, any choice of a theory or model can be 'explained' as being the result of a maximization process in which the objective function is an accepted measure of 'truthlikeness' and the constraint is the set of available alternative theories or models. To choose the best theory is to choose the one which maximizes some desired attribute. Over the last forty years, several different criteria or objective functions have been mentioned. The most well-defined have been 'simplicity', 'generality', 'verifiability', 'falsifiability', 'confirmability', 'and 'testability'. Less well-defined are 'empirical relevance', 'plausibility' and 'reasonableness'.

Each of these criteria has its advocates and its critics. Those advocates who wish to remain consistent with the dictates of Conventionalism will not claim that their explanation of the choice of any particular theory in any way constitutes a proof that the theory is actually true. If by chance the chosen theory is 'best' by all criteria, there could never be an argument. But usually competing theories are best by one criterion and not by another, and in such cases critics, who may also wish to remain consistent with Conventionalism, are thus forced to quibble over a choice between criteria [e.g., Samuelson, 1967; Lucas, 1980; cf. Boland, 1970b].

Limitations of choice criteria

Those critics who are not bound by the dictates of Conventionalism can take a different approach. One line of criticism [e.g., Boland, 1980] is to reject Conventionalism by arguing that each criterion is based on an allegedly absolutely *true* theory of the nature of any true theory of the phenomena in question. For example, choosing a theory which is the 'most simple' presumes that the real world is inherently simple, thus any true theory of the real world must also be simple, and that furthermore, although the truth of one's theory may not be provable, the simplicity of competing theories can be established if the measure of simplicity is well defined. A similar argument can be raised against the version of Conventionalism which judges theories on the basis of the criterion of generality.

Advocates of any Conventionalist criterion might wish to deny that they have assumed that their theory of the world is true, since such an assumption violates the requirements of Conventionalism. But, if the advocacy of a particular criterion is not based on the presumed true theory of the essential nature of the world which the theory 'explains', then the use of the criterion either leads to an infinite regress or opens the choice to a charge of arbitrariness. Specifically, one can always question the choice of the choice criterion. If a true theory of the world is not presumed, then we are right back at the doorstep of the Problem of Induction.

Conventionalist criteria other than simplicity or generality would seem to be less vulnerable. Unfortunately, there are still problems. One of the first Conventionalist criteria was verifiability, but that criterion is no longer taken seriously, as it has not fared well against the logical criticism of Popper and others who argue that all informative, non-tautological theories are unverifiable [Popper, 1934/59]. For Popper, theories are informative only if they are falsifiable. He seems successfully to have destroyed the belief in verification, as falsifiability and testability are now widely accepted as a minimum condition for the acceptability of any theory or model in economics [pace Hutchison, 1938 and Samuelson, 1948]. This is unfortunate, as 'theory choice' criteria, falsifiability and testability are still quite arbitrary. But worse, those critics *not* bound by Conventionalism can also argue that the true theory may not be the most falsifiable nor the most testable of the available alternative theories [Wisdom, 1963; Bartley, 1968].

Validation, confirmations and disconfirmations

For some purists, the acceptance of the criteria of verifiability or falsifiability might seem a little inconsistent if one still accepts Conventionalism and its denial of a (non-tautological and non-self-contradictory) theory being either true or false. If a theory cannot be false, what does 'falsifiable' mean? These purists find refuge in a set of weaker criteria for the lesser purpose of 'validation' [Stewart, 1979]. The most widely used criterion is 'confirmability', and rather than seeking to verify a theory or model we are said to be only seeking its confirmation. For example, the universal statement 'All swans are white' may be said to be confirmed (but not proven) when a very large number of 'white swans' have been observed in the absence of any 'non-white swans'. Those who accept Popper's criticism of the purpose for verification may opt for the criterion of 'testability' where the objective is to select only theories which in principle could be 'disconfirmed' [Hempel, 1966, ch. 4].

Unfortunately, such validation criteria have their limitations, too. For example, a highly confirmed theory may still be false. But purists can counter with the observation that this is not a problem, since any theory which does not violate the axioms of logic (i.e., one which is logically consistent) cannot be considered false even in the presence of a reported refutation (an observed counter-example) because any refuting fact is itself theory-laden - that is, any proponent of the 'refuted' theory can defend it by questioning the alleged truth of the observed counter-example [cf. Agassi, 1966a]. This example highlights one of the prominent features of logically consistent Conventionalism. In place of the concepts of 'true' and 'false', Conventionalism uses 'valid' and 'invalid'. And furthermore, the only *objective* and non-arbitrary test to be applied to theories or models is that of logical consistency and validity. Even if we cannot prove a theory or model is true, at the very minimum to be true it must be logically consistent.

The concept of confirmation is not without its logical problems, too. In its simple form it equates a probability of truth with a degree of confirmation. Following Hume, some might claim that although objective inductive proofs may be impossible, it is still possible to argue inductively, and the outcome of such an argument will be a 'degree of probability of truth'. Such a 'degree' concept presumes that a greater quantity of positive evidence implies a higher degree of probability of truth. Unfortunately, with this simple concept one has merely assumed what one wished to establish [Boland, 1980].

Recall that an inductive argument proceeds from particular positive statements - e.g., observation reports such as 'A white swan was observed in British Columbia today' - to general statements such as 'All swans in BC today are white.' In the absence of refuting observations, the general statement's probability of truth is measured by the ratio of the number of confirming observations to the unknown but finite number of possible observations - such as the ratio of observed white swans (without double-counting) to the number of all swans in BC today. So long as we specify which day 'today' is, this general statement is both verifiable and refutable. (Note that what Popper objected to was the verification of strictly universal statements where the quantity of possible observations were not finite.)

The only question of empirical significance here is whether subsequent observations of confirming evidence (e.g., more white swans) *necessarily* increase the degree of confidence in the general statement *as opposed to its denial* (e.g., the statement that there is at least one non-white swan in BC today). Based on the quantity of evidence available, what degree of confidence does one have that the *next* swan observed will be white? Advocates of the confirmability criterion would have us believe that each past observation of a white swan necessarily increases the probability that all future swans observed will be white. This alleged necessity is actually based on a prior, and unsupported, assumption that the general statement is true (or that its ultimate probability is one).

Since the criterion of confirmability is so widely used in econometrics, perhaps we should offer an explanation for our claim. If you think the general statement 'All swans in BC today are white' is *false*, your confidence in the *denial* will also be increased by the observation of each *white* swan. In other words, the probability that the next swan observed will be non-white (hence proving the falsity of the general statement in question) will increase as each white swan is observed (and tagged to avoid double-counting); that is, the ratio of the number of as yet unobserved non-white swans to the number of all unobserved swans increases as each white swan is counted. Thus, we think we can conclude that the significance of one's confirmations is based solely on one's *prior* assumptions. You will see confirming evidence for your empirical generalizations only because you have already assumed that they are true!

It must be realized that not all advocates of confirmation rely on a probability construct. But avoiding any reliance on probability will not circumvent the more well-known logical problems of confirmation. All conceptions of a logical connection between positive evidence and degrees of confirmation suffer from a profound logical problem called, by some philosophers, the 'paradox of confirmation' [see Gardiner, 1976].

The philosopher's paradox of confirmation merely points out that any evidence which does not refute a theory consisting of a simple universal statement (for example, 'All swans are white') must increase the degree of confirmation. The paradox is based on the observation that this example of a simple universal statement is equivalent to the statement 'All non-white things are non-swans.' Positive evidence consistent with the latter statement would have to include red shoes as well as black ravens, since in both cases we have non-white things which are not swans. But even worse, the set of all confirming instances must include all things which are not non-white swans. This merely divides the contents of the universe into non-white swans and everything else [Agassi, 1966b; Hempel, 1966].

The Remnants of Inductivism

For the most part neoclassical economics has ignored the alleged problems with conventional choice criteria. Today, almost all econometric hypothesis testing involves the use of one or more of the criteria discussed above. And, among methodologists there is still considerable discussion of falsifiability as a minimum condition for the acceptability of any theory or model. So one might wish to conclude that Conventionalism has completely supplanted Inductivism in economics. Such a conclusion would be somewhat mistaken, as there still remain many remnants of the vanquished Inductivism!

The most popular remnant is the alleged hierarchy which consists of 'hypotheses', 'theories' and 'laws'. In the tradition of Inductivism, every science was developed in stages. Each supposedly began with an 'hypothesis' which had been previously formed only by examining empirical data. The next step was the submission of the hypothesis to experimental testing. If the hypothesis passed the test, it was to be elevated in status to a 'theory'. Eventually, if it somehow reached the ultimate status, it was crowned a 'law'. It is difficult to take such a view seriously these days. Nevertheless, one still finds distinctions being made as if there were some significant difference among hypotheses, theories and laws. And related to this is a ban on speculations - 'one must not jump to conclusions until the facts are examined.' If Inductivism were actually completely abandoned, it would be difficult to see any reason for the continued promotion of the hierarchy or for a ban on conjectures and speculations.

Even if methodologists today avoid promoting the hierarchical distinctions of Inductivism, the dominant methodological perspective is that the fundamental problem facing all economists is one of choosing the one 'best' theory or model. It is this choice problem which is the primary remnant of Inductivism and the related presumption that we must deal with the Problem of Induction.

2

The Explanatory Problem
of Individualism

For theory it is irrelevant *why* people demand certain goods: the only important point is that all things are demanded, produced, and paid for because individuals want them. Every demand on the market is therefore an individualistic one, altho, from another point of view, it often is an altruistic or a social one.

The only wants which for the purpose of economic theory should be called strictly social are *those which are consciously asserted by the whole community....*

Many writers call production, distribution, and exchange social processes, meaning thereby that nobody can perform them - at least the two last named - by himself. In this sense, prices are obviously social phenomena....

We seem to be faced by this alternative: either we are to assume social utility curves, - in which case society must be the sole owner of capital and land, the society is communistic, and no rent or interest will be paid to individuals; or rent and interest are paid, in which case there are no social values, but only individual ones, and society as such does not control production....

Joseph Schumpeter [1909]

All human conduct is psychological and, from that standpoint, not only the study of economics but the study of every other branch of human activity is a psychological study and the facts of all such branches are psychological facts. ...The principles of an economic psychology ... can be *deduced* only from facts.... A very general view of common well-known facts gave English writers the concept of a 'final degree of utility,' and Walras the concept of 'rarity'.... From the examination of the facts we were led, by induction, to formulate those notions....

Vilfredo Pareto [1916/35]

individualistic atoms of the rare gas in my balloon are not
isolated from the other atoms. Adam Smith, who is
almost as well known for his discussion of the division of
labor and the resulting efficiency purchased at the price
of interdependence, was well aware of that. What he
would have stressed was that the contacts between the
atoms were *organized* by the use of markets and prices.

Paul Samuelson [1963/66, p. 1411]

Individualism as a Research Program

Individualism vs. holism

Methodological individualism, the research program outlined by
Schumpeter, has recently been identified by Mark Blaug as the 'view
that social theories must be grounded in the attitudes and behavior of
individuals, as opposed to "methodological holism", which asserts that
social theories must be grounded in the behavior of irreducible groups of
individuals' [1980, p. 266]. The view that neoclassical economics is firmly
grounded on a research program of 'methodological individualism' is today rather commonplace [e.g., Samuelson, 1963/66; Albert, 1979]. In our
terms, methodological individualism is the second main item on the hidden agenda of neoclassical economics. For future reference, let us specify:

> *Methodological individualism* is the view that allows *only* indi-
> viduals to be the decision-makers in any explanation of social phe-
> nomena.

Methodological individualism does not allow explanations which involve non-individualist decision-makers such as institutions, weather
or even historical destiny.

From the viewpoint of methodology, we need to examine the
reasons why methodological individualism is a main item on the neoclassical agenda. Unfortunately, the reasons are difficult to find, as
there is little methodological discussion of why economics *should*
involve only explanations that can be reduced to the decision-making
of individuals - except, perhaps, for Hayek's arguments for the informational simplicity of methodological individualism [1937/48; 1945/
48]. Our task in this chapter is to provide a rudimentary examination of
the nature and purpose of methodological individualism in neoclassical theory. Along the way we will review some recent developments in
the understanding of this agenda item.

An examination of the reasons for the presence of methodological
individualism on the agenda is more complicated than it might at first

appear. Supposedly [e.g., Schumpeter, 1909; Blaug, 1980], there is a built-in dichotomy which allows only two options - methodological individualism vs. methodological holism. Given the individualism-holism dichotomy, the reasons for promoting methodological individualism may be rather negative. The social-philosophical basis of neoclassical economics is dominated by the eighteenth-century anti-authoritarian rationalism that puts the individual decision-maker at the center of the social universe. A rejection of individualism would be tantamount to the advocacy of a denial of intellectual freedom. For intellectual reasons, we would need to promote the view that individuals are free to decide their own fate in order to avoid endorsing authoritarianism. For political reasons, it would seem we have to favor individualism in order to avoid inadvertently advocating any ideology based on 'holism' - e.g., communism, socialism, Marxism, etc.

Adding to the confusions caused by the acceptance of the (possibly false) dichotomy between individualism and holism, there is the confusion raised by the alternative view of individualism promoted by Popper in his *Open Society*. Specifically, there is his version of 'methodological individualism' [Popper, 1945/66, p. 91], which does not accept the individualism-holism dichotomy and thus is apparently more general than the individualism defined by Schumpeter (and Blaug). In Popper's terms, Schumpeter's 'methodological individualism' should be called 'psychologistic individualism' and Blaug's 'methodological holism' should be called 'institutional holism', while Popper's 'methodological individualism' should be called 'institutional individualism' [Agassi, 1960; 1975]. Unfortunately, this approach only adds a second dichotomy - psychologism vs. institutionalism. It does not automatically give us an explanation for the advocacy of individualism.

In order to explain why neoclassical economics is based on methodological individualism, one can, of course, point to obvious questions of ideology [cf. Weisskopf, 1979] but as an explanation this only begs the question at a different level. If the decision to adopt methodological individualism is based on ideological considerations, how do individual economists choose their ideologies? Must our explanation of the choice of ideologies be constrained by the prescriptions of methodological individualism? To what must the explanation of the choice of ideologies be reduced? To avoid an infinite regress, it cannot be an ideology.

Individualism and explanations
Pareto's candid comments (quoted above) suggest a very different approach: one that connects psychology with induction. This approach will be examined in the remainder of this chapter. We shall argue that

there is a close connection between the Problem of Induction and the research program of methodological individualism. Specifically, for neoclassical economics, methodological individualism is a research program that is designed to facilitate a *long-run* solution to the Problem of Induction.

To examine the relationship between Inductivism and individualism in neoclassical theory, we need to consider another aspect of Pareto's comments. What Pareto, and John Stuart Mill before him, presumed was that there are rules of explanation that prescribe the existence of an irreducible set of acceptable 'primitives'. Since the time of Mill, most economists have accepted the view that for individualism to be the basis of all explanations in social theory, the irreducible minimum must be the given psychological states of the decision-makers [see also Scitovsky, 1976]. Today we might simply say that the psychological states of all individuals are *exogenous*, but Popper sees something more in the view of Mill, which he calls 'psychologism' [1945/66, ch. 14] We must be careful here to distinguish psychologism from individualism, as it is possible to form a psychologistic methodology which is 'holistic' and with which, for example, explanations are reduced to 'mob psychology' or 'class interest'. For reference we shall define the more general methodological principle as follows:

> *Psychologism* is the methodological prescription that psychological states are the *only* exogenous variables permitted beyond natural givens (e.g., weather, contents of the Universe, etc.)

And we shall always use Agassi's term 'psychologistic individualism' to identify the Mill-Pareto prescription as a special form of methodological individualism. Specifically,

> *Psychologistic individualism* is the version of psychologism which identifies the individual with his or her psychological state.

We should note immediately that the implications of adhering to a psychologistic individualist version of neoclassical theory means that everything or every variable which cannot be reduced either to someone's psychological state or to a natural given must be explained somewhere in the theory. We should also note that a theory can conform to methodological individualism without conforming to psychologistic individualism only if the requirements of psychologism are abandoned.

Reductive individualism

In light of the proscription of non-individualist and non-natural exogenous variables, the key methodological obstacle for neoclassical theories of economic behavior is the specification of an appropriate conception of the relationship between institutions and individuals. On the one hand, social institutions are consequences of decisions made by one or more individuals. On the other hand, individual decision-makers are constrained by existing institutions. If any given institution is the result of actions of individuals, can it ever be an exogenous variable? That is, can institutions really be constraints? If institutions limit the range of choices facing any individual, are the individual's choices really free? If any institution is a creation of groups of individuals, can it have aims of its own or must it merely be a reflection of the aims of the individuals who created it?

These questions are not often discussed in the economics literature because the psychologism of Mill or Pareto is simply taken for granted. Thus, whenever anyone feels bound by methodological individualism, he or she is immediately bound also by the psychologistic individualism. As a result, in any economics explanation in which institutions are recognized, they are always to be treated as mere epiphenomena. That is, institutions are to be analogous to pictures printed in the newspaper. What appears in any newspaper picture as a person's face is actually only a collection of black and white dots. One can explain the appearance of a face by explaining why the dots are where they are.

The explanatory obstacle posed by the existence of institutions exists regardless of the prescriptions of psychologism. Methodological individualism alone leads to two primary methodological requirements. First, no institution can be left unexplained and, moreover, every institution must be explained in individualist terms. Second, any conceived institution must be responsive to the choices of every individual. The first requirement begs a fundamental methodological question about what constitutes a successful explanation. Is there a set of automatically acceptable givens? The second raises the thorny question considered in Arrow's (Im)Possibility Theorem. Can the choice of an institution be rationalized in the same manner as we rationalize an individual's choice of a bundle of goods? If it can, then the social utility (welfare) function used to make the social choice must also be a social institution - one which, like the picture on the newspaper page, must be an epiphenomenon. Either the social choice is nothing more than the logical consequence of individual choices, or the social utility function must be perfectly responsive to changes in any individual's utility function.

Now, it is commonly accepted that all explanations require some givens - i.e., some exogenous variables. In a fundamental way, specification of the exogenous variables is probably the most informative theoretical assertion in any theoretical model [Boland, 1975]. The various competing schools of economics might easily be characterized on the basis of which variables are considered exogenous. Marxian models take 'class interest' and 'rates of accumulation' as exogenous givens. Some institutional models take the evolution of social institutions as a given and use it to explain the history of economics. Many neoclassical models would instead attempt to explain 'rates of accumulation' and 'institutions' [Boland, 1979b], and it is conceivable that some might even try to explain 'class interest' as an outcome of rational decision-making. Whatever the case, no one model can explain everything; there must be some givens. For neoclassical economics today what the presumption of psychologism does is conveniently to restrict the list of acceptable givens. Given psychologistic individualism, the psychological states of the individuals in society are the irreducible givens.

The methodological view that there is but one permissible set of exogenous variables to which all successful explanations must be reduced is called 'reductionism'. Popper's methodological individualism has been specifically identified by Blaug as an example of a reductionist research program. Supposedly, theorists who are bound by reductive methodological individualism are obligated to explain away any non-individualistic variable which might appear to be exogenous, or any 'macroeconomic propositions that cannot be reduced to microeconomic ones' [p. 51]. Blaug recommends giving up methodological individualism rather than macroeconomics. We suspect that he has only psychologistic individualism in mind, since, contrary to what Blaug says, Popper's methodological individualism does not have to be a reductionist program; only the special version, psychologistic individualism, does. In Popper's version of methodological individualism - institutional individualism - individuals are not identified with psychological states but rather with their unique problem-situations. With his institutional individualism, the decision-maker is considered a problem-solver with specific aims which may not be psychologically motivated [Agassi, 1960; 1975].

Institutional Individualism

The conception of methodological individualism as a reductionist program can be somewhat misleading. It might not always be clear what constitutes a permissible individualistic exogenous variable. In any psychologistic individualist version of neoclassical theory, what constitutes the individualistic variable is easy to see: it is the individuals' psychological states. Specifically, individuals are always identified with their utility functions (as firms are often implicitly identified with their production functions [cf. Rowcroft, 1979]).

Viewing psychology as the foundation of all economics explanations raises some subtle questions and dilemmas. Would a psychological basis for all economics explanations imply that everyone will make the same choice when facing the same given price-income situation, or will there never be two individuals doing the same thing? The first option seems to deny individuality and free will, and the second is rather unrealistic. (Some may argue that the latter is not unrealistic since in the real world there is only a finite set of choice options which eliminates the possibility of complete individuality.)

In order to understand the methodological role of individualism we need to consider a key question: is it possible to construct an individualistic explanation which is not psychologistic? Or, similarly, is it possible to be in favor of individualism while at the same time being against psychologism? To answer these questions we need first to examine the nature of psychologism, then we will be able to consider Popper's alternative form of methodological individualism which denies psychologism.

Psychologism

Psychologism is primarily a basis for explaining the behavior of both individuals and social institutions and as such it can too easily be made a part of a specification of the second main item on the neoclassical hidden agenda. Along these lines, psychologism might be considered a mere arbitrary reductionist program in that it may only provide the minimum conditions for the acceptability of any given theory. Although it does make methodological individualism a reductionist program and it does specify an acceptable set of exogenous variables - only psychological states and natural constraints to be allowed - this narrow conception of psychologism as a convenient methodological tool would seem to us to be a bit superficial. Reliance on psychologism is more than a methodological ploy to solve the Problem of Conventions because psychologism implicitly involves a specific theory of society and the individual.

The basis of psychologism is a theory that there is something which all individuals have in common. The common element is sometimes called 'Human Nature'. The accepted view of what constitutes Human Nature has changed considerably over the last two hundred years. Today, it is merely asserted that all individuals are governed by the same 'laws' of psychology. In its simplest form psychologism would have us believe that any two individuals facing exactly the same situation would behave in exactly the same way. With simple psychologism, whenever two people are behaving differently, they must be facing different situations. In this light it would appear that, as a program of explanation, simple psychologism is very versatile; it can serve as the basis for Freudian psychoanalysis [Popper, 1945/66, ch. 25], for anthropological explanations of the differences between primitive tribes [Jarvie, 1964], and even for economics [Stigler and Becker, 1976].

Although psychologism would seem to be a straightforward specification of methodological individualism, in its simple form, surprisingly, it actually precludes individuality! Methodologically speaking, simple psychologism allows differences between the choices of individuals to be explained only in terms of the differences between the nature-given situations facing the two individuals. All individuals are, in effect, identical. Obviously, simple psychologism does beg an important philosophical question. If everyone were governed by the same psychological 'laws', what would be the basis of individuality?[1]

It is interesting to note that even though neoclassical theories are usually based on psychologism, they seem to have overcome this last question by being able to have it both ways. (However, they do so by stopping short of complete reduction.) Consider demand theory. Individuality is preserved by saying that individuals can have any utility function they wish. However, psychologism is also preserved by saying that all individuals' utility functions do have one common feature. Every utility function exhibits a negatively sloped marginal utility curve.[2] Although the slopes of their respective marginal curves must all be negative, the individual utility functions differ in that there is an unlimited number of possible (negative) magnitudes for the slopes of their marginal curves. Thus it would seem that there is wide scope for individuality, yet the essential commonality for the purposes of psychologistic economic theory is still provided. Again, it is the combination of universal constraints (natural givens) and psychological differences that is the basis of neoclassical explanations constructed in accordance with psychologism. However, one might wonder whether psychologism is actually a necessary element in neoclassical theory. We shall argue that it is not.

Psychologism is very versatile. In the short run it satisfies the needs of Conventionalism in that it provides at least one criterion for the acceptability of alternative theories or models in terms of the prescription of acceptable exogenous variables. In the longer-run perspective of Pareto or Mill it also focuses on one source of atomistic facts in order to imitate inductive science. It is unlikely that anyone ascribes to this long-run perspective anymore. Instead, we shall argue that psychologism is retained because it is a part of the Conventionalist program to deal with the Problem of Induction.

Sophisticated psychologism

As long as neoclassical economics is based on a reductive methodological individualism, some form of psychologism must be retained to stop a possible infinite regress. But, as we explained above, there is a problem with simple psychologism, as it seems to deny individuality in order to satisfy the methodological needs of reductionism. That neo-classical economics is an intellectually impressive solution to the problem of simple psychologism is not widely recognized. Instead, those who recognize that there is a problem with simple psychologism can opt for a more sophisticated form of psychologism.

The most common sophisticated alternative to simple psychologism merely denies the uniformity of Human Nature and instead claims that there are different types of people. Thus, when two individuals face the same situation but respond differently, one could explain the difference as the result of the two individuals being of different psychological types. Sometimes people will be said to have different 'mentalities', which amounts to the same thing.

This form of psychologism is probably the most widely accepted today. It is used to explain all sorts of happenings. There are supposedly many different types of individual. For example, there are 'criminal mentalities', 'extroverts', 'introverts', 'artistic types', 'mathematical minds', and so on. The methodological basis of Thomas Kuhn's famous book *The Structure of Scientific Revolutions* relies on a form of sophisticated psychologism. Kuhn presumes that the reason why the structure of science is different from other disciplines is that scientists have a different mentality [1971, pp. 143ff.].

Unfortunately, sophisticated psychologism, while allowing for individuality, opens the door to an infinite regress. Instead of asserting the existence of a Human Nature consisting of a uniform psychological type (e.g., a set of needs shared by everyone), sophisticated psychologism asserts a set of possible categories of types. One of the more sophisticated forms says that there is a hierarchy of needs and that people differ only because they rank them differently [e.g., Maslow, 1954]. Given a finite number of needs, there would then be a finite (but larger) number of possible rankings to use to explain differences between individuals. For example, if there were three human needs, then there would be six possible rankings and hence six different types of individuals.

The key issue concerning the existence of Human Nature is whether or not there is something uniformly attributable to all individuals. If we try to avoid simple psychologism by saying there are many different psychological types, then to complete a reductive use of psychologism we would have to explain why people are of different psychological types. This immediately leads to an infinite regress which can be stopped only by asserting the existence of some deeper uniform attribute of Human Nature. In other words, a reductive methodological individualism based on psychologism can only lead to some form of simple psychologism. Otherwise, it is completely arbitrary.

Institutions and the aims of individuals

We mentioned earlier that the key question for the explanatory problem of methodological individualism is the explanatory relationship
between institutions and individual decision-makers. This is also the
key question for distinguishing the individualism usually presumed in
neoclassical theory from the version which Popper offered in his book
The Open Society and its Enemies. The relationship between Popper's
version of individualism and other forms, as well as the relationship
between individualism and holism, was developed by his student
Joseph Agassi [1960, 1975]. In order to understand the nature of
psychologism, the Popper-Agassi alternative view will be presented in
this section.

The central feature of psychologistic individualism is its insistence
that only individuals can have aims and that aims are considered
psychological states. Popper and Agassi reject the identification of
aims and psychological states. Individuals do have aims, but they need
not be psychologically given. Aims may be changed, yet at any point in
time they may still be givens. If any individual treats an institution as a
constraint, then institutions must be included in the set of permissible
exogenous variables. Thus, Popper and Agassi reject the limitation on
acceptable exogenous variables. Institutions are to be included among
the explanatory variables along with the aims of individuals. It is for
this reason that Popper's alternative is called 'institutional individualism'. Unlike psychologistic individualism, institutional individualism
is not necessarily a reductionist research program. The existence of
given institutions in any explanation is not a threat to its individualism.
Institutions are still the creations of individuals - e.g., creations of past
decisions of individuals - yet, for the purpose of real-time decision-
making, some institutions have to be considered as given [Newman,
1976, 1981].

To some observers, institutional individualism may appear to be
either a paradox or an impossibility. But such a perception might only
betray their belief in the reductionist version of individualism. Nevertheless, there is something missing. How can a minimally satisfactory
Popper-Agassi explanation consider institutions as givens and yet
consider them to be creations of individual decision-makers? Neither
Popper nor Agassi has answered this question.

For students of Marshall's neoclassical economics, however, the
answer to this question is rather simple. The overlooked element is
'time'. In any particular real-time situation, institutions are included in
the list of 'givens' simply because any one individual decision-maker
cannot change all of them [Newman, 1981]. In fact, in many cases it is
easier for individuals to change their aims than to alter some of their
givens. In some cases it is simply not possible to change some of the

givens. In other cases, the individuals have chosen not to change some of them. In other words, the exogeneity of some givens may be a matter of the decision-maker's choice. No two individuals may choose to face the same situation. Even if they did, they may choose to have different aims. Stating this in terms more consistent with neoclassical economics, there is no reason to consider psychological states as givens, since sometimes they, too, may be a matter of choice.

Individualism as an Explanatory Problem

Institutional individualism is an interesting perspective for the study of neoclassical research programs for the following reasons. On the one hand, institutional individualism can be a way of dealing with the explanatory problem of methodological individualism without having to endorse psychologism. On the other hand, psychologism is not a *necessary* attribute of neoclassical theory. Specifically, if we strip away the psychologism that is traditionally presumed in neoclassical economics, we will find an approach to explanation that comes very close to that promoted by Alfred Marshall in his *Principles*. In Marshall's short run, virtually all variables but the quantities of labor and output are fixed and given. In the longer run, more things are variable (and, thus, subject to choice), but there are still some things, such as 'social conditions' or the 'character' of some individuals, that take generations to change [Marshall, 1926/64, p. 315, and Book VI] - we might even say that things that are 'fixed' are merely things which take an infinity of time to change [Hicks, 1979]. It is unfortunate that his optimistic Victorian view that even personal character was not immutable was lost somewhere along the way. This raises an interesting methodological question: why has psychologism - which has its origins in Hume's Romantic accommodation of the Problem of Induction - been able to survive even the overwhelming dominance of Marshall's Victorian economics?

Explanation and rational decision-making
The reason why psychologism survives is that it is supported by the common presumption that rationality is a psychological process. This presumption, in turn, has a tradition based on a belief that Hume was able to overcome the Problem of Induction [see Popper, 1972, ch. 1]. It is also supported by the older view that rational decision-making must in some way involve inductive rationality.

As Popper explains, Hume's 'solution' to the Problem of Induction (and the 'problem with induction') is to say that although there is no objective inductive rationality, there is a subjective one which allows people to think inductively. In other words, people do things in their heads which they cannot do on paper. This psychologistic view of rationality led to a long history of attempts to understand the psychological processes of knowing and learning.

Surprisingly, this psychologistic view of rationality is even accepted by the many critics of the use of the assumption of rational decision-making in economics [e.g., Shackle, 1972; Simon, 1979]. These critics do not deny the psychologistic view of rationality; instead they deny the possibility of collecting sufficient facts to acquire inductively the knowledge necessary to make a rational decision. In other words, they do not deny Inductivism, only the feasibility of inductive knowledge. This leads them to argue that neoclassical economics is wrong in assuming that individuals are maximizers, since the supposedly needed inductive knowledge of the successful decision-maker is a practical impossibility. If one were to deny Inductivism, then their critiques lose their force [see Boland, 1981b].

How can one explain behavior on the basis of rational decision-making without endorsing or presuming either Inductivism or a psychologistic view of rationality? This is a problem which has not been dealt with in economics, but it will have to be if economists are going to avoid the criticisms of Simon and Shackle or give Popper's views more than a superficial gloss.

The view that rationality is a psychological process is a relic of the late eighteenth century. Even today, it is still commonplace to distinguish humans from other animals on the basis that humans can be rational. Thus any criticism of a psychologistic view of rationality might be considered dangerous. Nevertheless, the psychologistic view is based on a simple mistake. It confuses one's *argument* in favor of an individual's decision with the *process* of making the decision. It also confuses being rational with being reasonable - the latter only implies the willingness to provide reasons for one's actions. The reasons may not always be adequate.

The case against psychologistic rationality is rather straightforward. Simply stated, humans cannot be rational - only arguments can be rational. An argument is rational only if it is not logically inconsistent (i.e., only if it does not violate the axioms of logic [see Boland, 1979a]). But, most important, whether an argument is rational can be decided independently of the process of its creation or the psychological state of its creator. Since there is no inductive logic, our knowledge of the process of creating a theoretical argument cannot provide the argument with logical validity if it is one which is otherwise invalid. Popper puts it quite simply, 'what is true in logic is true in psychology' [Popper, 1972, p. 6]. Psychologistic rationality cannot be more than what is provided by logical arguments. Thus, any discussion of rational decision-making need not involve psychology. So we ask again, why is psychologism still commonly accepted?

Psychologism and induction in the long run
There is one important reason why the adherence to both psychologism and Inductivism never presents a problem in neoclassical economics. It is simply that neoclassical models liberally use long-run analysis. A reductive psychologistic individualist explanation is successful *only if* all non-individualistic exogenous variables can be made endogenous (i.e., explained), leaving only natural constraints or psychological states (i.e., individuals). In neoclassical economics, a variable is endogenous only if it can be shown to be the consequence of a maximizing choice. If a variable is an externally fixed constraint, it cannot be a matter of choice. Thus, a minimum requirement for maximization is that the object of choice be representable as a variable point on a continuum [Lancaster, 1966]. This would mean that all short-run constraints which are neither natural nor psychological givens must eventually be explained. If one allows sufficient time, then everything can be changed. Thus, it is easy to see that in the long run - when everything (except the permitted exogenous variables) is variable and thus subject to maximizing choice decisions - reductive psychologistic individualism is at least possible.

The same claim could have been made for induction. If we allow a sufficiently long time, perhaps all the facts needed for an inductive proof might be found. We must remember, though, that whenever 'a sufficiently long time' really means an infinity of time, we are dealing with an impossibility. One way to say some task is impossible is to say that it would take an infinity of time to complete it. Conversely, if we do not mean an infinity of time, then it is an open question whether all the facts have been provided or whether no counter-facts exist anywhere. In other words, in the long run the Problem of Induction is non-existent.

Individualism as an Agenda Item

We can now attempt to explain why individualism is an item on the hidden agenda of neoclassical economics. The explanation we will give is that individualism is on the agenda because it has been viewed as a means of providing the basis for a long-run inductive research program. Perhaps it may be possible to identify other reasons for being in favor of an individualist theory of society but, it will be argued, they only add support. This is to say, it is possible to be in favor of an individualist society without advocating an Inductivist view of explanations - but without Inductivism the individualist view may seem rather weak.

It would appear, then, that Blaug was correct in identifying the methodological individualism of neoclassical economics as a reductionist research program. However, reductive methodological individualism is inherent not in neoclassical theory but only in the aims of individual neoclassical theorists. In effect, neoclassical theory is an institution which has its own aims - namely, to demonstrate that it is possible to view society as the consequence of decisions made only by individuals. It does not necessarily have the same aims of some neoclassical theorists - for example, of those who wish to show that society is the consequence of decisions which logically follow only from the psychological states of individual decision-makers and that there is no need for holistic ideologies.

Attempting to explain the nature of neoclassical theory as that of an institution raises all of the questions we have been discussing in this chapter. For our explanation of neoclassical economics to be correct, must we argue that neoclassical economics is an epiphenomenon reflecting only what individual economists do, or are we allowed to argue that neoclassical economics has a life of its own, which is independent of what particular economists do? We see immediately, then, that the explanation we are offering still may not satisfy those who only accept reductive (i.e., psychologistic) individualist explanations.

Individualism as Inductivism
When explaining why individualism is on the agenda of neoclassical economics, we must be careful to distinguish between the general research program of any neoclassical theory and the specific research program of individual neoclassical theorists. Since our primary concern in this book is to understand the methodology of neoclassical economics, we should only be concerned with the specification of neoclassical research programs. So how do we accommodate the specific aims of individual economists? Was Jacob Viner correct when he (supposedly) said, 'Economics is what economists do'?

Can economics be something other than exactly what contemporary economists do? If we are limited to a reductive individualist explanation of the institution of neoclassical economics, then we would have to agree with Viner. Furthermore, it would seem, if we wish to learn anything about neoclassical economics we will have to form our conclusions only from specific examples of what economists do. That is to say, reductive individualist explanations can only be inductive explanations.

A reductive individualist explanation of the nature of neoclassical economics (such as Viner's) raises certain questions. If we find some 'economist' who is not behaving as other economists do, must we question whether that person really is an economist? How do we decide? Which came first, the nature of neoclassical economics or the behavior of neoclassical individual economists? Such questions arise whenever one is bound by the reductive individualist research program. One could instead choose to explain institutions according to that which is allowed by a non-reductive program such as institutional individualism. Given that neoclassical economics existed before most of today's neoclassical economists were born, it would be possible to argue that neoclassical economics continues to follow reductive individualism only because today's economists choose to accept such a hidden agenda as their exogenous guide. (Perhaps this is because no individual neoclassical economist could ever hope to change the *hidden* agenda in his or her lifetime.) In this sense, neoclassical economics is an exogenous element whenever the individual economist is choosing a specific research program.

The only thing at issue, then, is whether reductive individualism is an *essential* element of neoclassical methodology. To decide this we would need to determine whether or not the conclusions of today's neoclassical economics require reductive individualism. If the conclusion of any neoclassical article can be shown to be independent of any reductive individualism - e.g., it may presume the existence of exogenous non-individualistic variables other than natural constraints - then we will have to conclude that reductive individualism is not essential. For now we will leave this question open (alternatively, see Newman [1981]).

Now we assert, perhaps perversely, that the methodological individualist agenda item of neoclassical economics is, as Blaug claims, a reductionist version. However - and this is where we are perverse - the reason why it is a reductionist version is not because neoclassical economists or neoclassical economics are essentially Inductivist but only because economists have not endeavored to purge the unnecessary Inductivist and reductionist elements in neoclassical economics. In other words, neoclassical economics is based on reductive methodological individualism by default.

This view only raises another question. Why have economists not purged the reductive individualism and instead adopted the more modest individualism which Marshall was promoting (which simply accepts short-run non-individualist and non-natural constraints such as the amount of physical capital)? The answer to this question is the key to our argument here. Reductive individualism has not been purged because it is thought to be the means of providing the 'atoms' or minimal facts from which one is to 'induce' the 'laws of economics'. Supposedly, if one knew the utility functions of all individual consumers in society and the production functions of all individual firms in society then, given only the natural constraints (e.g., resource endowments), we could derive (and thus explain) all prices, quantities, and institutions. Few neoclassical economists would disagree with such a supposition. However, they might admit that obtaining all the necessary knowledge is a virtual impossibility. But again, this admission may only reflect a belief in the necessity of induction. In short, neoclassical economics today is based on reductive individualism because economists have not yet chosen to reject the need to deal with the Problem of Induction.

Psychologism and Conventionalism

As we have argued above, economists not only accept the reductive individualist research program, but they compound this when they also accept psychologism by the identification of individuals with their respective utility functions, that is, with their respective psychological states. We argue that since individualism is too often presumed only for the philosophical purposes of dealing with the Problem of Induction, we need to examine the role psychologism plays in the individualist agenda item.

Again we have to be perverse. On the one hand, psychologism is accepted because it facilitates a reductive individualist research program to deal with the Problem of Induction. On the other hand, psychologism is also accepted as an arbitrary means of solving the Problem of Conventions, as we explained in Chapter 1. It may seem that psychologism is being used to solve contradictory problems, since Conventionalism is considered an alternative to Inductivism. But there is no contradiction here. Conventionalism is based on Inductivism in the following sense. Conventionalism accepts the impossibility of an inductive proof of the truth of any theory. Another way of stating this is that Conventionalism accepts that an inductive proof would require an infinity of time to complete. Thus, in the short run, Conventionalism attempts to establish rules of acceptance for choosing between competing theories. Invoking psychologism provides one of the rules of acceptance, namely, that the allowable exogenous variables in any acceptable theory must not include any givens other than the natural givens and the psychological states of the individuals. Other variables may be temporarily fixed (e.g., institutional constraints) but not exogenous. That is, it must be possible to explain them, in principle, by allowing for an artificial passage of time. But true to Conventionalist principles, any choice based on an hypothetical passage of time cannot be construed as a proof.

This point needs to be stressed in order to understand the role of psychologism. As explained in the last section, if we were to allow for an infinity of time, induction might not be impossible. If we were to allow for an infinity of time, then all artificial, non-individualist constraints could be relaxed so that the only exogenous givens would be individualist variables. In other words, in the very long run both Inductivism and psychologism would be feasible. However, no one could claim that a long-run argument constitutes an *inductive* proof. Rather, what is provided by long-run arguments (which are consistent with psychologism and Inductivism) is only a demonstration of the hypothetical possibility of an inductive proof and a complete reduction to psychological states. In other words, fixed non-individualist constraints are allowable in the short run only if it can be demonstrated that it is the *natural* shortness of the run which alone explains their fixity. Such a demonstration is provided by every long-run model.

To a great extent, then, given that Conventionalism does not allow proofs of absolute truth, psychologism would seem to be a successful, albeit arbitrary, means of solving the Problem of Conventions. By legislating psychological states as the only accepted set of non-natural exogenous variables, we are allowing conditional explanations to avoid the infinite regression that would seem to be required of an absolutely true explanation. By taking psychologism and Conventionalism as methodological givens, we are never expected to explain the individual's psychological state.

Notes to Chapter 2

1. At first the possibility of two identical situations would seem unlikely, but what about identical twins? Surely we could test the plausibility of simple psychologism by examining the behavior of identical twins. Could we use identical twins to test whether an individual's psychological make-up is truly exogenous - that is, not influenced by non-psychological, environmental factors? For many years it was believed that the exogeneity of psychology had been established using identical twins. Specifically, it was claimed that identical twins are bound to be identical in everything, including psychological make-up. Thus, if a pair of twins were separated at birth but were later reunited and given the same test (e.g., for IQ) they would score the same despite having lived separately in different environments. Supposedly, this had even been established by extensive scientific analysis. As it turned out, the evidence had been falsified [Kamin, 1974; Hearnshaw, 1979]. Of course, psychologism would never fail this test, since advocates could always explain away differences as being the results of the practical problem of actually presenting the identical twins with exactly the same test situation. So a test of simple psychologism now seems impossible.

2. Or any logical equivalent not based on calculus concepts.

PART II

METHODOLOGY IN NEOCLASSICAL ECONOMIC THEORY

3

Psychologism vs.
Disequilibrium Models

---

it really is assumed ... that what you see when you look
out the window is an economy in ordinary general
equilibrium....
This view has obvious (and intended) affinities to
nineteenth-century economic thought, Say's Law, and
all that. Like that tradition, the new equilibrium school
faces a basic problem: how can it account for the 'obvious' large-scale divergences from equilibrium that we
think we see, especially in prolonged depressions?
Robert Solow [1979, p. 341]

Every explanation of economic crises must include the
assumption that entrepreneurs have committed errors.
But the mere fact that entrepreneurs do make errors can
hardly be regarded as a sufficient explanation of crises.
Erroneous dispositions which lead to losses all round will
appear probable only if we can show why entrepreneurs
should all simultaneously make mistakes in the same
direction. The explanation that this is just due to a kind
of psychological infection or that for any other reason
most entrepreneurs should commit the same avoidable
errors of judgement does not carry much conviction. It
seems, however, more likely that they may all be equally
misled by following guides or symptoms which as a rule
prove reliable. Or, speaking more concretely, it may be
that the prices existing when they make their decisions
and on which they had to base their views about the
future have created expectations which must necessarily
be disappointed. In this case we might have to distinguish
between what we may call justified errors, caused by the
price system, and sheer errors about the course of external events.
Friedrich Hayek [1933/39]

The Current Problem-Situation of Neoclassical Theory

We have been arguing that all neoclassical research programs are based on a hidden agenda consisting of two main items. One is the acceptance of the need to deal with the so-called Problem of Induction either directly or, what is more common, indirectly by dealing with its variant, the Problem of Conventions. The other item is the requirement of methodological individualism - that every explanation must assume that only individuals make decisions. However, we also pointed out that at present neoclassical theory is based on a reductive version of methodological individualism - specifically, one which identifies the individuals with their exogenous psychological states (such as their given utility functions). The strict reliance on the reductive version - that is, on psychologistic individualism - always presents a general problem of explanation which we have called the problem of simple psychologistic individualism: if everyone is governed by the same laws of psychology, then there is no psychological basis for individuality. We noted that neoclassical theory provides a solution to this problem by restricting the laws of psychology to only that which specifies that everyone faces diminishing marginal utility (or its equivalent). This solution allows people to have different utility functions; hence it provides a means of solving the more general explanatory problem of methodological individualism as well as the Problem of Conventions. The reductive methodological individualism of neoclassical economics accepts only models which exclude all exogenous variables except psychological states and natural givens.

We thus note that the two agenda items are not independent, as the latter one is sustained partly because it supports the former. That is, it would be difficult for most neoclassical economists to give up their reliance on psychologistic individualism and their solution to the problem of simple psychologism because that would entail the lack of a means of dealing with the Problem of Conventions. Furthermore, this difficulty is compounded by the fact that most neoclassical economists take the Problem of Conventions for granted; hence it is difficult to see that there may be a need to deal with any of these problems.

It is not our job to form a final judgement or 'methodological appraisal' of the existing neoclassical research program, as some might wish [e.g., Blaug, 1980]. Instead, our purpose is to establish a clear understanding of what neoclassical economics is rather than to determine what some philosophers think it should be. We also wish to examine what practicing economists think economics should be while recognizing that they may not all share the same view. Although some of what we shall argue is critical of certain aspects of some neoclassical models, we do not intend to present a destructive criticism of neoclassical economics. If we did intend a destructive criticism at this stage, we would immediately set about eliminating the Problem of Induction, which would appear to eliminate the more impressive aspects of neo-classical theory. But our purpose is quite different. In particular we wish to understand the methodological nature and purpose of existing neoclassical research programs which accept the items on the hidden agenda, and thus for our purposes we have to take the two items as givens. Besides, as we shall argue, *although the hidden agenda is necessary for the explanation of neoclassical methodology, it is not necessary for neoclassical economic theories.*

When we say that we take the hidden agenda items as givens it does not mean that we are thereby accepting them. On the contrary, we shall be arguing that, paradoxically, it is the acceptance of the two items which gives rise both to the many theoretical problems that avant-garde economists find fascinating and to the obstacles which block their solution.

We will begin by considering the neoclassical research programs which are based on the acceptance of the neoclassical solution to the problem of simple psychologistic individualism - e.g., those which are based on the view that the only psychological law affecting all indi-viduals is the negative slope of their marginal utility curves and that individuality is provided by there being an infinity of utility curves satisfying this requirement. Although we have argued before that psychologistic individualism is accepted by some 'conservative' metho-dologists because it is viewed as one way of providing the 'atoms' for a long-run inductive science, we shall postpone consideration of the direct effects of the Problem of Induction until Chapter 4. Instead, we will examine the short-run theoretical consequences of attempting to deal with the Problem of Conventions within the confines of the problem of simple psychologism.

The Price System and Psychologistic Individualism

By saying that neoclassical economics is based on psychologistic indi-vidualism, we are saying specifically that neoclassical theories or analyses must permit only two types of exogenous variable: natural constraints and psychological states. Of particular concern is the psychologistic individualist requirement that no social institution that appears in our explanations must be allowed to play the role of an exogenous given. For reference, let us call this particular requirement the 'problem of social institutions'. Specifically:

The *problem of social institutions* is: how do we assure that every institution which is introduced as a given in the short-run (or partial

equilibrium) version of a model can be explained in terms that
include only the exogenous variables permitted in the long-run (or
general equilibrium) version of the model?

The Price system as a social institution

To begin, let us consider what Schumpeter noted: 'prices are obviously
social phenomena' [1909]. What does this mean? Does this mean that
the price system is an exogenous social institution? Or is it merely an
epiphenomenon of the psychological states of the individuals in society? If, as required by psychologistic individualism, it is only an epiphenomenon, then it must be true that (1) the actual price system can be
influenced by each individual, and (2) in our explanation of the price
system, the value of all prices can be determined only by reference to
all exogenous variables, namely, the natural givens and the psychological states of *all* individuals.

Condition 1 is the basis for some of the interesting theoretical
questions raised by Kenneth Arrow [1959]. Specifically, in what circumstances is it *possible* for all individuals to be influencing the determination of the market price, yet at the same time for no one individual
alone to determine the actual price and thereby deny the influence of
all other individuals? Arrow argued that condition 1 is satisfied only
when the market is in equilibrium. When the market is in equilibrium
all individuals influence the price by their participation on the demand
side or the supply side, since if they withdrew from either side, the
price would change. Also, in equilibrium no individual can force the
price to change to a specific price other than the value of the equilibrium price, since any effort to do so would cause a disequilibrium. We
see then that according to the neoclassical (i.e., psychologistic) view of
the market determination of actual prices, the individual's 'influence'
on the price level is only indirect or 'unintended'. Given this, all that is
required for the logical adequacy of this view is that the states of all the
permitted exogenous variables do indeed entail a determinant price
system (i.e., all markets are potentially stable). This is the requirement
that for any model of the price system there must exist a solution for the
values of all the prices - i.e., we must be able to provide a so-called
'existence proof' [see Boland, 1970a].

Over the last fifty years the mathematical requirements for any
existence proof have been explored and analyzed in excessive detail, to
the boredom of most economists. Such proofs are no longer the basis
of research programs in economic theory, although it could be argued
that the existing proofs still require too much of the real world [Bo-
land, 1975]. There nevertheless remains an unanswered part of
Arrow's argument. What happens to the methodology of psychologistic individualism when the market is not in equilibrium? Arrow argues

that in order to explain the determination of prices, we violate the requirements of psychologistic individualism, since in order to get the price to return to the equilibrium, at least one individual (i.e., the bidder) must set the price, and that means that at least one individual is determining the price! This observation of Arrow has led to two schools of thought. One argues that we need a theory of 'disequilibrium trading' [e.g. Clower, 1965]; the other argues that we need a neoclassical theory of the individual bidder [Gordon and Hynes, 1970]. Neither school has been completely successful, thus Arrow's challenge still stands.

We shall argue here that the theoretical puzzles based on condition 1 are the direct consequence of the acceptance of the methodological requirements of psychologistic individualism and, in particular, of condition 2 - the requirement that all institutions must be endogenous. It will be easy to see that in any case the problem of social institutions has immediate consequences for our concept of the price system as a social system which *endogenously* coordinates all individuals, and in which they are all presumed to be engaged in independent, rational decision-making.

The concept of a social institution is not often specified in economic models, although a few writers have discussed some of the important attributes of institutions from the perspective of neoclassical models [Buchanan and Tullock, 1962; Davis and North, 1971]. An obvious example might be the legislated 'ground rules' that define property rights. Generally, it is accepted that institutions exist potentially to constrain all individual decision-makers. But what makes institutional constraints important is that they are not naturally given but have themselves been created by other individuals acting in concert. That any institution may effectively constrain only one individual is not the issue here; rather, the issue is that its existence is dependent on the activities of many individuals, including any individuals who may be constrained by the institution.

In order to distinguish institutions from individual actions in the most general terms, we are saying that any constraint, the establishment of which requires the implicit or explicit participation of many individuals, is in some sense an institution. For this reason, some economists might consider a system of all market-determined prices to be an institution whose function is to provide the decision-maker with a 'summary of information about the production possibilities, resource availabilities and preferences of all other decision-makers' [Koopmans 1957, p. 53]. In the neoclassical market everyone faces the same price, and in this way the price is an institution with which individuals' social behavior can be coordinated.

Individualism vs. coordination

Methodologically speaking, the neoclassical theorist cannot rest until it is shown that the nature of any institution is what it is only because people have directly or indirectly chosen that it should be what it is [Boland, 1979b]. Recognizing the price system as an institution is interesting in this sense because the price system serves a dual purpose. On the one hand, it has to be *responsive* (no matter how small the degree) to every individual's psychological state and, on the other, it has to be a relatively *stable* signal indicating to every individual decision-maker the wishes of every other individual in society. How can a social institution serve such a dual purpose? How can something be both volatile (i.e., responsive) and stable?

To answer these questions, we need to understand the neoclassical conception of market-equilibrium prices (i.e., socially coordinated prices). Specifically, we need to understand how prices would have to be determined in a neoclassical model in a manner consistent with psychologistic individualism. As Arrow argued, in a consistent neoclassical model, prices are determinant only when the influences of *all* individuals are, in some non-accidental way, *in balance*. But, as suggested by Koopmans, if prices are to fulfill the requirements of a social institution, not only must we assure the possibility of such a balance being a stable institution, but that balance must *also* be an *equilibrium*. That is, any accidental disturbance of the balance will be corrected without the extraordinary influence of any one individual or institution. Any going price will be the one price at which the influence of individuals (through their willingness to demand or supply some of that good) are in balance. What the existence of an equilibrium implies is the following. The going (observable) price of a good is not an accidental price. It is not accidental because had it been higher or lower there would have been *reasons* for it to return to the balancing price [see further, Boland, 1977b].

Unfortunately, an existence proof does not usually provide behavioral reasons for the occurence of an equilibrium. All of the mathematical studies concerning existence proofs have only assured the existence of a possible *balance* (for example, as a solution of a system of simultaneous equations representing demand and supply functions). Nothing more was intended [Hahn, 1973]. The question still may be open as to whether a potential balance is also an equilibrium. To many, the distinction between a balance and an equilibrium may not appear to be very significant because in economics textbooks the concept of equilibrium is often confused with that of a balance. But the distinction is essential to an understanding of avant-garde theoretical research programs.

To understand this distinction, consider a coin balanced on its edge.

If it is tilted slightly to either side, its physical position will permanently change. That is, there is no reason for the coin to bring itself back into the original upright balance. Textbooks would say that this is an unstable equilibrium, but, more correctly, it is an unstable balance - the concept of an unstable equilibrium is self-contradictory. Similarly, textbooks would say that an equality between supply and demand is an equilibrium when actually it is only a balance. For an equilibrium, more is required.

If there are reasons why a balance is not accidental (e.g., if it is the result of competition), then those reasons imply that the balance is stable, i.e., it is an equilibrium. In neoclassical theory this is of particular importance to the concept of equilibrium prices. The equilibrium price can be thought to be determined by the reasons which guarantee that demand and supply will be in balance, because these are the reasons which guarantee the existence of a stable balance. But to accommodate psychologistic individualism, the reasons must be related to individuals' psychological states.

Equilibrium and psychologism

Now let us consider how the acceptance of psychologistic individualism affects the neoclassical concept of a market equilibrium. The psychologistic individualist explanation of equilibrium goes as follows. On the basis of a posited relationship between the quantity demanded of a good and its going market price, and of a posited relationship between the quantity supplied of that good and the *same* going price, the equilibrium price will of necessity be the one price that brings into balance these two quantities as an unintended consequence of competition. What that price will be depends on the two posited relationships. Generally, if either relationship changes, the result will be a new equilibrium price. It is the sensitivity of the demanded (or supplied) quantity's relationship to the price which assures the responsiveness of the equilibrium price to changes in individual psychological states. In neoclassical theory the relationship is merely a consequence of maximization based on given utility functions. Changes in the psychological state of any individual must have some effect on the equilibrium price (even though, when there are many individuals, the result may appear to be negligible) if psychologistic individualism is to be maintained.

Formally, one part of the psychologistic individualist explanation is easy to provide. As we have just stated, the relationship between the quantity demanded (or supplied) by any individual is asserted to be the consequence of maximization (i.e., rational decision-making). One aspect of maximization is that its consequences are usually determinant (and non-arbitrary); that is, it leads to a unique quantity for any given price (for the given budget). If we are given the going price, then theoretically we can calculate the quantity demanded and supplied for any good. If there is a discrepancy between the quantities demanded and supplied, then it must be the case that at least one individual is not maximizing! For example, for the usual case in which the demand curve is negatively sloped and the supply curve is positively sloped, if the price were lower than that which would clear the market, then the transacted quantity must be less than the quantity which would maximize every individual's utility (at that price). In other words, whenever the market is not in equilibrium not all individuals can be maximizing according to their psychologically given utility functions (recognizing that a profit function is also the result of a psychological desire to maximize profits or to survive [Alchian, 1950]).

Equilibria and incentives
This point needs to be stressed, since it is the center of the methodological problem facing many theorists today. *The neoclassical theory that all individuals are maximizers can be true only if all markets are in equilibrium*. For an equilibrium to exist, there cannot be any incentive for individuals to change their behavior, that is, change their choices. If an incentive does exist, then we would have to explain why it has not been pursued. If the individual chose not to pursue it, it could not have been an incentive. If the individual is in any way constrained from pursuing it, then additional constraints must be included among the exogenous variables of our explanation. This leads to the central theoretical problem of neoclassical economics today. How can there be any disequilibria? Would anyone choose a state of disequilibrium?

Before discussing the methodological problems of disequilibria, let us be clear about the more elementary relationship between equilibria and incentives. Basically, a true equilibrium says that all possible gains from trade or from adjustments to behavior have been exhausted. If there were possible gains available, then there would be reasons for change. In a state of market equilibrium there cannot exist any incentives for change. This does not mean that there are no constraints, but only that all operative constraints must be beyond choice.

Psychologism and the World of Adam Smith

Self-interest vs. social optima
For the purposes of psychologistic individualism, it is essential that all incentives be individualist and not social. Consider, for example, the profits of the firm in a competitive economy. We say that excess profits must in the long run be zero. Perhaps from the social point of view this

may be desirable, but to be consistent with psychologistic individual-ism we must not allow social objectives to be imposed on individual firms. Even from the social point of view, profit itself is not necessarily interesting. As Schumpeter pointed out, 'as the rise and decay of industrial fortunes is *the* essential fact about the social structure of capitalist society, both the emergence of what is, in any single instance, an essentially temporary gain, and the elimination of it by the working of the competitive mechanism, obviously are more than "frictional" phenomena, as is that process of underselling by which its achieve-ments result in higher real incomes all round' [1928, pp. 380-1]. The point of Adam Smith's classical vision is that the pursuit of private interest (i.e., 'selfishness') *unintentionally* produces a social good. It does this only in a world of competition where profits are indirectly eliminated. Zero profits are an 'unintended consequence' of the com-bination of profit maximization and competition.

The only individualist incentive we use to explain the behavior of a firm in the short run is the maximization of profits - the difference between total revenue and cost. When costs equal revenue, average cost must equal average revenue. For a profit maximizing firm, howev-er, average cost and revenue is irrelevant *with regard to maximization*. As is well known today, it is marginal revenue and marginal cost that matter.

The firm can respond to its incentives (possible improvements in its profits) in two different ways. Primarily, it can internally and indepen-dently alter its output to adjust its costs and revenue. If it is maximizing its profits, then, of course, marginal revenue must just equal marginal cost. But also, if it is maximizing profits, any increase in output must produce a situation in which marginal cost exceeds marginal revenue. So long as the firm is not incurring losses, there is no incentive for it to change its output. Secondarily, it can also deal with its situation by altering its external situation - but only if there exist other possibilities. If it is making losses (even though it may be minimizing them), it can do nothing to change its situation unless there exist better alternatives. But such contingencies are beyond its control in a competitive eco-nomy. Either a losing firm eventually quits or it switches to another industry. Its decision is a private matter.

The assumption of profit maximization, then, only assures that marginal cost equals marginal revenue. Which of the individualist variables assure the attainment of zero profits? If some firms in one industry are making profits while firms in another are making losses, then there is an incentive for the losing firms to change industries. In doing so the firms entering the profit-making industry only drive the market price down or reduce every other firm's share of the market and, either way, reduce everyone's profits. Even so, the existence of profits is an incentive for individual entrepreneurs to enter. The incentive to enter disappears only when profits are driven down to zero - however unintentionally.

So the individual's pursuit of self-interested profits internally and externally eventually leads to zero profits. But zero profit combined with profit maximization does not necessarily mean that the social goal of optimum resource allocation has been served. Or does it? It does whenever all maximizers are also price-takers.

Social optima as forced, unintended consequences

The allocation of resources is optimum only if there is no possibility of reducing their utilization without reducing outputs. Traditionally, this is illustrated by a U-shaped average cost curve which represents all the possible levels of the cost of the resource used per unit of output. If average cost can be decreased by producing more, then the current output is not efficiently produced. Maximum efficiency in this sense then occurs only at the level of output where average cost is minimum. This is the key to connecting the individual's concerns to the social objective. It is also the key to understanding the role of natural constraints.

Since the individual maximizer is only concerned with marginal values, we need to note an elementary point: the behavior of the average is not independent of its relationship to the margin. Specifically, to cause the average to fall, the margin must be below the average. Similarly, if the average rises, it can only be because the margin is above the average. Thus, with this elementary point in mind, we see that whenever the average is at a true minimum and thus temporarily unchanging with respect to output, the margin equals the average. So, in order to get the firm to use its resources efficiently, we need only have the firm produce where the marginal cost equals the average cost.

But profit maximization, our individualist incentive, only assures the equality of marginal cost with marginal revenue. Similarly, reducing profits to zero only assures that average cost equals average revenue. There is nothing here to bring average and marginal cost into equality. Now here is where the idea that firms (and buyers) are price-takers becomes crucial. If a firm is a price-taker - that is, the price is given and does not change in response to the firm's behavior (such as when there are very many small firms or prices are externally fixed) - then marginal revenue will necessarily equal the average revenue (which is the price). In this special case, if the individual firm's profit is maximized, the price (marginal revenue) will equal its marginal cost. If the individual firm inadvertently causes profits to be reduced to zero, the price (average revenue) will equal its average cost. Thus, indirectly we obtain the desired efficiency; the firm's marginal cost will equal its average cost *without the deliberate action by any individual* in that regard!

Do we need Adam Smith's World?

What has to be seen is that in an individualist world of price-takers (that is, where no one individual or small group can set the price for everyone else), it is the combination of zero profits and profit maximization that implies the achievement of an optimum allocation of resources - maximization of efficiency, so to speak. While we can see that an individual firm might wish to maximize profits, no individual would want to eliminate profits. This is both the perversity and the beauty of Adam Smith's world. No individual has to have zero profits as his or her goal. It is the free pursuit of private interest which, unintentionally, is *sufficient* for the provision of the social good.

Adam Smith's world of greed and virtue

If one examined only the sufficient conditions for an economy which is in a state of psychologistic individualist equilibrium, the beauty of Adam Smith's world would be lost. Surely any entrepreneurs who took a broad perspective (or a course in the principles of economics) would see that the outcome of any promotion of free competition must lead to the situation in which, without further changes in the natural constraints, everyone ends up making no profits beyond the costs of production. With this realization, it is easy to see why some critics of neoclassical theory [e.g., Robinson and Eatwell, 1973] might argue that the real incentive for any entrepreneurs is to restrict competition or eliminate their competitors so as to create so-called monopoly profits. Although they are correct about a realistic world of governmental regulations and patents, this view completely misses the point of Adam Smith's unregulated world.

What Smith's world provides is an incentive for entrepreneurs to alter their technological constraints [see further, Schumpeter, 1942/50]. For example, if we are all in a state of long-run equilibrium - in which everyone's supply price just covers his or her production costs - one way to get ahead is to improve one's technology of production in order to reduce the costs and thereby create short-run profits. The profits will be only short-run gains because in Adam Smith's world, where there are no patents, no marketing boards, etc., other producers will attempt to duplicate the cost-reducing technologies, and in this way everyone (i.e., each consumer) benefits from the original entrepreneur's 'greediness'- so long as free competition prevails. This is how 'virtue' is unintentionally the outcome of greed or 'selfishness' in Adam Smith's world.

Freedom vs. necessity

We have noted that Adam Smith's world is concerned with the sufficiency of free competition when combined with rational decision-making for the achievement of a social optimum. We wish to point out that some neoclassical theorists have also been concerned with its necessity. Hayek [1937/48] specifically wished to show that other world-views (e.g., 'collectivism') were not sufficient. His argument was that exogenous social institutions were informationally inefficient. Specifically, in Adam Smith's world the individual only needs to know his or her own situation (tastes, prices, income, and the location of the market). In the contrasting liberal socialist world, for example, where a central authority may plan the workings of the entire economy, made up of individual but constrained decision-makers, the central authority would have to know the same information but for all individuals!

The primary message of Hayek's view is that if one realizes that all decisions require information and one assumes that the objective of every socialist economy is the achievement of a social optimum, then, if one adopts both psychologistic individualism and Hayek's view that only individuals know what is best for them, the determination of the social optimum must depend on the psychological states of all individuals. Hayek asserts that there is no way a socialist central planner could ever be able to calculate the social optimum in order to implement policies to reach it. What he presumes is that in a psychologistic individualist world there are private facts that affect each individual's view of what is best for him or her. Such private facts are by definition beyond the acquisition of any central planner, yet they are necessary for the calculation of the social optimum. Thus, with Hayek's view, we can see that, *given psychologism*, Adam Smith's world is a necessity, as all other world views would give a role to an exogenous institution which would necessarily have insufficient knowledge to formulate adequate policies.

One has to admit that Adam Smith's view is magnificent, almost magic. But there is no magic here, only simple arithmetic. What is magnificent is the total reliance on individual decision-making. No social institution would seem to be necessary. The final outcome is the result only of the actions of individuals. But there may seem to be a paradox here. The key element to yielding the optimum (beyond maximization) is the inability of one individual firm or consumer to affect the price; that is, competition must be perfect. Nevertheless, individuals are not powerless, since they are allowed to make their personal contribution to supply or demand. The end result is both a social optimum and an equilibrium. All this can exist without any recourse to either non-natural or non-individualist variables or constraints. The only assumption in this neoclassical vision of Adam

Smith's world is that every individual is an independent (i.e., self-interested) maximizer. If one could show that the existing world is possibly an instance of an Adam Smith world in long-run equilibrium, then one would have proven the logical feasibility of a psychologistic individualist research program. But what about the assumption that all decision-makers are price-takers? And how do we know when the world is in long-run equilibrium?

Psychologism and Long-run Equilibria

Equilibrium vs. imperfect competition

Theorists either explain why something exists or they explain it away [cf. Agassi, 1977; Solow, 1979]. For those theorists bound by psychologistic individualism, disequilibria must be explained away. In the absence of constraints, neoclassical theory would argue that an equilibrium must exist, since without constraints universal maximization is entailed. If there is a disequilibrium, then it follows that there must be an operative constraint somewhere. Thus, for psychologistic individualism, it must be shown that what appears to be a disequilibrium is really a chosen event or the consequence of a natural constraint. This is because the only allowable exogenous (i.e., non-chosen) variables are natural constraints and psychological states.

The concept of equilibrium is a contingent proposition. There is a disequilibrium only if there are unexploited gains that *can* be obtained. Is it always a question of assessing the (transactions) cost of obtaining the gains? But, possibly more important, how do we measure the potential gains? Too often the alleged gains are an illusion caused by comparing the existing state with an ideal state. As Coase put it,

> very little analysis is required to show that an ideal world is better than a state of laissez faire, unless the definitions of a state of laissez faire and an ideal world happen to be the same. But the whole discussion is largely irrelevant for questions of economic policy since whatever we may have in mind as our ideal world, it is clear that we have not yet discovered how to get to it from where we are.... [1960, section 10]

The question here is whether the state of *laissez-faire* can be one in which there is imperfect competition. The approach offered by Coase allows us to argue that the ideal world is the one with perfect competition - that is, the one where the achievement of private goals indirectly assures the achievement of social goals. However, it may cost us too much to have that much competition. Imperfect competition may be the realistic *laissez-faire* optimum.

If this approach is taken in order to explain away the disequilibria (relative to the ideal world), then we would need to show that the resulting *laissez-faire* equilibrium (i.e., the imperfectly competitive equilibrium) is the result only of individuals' pursuits of their private interests. The question for us then is: how can an imperfectly competitive equilibrium be seen as a social optimum? To be an equilibrium, there should not be any possibility of an improvement, that is, there should not be any incentive. This is assured only if everyone is maximizing with respect to every variable of choice.

This is where the old problem of increasing returns comes in [cf. Sraffa, 1926]. The textbook diagram of an imperfectly competitive equilibrium clearly shows the firm's profit maximizing output to be at a level where the average cost curve is negatively sloped (i.e., to the left of the bottom of the U-shaped average cost curve). If the output is at such a level, it is possible to reduce the average cost (hence the average use of resource inputs) per unit of output - that is, to reduce the ratio of inputs to outputs. If that ratio can be reduced, then its inverse - the returns for each unit of input - can be increased. This possibility is sometimes called a situation of increasing returns. Any situation in which there are increasing returns would seem to indicate the possibility of reducing costs, which would benefit everyone in society. From the perspective of society, increasing returns imply disequilibria, since the existing potential cost reduction is an unexploited incentive, hence increasing returns imply that we have not yet reached a social optimum. Yet an imperfectly competitive *equilibrium* appears necessarily to entail increasing returns.

Although this is an elementary point of price theory, we must treat it with care. Let us then look again at imperfect competition from the perspective of the individual decision-maker who is supposed to pursue profit maximization. If a firm is an imperfect competitor, then by definition it cannot be a price-taker, since its output decisions affect the price. Whenever the price varies with the level of output, marginal revenue is not equal to the price. Furthermore, since it is always assumed that the demand curves are downward-sloping, marginal revenue is always less than average revenue. Now, keeping this in mind, recognize that profit maximization implies the equality of marginal revenue with marginal cost. If we also recognize that a competitive equilibrium painted in any color implies the absence of excess profits (over the cost of producing the chosen level of output) - the absence of incentives for new firms to enter the competition - then the price must equal average cost. Putting all these implications together means that profit maximization with competitively imposed long-run zero profits does not entail the lowest possible average cost. In particular, since marginal revenue is below the price and since profit maximization means that marginal revenue equals marginal cost, then necessarily marginal cost is below average cost - which means that average cost must be falling (i.e., there are increasing returns) whenever there is an imperfectly competitive *equilibrium*.

The conjunction of these implications forms the textbook picture of an imperfectly competitive equilibrium - a tangency between the demand curve and the average cost curve - and since the demand curve is negatively sloped, so must the average cost curve be downward-sloping. If the average cost curve is necessarily falling for a competitor facing the usual downward-sloping demand curves, then *in equilibrium* there must exist the possibility of reducing average cost further. Thus, whenever there is an imperfectly competitive equilibrium, there appears to be a necessary conflict between the individual decision-maker's optimum (profit maximization) and what might be society's optimum (minimizing average cost).

How can the imperfectly competitive equilibrium ever represent a social optimum? If the individual firms' average cost could be reduced, society would benefit, since the available resources could seem to be made to produce more output for the same input. Thus, the possibility of social benefits (reduced average cost) coexists with the absence of any incentive for the producer to change its behavior, since profits are both maximum and zero. But, on the other hand, if every producer is maximizing profits and profits are zero (and the demand curve reflects utility maximization by all individuals), how can there be any disequilibrium? The common view of an imperfectly competitive equilibrium as a social disequilibrium may be only an illusion created by comparing it to an unrealistic ideal world that nobody really wants. If any imperfectly competitive equilibrium is a *laissez-faire* equilibrium (i.e., the consequence of everyone's pursuit of profit or utility maximization), then there is no disequilibrium (unexploited gains) in the real world.

Imperfect competition vs. psychologistic individualism
Let us consider the implications for possible theories of the imperfectly competitive firm - the firm which either is not a price-taker or has such a large share of the market that its output decisions do affect the price. The general question is: in the long run, when ultimately the firm's profits are driven down to zero but are still maximized for its non-negligible share of the market, can the firm really be considered to be in equilibrium? Following the works of Robinson [1933] and Chamberlin [1934], most textbook theories say yes. But, unlike the perfectly competitive world where anything goes, the imperfectly competitive world seems to be based on an arbitrary institutional assumption that restricts competition. That is, the nature of the market situation has

been exogenously given. Unless the degree of non-perfect competition is explained, it may be an unacceptable given in our explanation. Does this mean that one cannot complete a psychologistic individualist program if one attempts to develop a theory of an imperfect competitor in equilibrium? Or does this merely mean that an imperfectly competitive equilibrium is an illusion and thus that the imperfectly competitive firm is doomed to perpetual disequilibrium? Can an imperfectly competitive firm ever be in equilibrium and thus be explainable?

In order to explain how there can ever be an imperfectly competitive equilibrium, we only need to explain why the possibility of internally reducing average cost would be ignored. The explanation is that if average cost and average revenue are equal and if average revenue will fall faster (rise more slowly) than average cost, then there would be no incentive to reduce cost further. What does this explanation say about the 'apparent' increasing returns? It says that they never really existed or, more generally, that the assessment of costs and benefits is misleading.

This raises an interesting theoretical question. How do we know there are increasing returns? What is the source of the increasing returns? So as to avoid repeating all of the volumes of articles devoted to the puzzle presented by the concept of increasing returns, let us bluntly state the analytical case concerning the existence of increasing returns for a given production function, say f, where f is defined as

$$\text{Output} = f \text{ (labor, capital).} \qquad [1]$$

If we were to double both factors and the result is that the output more than doubles, then we would have a case of 'increasing returns'. But how is it possible for there to be increasing returns? If the doubling process has merely meant building an identical plant next door, what is the source of the increase in output beyond the level of the original plant? Either the source is external or the production function has been misspecified, since there must be some third factor which has been more than doubled to account for the increased output. These two possibilities are really the same thing. Some constraint was not stated in the original production function. It should have been,

$$\text{Output} = f \text{ (labor, capital, } X). \qquad [2]$$

where X is the missing factor. As Harvey Leibenstein would probably say, there could only have been the possibility of increasing returns because one of the factors (namely, X) was previously being used inefficiently; that is, the optimum quantity of X was not chosen. Stated another way, there could be the possibility of increasing returns only because the original plant was not maximizing profits with respect to *all* inputs.

Any attempt to explain the existence of increasing returns only brings into question the true nature of the production function [Samuelson, 1947/65, p. 84]. If everything is variable, then exact duplication is possible; hence no production functions can exhibit increasing returns. If increasing returns are possible, then there must be something constraining the variability of one or more of the factors so as to create the possibility of improving efficiency. But if there is something constraining the factors, then there is something which should have been included in the specification of the production function, that is, a missing factor. If it is not included, then we have the methodological problem prescribed by psychologistic individualism. Any non-natural, non-individualist constraints must be explained away.

Explaining disequilibria away
Attempts to explain imperfectly competitive firms raises the key dilemma facing modern theorists. On the one hand, if one is to fulfill the commitment to the psychologistic individualist program, then there cannot be any unexplained non-natural, non-individualist constraints. That is, there cannot be any disequilibria, since a disequilibrium is only possible because something is constraining the attainment of an equilibrium by constraining universal maximization. On the other hand, if imperfect competition exists, then there is something which is constraining competition, and thus something is left unexplained. Even worse, some may say that an imperfectly competitive equilibrium is still a disequilibrium in terms of perfect competition. Only in a perfectly competitive equilibrium is it possible to fulfill all of the requirements of a psychologistic individualist research program.

The key question here is the following. If we accept that a realistic concept of the existence of disequilibrium implies the existence of an endogenous constraint, do we also have to accept the reverse, namely, that the existence of an endogenous constraint implies the existence of a disequilibrium? If one considers the reverse, then the way is open to explaining away disequilibria. One can simply deny the existence of permanent (long-run) endogenous constraints. And if disequilibria can be explained away, then psychologistic individualism will be a feasible research program.

One way disequilibria are explained away is to show that all non-natural constraints are matters of choice. Thus what appears to be a disequilibrium is really an equilibrium, as there are no real possibilities of improvement [e.g., Coase, 1960]; if there were, they would have been pursued. This way may not appeal to everyone, since this is really an indirect argument that in some way assumes what it is supposedly proving. There is another way which, while more mysterious, is at least direct. It argues that the formal transaction prices do not reflect the actual prices. The actual price is the sum of the formal price and the average cost borne by the *buyer*. For example, many people will wait in a queue to save money at a price-reduction sale. Those who do not wish to wait may go elsewhere and pay a higher price [e.g., DeVany, 1976].

This 'invisible-price' approach can go a long way towards explaining why some may see increasing returns when there really are none. The actual average cost curve may be minimum at the output level corresponding to the textbook's imperfectly competitive long-run equilibrium. The actual demand curve may be perfectly elastic, since all reductions in prices are compensated by offsetting increases in transactions costs. If this is the case, then the formal imperfectly competitive long-run equilibrium is actually a perfectly competitive equilibrium! Even more important is the consequence that the price any individual pays is no longer a social institution. Every individual's actual price is specific to that individual's psychological state concerning willingness to wait. This invisible-price approach gives new meaning to Hayek's view of the impossibility of a successful social planner.

Psychologism in the Short Run

Although in the long run *we* may all be dead, in any long-run equilibrium psychologism and Inductivism live. It is easy to see that psychologism is not jeopardized if we can adopt a view of the world where everything is in long-run equilibrium. Does this mean that if one wishes to build more realistic short-run models, one must abandon the psychologistic individualist research program in favor of a more complicated disequilibrium approach?

The consensus among avant-garde theorists today gives a negative answer to this last question. That is, there seems to be agreement that a realistic short-run neoclassical theory must involve disequilibria that cannot be explained away, yet the requirement of psychologistic individualism must be retained. We would argue that, methodologically, this is self-contradictory - disequilibria imply the existence of non-natural and non-individualist givens, while psychologistic individualism implies only individualist or natural givens. The problem facing contemporary theorists is to find a way either to explain the existence of disequilibria even though individuals are seen to be free to follow only their self-interest or to explain disequilibria away. And so, theorists solve the problem by depending primarily on expectational errors as the prime source of divergences from full equilibrium. Economic agents optimize subject to what they perceive to be their circumstances.... Agents have to form expectations about ... unknown or imperfectly known circumstances. One necessary part of the definition of equilibrium in this kind of world is that those expectations be confirmed, at least in some reasonable statistical sense. The way is now open to explain major departures from equilibrium as mainly the result of unusually large and/or unusually prolonged expectational errors. [Solow, 1979, p. 341]

In the next chapter we shall examine this 'expectational errors' approach to short-run disequilibria. We shall argue that as a solution to the methodological problem of disequilibria it is an illusion, as it is based on the acceptance of Inductivism.

4

Rational Expectations and Theories of Knowledge

Expectations, since they are informed predictions of future events, are essentially the same as the predictions of the relevant economic theory....
The [rational expectations] hypothesis ...[is] that expectations of firms ... tend to be distributed, *for the same information set,* about the prediction of the theory....

John Muth [1961, p. 316, emphasis added]

At the logical level, Benjamin Friedman has called attention to the omission from MREH [macro rational expectations hypothesis] of an explicit learning model, and has suggested that, as a result, it can only be interpreted as a description not of short-run but of long-run equilibrium in which no agent would wish to recontract. But then the implications of MREH are clearly far from startling, and their policy relevance is almost nil. At the institutional level, Stanley Fischer has shown that the mere recognition of long-term contracts is sufficient to generate wage rigidity and a substantial scope for stabilization policies. But the most glaring flaw of MREH is its inconsistency with the evidence: if it were valid, deviations of unemployment from the natural rate would be small and transitory - in which case *The General Theory* would not have been written.... Sargent (1976) has attempted to remedy this fatal flaw by hypothesizing that the persistent and large fluctuations in unemployment reflect merely corresponding swings in the natural rate itself. In other words, what happened in the United States in the 1930s was a severe attack of contagious laziness! I can say that, despite Sargent's ingenuity, neither I nor, I expect, most others at least of the nonmonetarists' persuasion are quite ready yet to turn over the field of economic fluctuations to the social psychologist!

Franco Modigliani [1977, p. 6]

What is really surprising about rational expectations models is that they employ a 500 year-old theory of knowledge and at the same time ignore the 200 year-old refutation of that theory! It is also surprising that although 'expectations' are now considered a central concern of many mainstream theorists, there is virtually no discussion of the theories of knowledge which must support any concept of rational expectations. This is the case even for the critics of rational expectations. Contrary to Benjamin Friedman's view, all models that employ a Rational Expectations Hypothesis do have a theory of learning. Their theory of learning is not discussed simply because it is presumed that everyone understands and accepts it, since there are no recognized alternatives. Specifically, all such models implicitly presume an Inductivist theory of learning. Rational expectations are nothing more than the standard Conventionalist response to the realization that true induction would require an infinity of both time and information.

Knowledge, Expectations and Equilibrium

Knowledge and long-run equilibria

It was noted in Chapter 3 that one of the necessary conditions for (general) market equilibrium is that all demanders and suppliers are maximizing, which implies also that all potential gains from trade are being exploited. It follows then that equilibrium of all markets entails the successful acquisition of *adequate* knowledge for the purposes of maximization.

Now just what constitutes 'adequate knowledge for the purposes of maximization'? Recall Solow's comment, quoted above, that disequilibria are being explained away today by referring to expectational errors. Specifically, he noted that optimization requires the formation of expectations about 'prices that rule in the future, as well as other facts about the future that cannot now be known'. If an individual or firm is ever going to be successful in maximizing utility or profit, the expectations must be correct. Expectational errors lead to failures to maximize. This leads us to ask what constitutes 'expectational errors'? And more perversely, can one ever expect to be able to avoid 'expectational errors'?

Knowledge and learning in the short run

Years ago Hayek argued that since the individual's acquisition of the (true) knowledge of his or her circumstances, the givens, is essential for any (stable) equilibrium, in order to explain how the economy changes over time we must be able to explain how individuals acquire their knowledge [1937/48, p. 47]. Hayek's concern was that there was no (inductive) way to show how any individual could ever acquire true knowledge. Hayek pessimistically confessed his inability to offer an explanation for even one individual's knowledge acquisition process [pp. 47-8]. Explicitly, he admitted that he could not specify 'assertions about causal connections, about how experience creates knowledge' [p. 47]; implicitly, he was merely admitting the impossibility of an inductive proof.

Today, neoclassical theorists are more optimistic. Their optimism is based on the acceptance of Conventionalism (and an ignorance of such things as the paradox of confirmation which we discussed in Chapter 1). Mainstream theorists today do not require that any individual decision-maker have absolutely true knowledge because they would readily admit that inductive proofs have always been impossible. Instead, it would be argued that nobody's knowledge is ever absolutely true but only 'true' according to some degree of probability. Thus, a more moderate view of knowledge would be asserted. Today many theorists would argue that absolutely true knowledge has a probability of 1.00 and that a realistic view of knowledge would say the actual knowledge of any individual or group of individuals has a probability of less than 1.00. Of course, the closer the probability is to 1.00 the better is the knowledge [Malinvaud, 1966]. Given this view of knowledge, it could be argued that learning takes place whenever the probability of one's knowledge is increased - for example, whenever the degree of confirmation has increased.

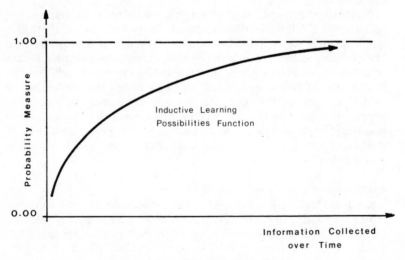

Figure 4.1 *Inductivist learning*

Let us illustrate this view of learning and knowledge with a simple diagram, Figure 4.1, in which the curve indicates that the inferred probability of one's knowledge increases as information is collected. We shall call such a curve the 'inductive learning possibilities function'.

It is a very short further step to argue that the probability of the truth of one's knowledge is like a utility function and that learning is only a matter of maximizing the probability. It is precisely this step that has been taken in the formation of the concept of rational expectations.

The Conventionalist theory of learning

The basis of virtually every neoclassical model that involves the recognition of limited or 'imperfect' knowledge is a Conventionalist theory of knowledge and learning - a theory which is merely a short-run version of the old Inductivist theory of knowledge and learning. When we say every neoclassical model we are including in this claim all models of rational expectations and efficient markets, as well as the theories of imperfect information and uncertainty.

Let us review the Inductivist theory of knowledge and learning which we examined in Chapter 1. Briefly stated, this old theory said that individuals learn by collecting (objectively provable) facts and when they have enough of them they are able to induce the true theory which would explain the phenomena encompassed by those facts. Inductivism, as we have said, presumes that such an inductive process is indeed possible. For any specific case the only question at issue is whether enough facts have been collected, or possibly whether the quality of those facts is adequate, or both.

Now the Conventionalist theory of learning, which we also discussed in Chapter 1, recognized that there really is no way to collect enough facts to prove absolutely the truth of any explanation. Instead, the best we can do is to maximize the quantity of facts collected or improve their quality (which sometimes turns out to be the same thing as collecting more facts). One learns either by improving the empirical support for one's theory or by finding a better theory. Switching to another theory would be considered a case of long-run learning, and improving the support of one's present theory would be considered short-run learning.

The important point to be realized here is that the Conventionalist theory of learning is merely a version of the Inductivist theory. The difference is only that absolute proofs (i.e., where probability equals 1.00) are no longer required. Learning, in a sense, has been quantified. Either one learns directly by collecting *more* information (i.e., information about additional variables deemed to be relevant), or one learns indirectly by collecting *more* secondary facts to improve the estimates contained in the present set of information.

The Conventionalist theory of information and knowledge

This leads to the Conventionalist theory of information. At any point in time, the current knowledge is a specific 'information set' (a collection of empirical hypotheses which summarize all information bits, i.e., all data) used to derive propositions about relevant decision variables [Hirshleifer and Riley, 1979]. The quality of the information in the information set is reflected in specific probabilities of the truth of those hypotheses, and thus the quality of information is a direct function of the quantity of evidence available to support the required information set. Thus 'more information' can mean two different things: either more supporting evidence for the hypotheses included in the present information set or an expansion of the information set to include additional variables and hypotheses.

From the perspective of Conventionalism, knowledge is merely a name which refers to the information set of the decision-maker. Knowledge can never differ from, or be anything more than, what is contained in the information set, which in turn is nothing more than what can be inferred from the available empirical evidence and logical analyses relating to the evidence. The more information we have, the better is our knowledge. For those who speak in terms of probabilities, the more information we have, the higher will be the probability that our knowledge is true because either there is more evidence or there are more ways to relate the evidence. There are some who draw an analogy between information and resources and thereby speak of information being efficient [see Hirshleifer and Riley, 1979]. That is, one information set can be more efficient than another if it provides a higher probability, given the same or a smaller quantity of supporting evidence

We have illustrated this theory graphically in Figure 4.2, in which the curve in Figure 4.1 has been modified by placing the quantity of information for a specific information set (e.g., for a given model of the economy) on the horizontal axis and the probability of our knowledge being true on the vertical. The Conventionalist theory of knowledge posits a specific relationship between these two, which is a monotonically increasing function that increases at a decreasing rate such that it approaches *asymptotically* the horizontal line drawn through the point representing a probability of 1.00. To illustrate the possibility of there being two different information sets (or models), there are two 'inductive learning possibilities functions', one for each information set. Each curve preserves two essential properties of the learning theory presumed in Conventionalism. Each curve is monotonically increasing in order to represent the inductive learning; and the Conventionalist denial of the possibility of inductive proofs is represented by the curve being asymptotic to the horizontal line through

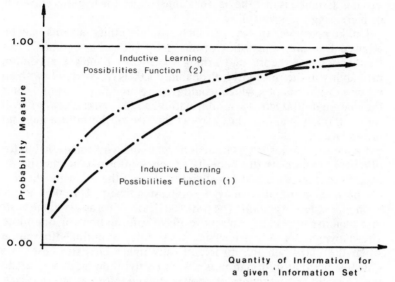

Figure 4.2 *Conventionalist learning*

1.00, which means that the probability can never reach a maximum for any finite amount of information.

The Economics of Knowledge and Information

Once one has put the relationship between the quantity of information and the probability of the truth of knowledge into the context of an input-output relation, the way is open to apply economic analysis to the status and acquisition of knowledge. We will suspend our disbelief in such a relationship for now and instead examine the 'economics of information acquisition'.

Given the conception of an informational input-output relationship, we next draw an analogy between it and the utility function of demand theory, in which probability plays the role of utility and information plays the role of the consumed good. Now this is the key: when we say the consumer maximizes his or her utility we do not mean that the absolute maximum is reached but only the highest level of utility that the consumer can afford. The same will apply to the neoclassical conception of a 'rational' acquisition of knowledge. We will see that the rational expectation hypothesis does not assume that the absolute maximum for the probability of one's knowledge is ever obtained.

What is assumed is that the 'learner' must assess the benefits and costs of increasing the probability.

Unlike consumer theory, in which absolute utility maxima may be allowed for finite quantities of any good (i.e., 'bliss points'), this Conventionalist theory of learning specifically denies a maximum probability in the real world. Probability 1.00 is reached *only* with an infinity of information which would require an infinity of time. Thus the marginal productivity of information, so to speak, is always positive, although it approaches zero as the size of the information set grows larger.

Perhaps for philosophers there is never enough information, but for practical economists the benefits of more information may be an insignificant increase in the probability of one's theory, while the cost of the new information may be quite significant. This then is the economics of information. The 'rational' learner has assessed the costs and benefits of seeking one more bit of information (or one more alternative model to consider) and has stopped acquiring information when the extra benefits no longer outweigh their extra cost. The obvious fact that information is always costly, then, adds support to this Conventionalist theory of knowledge and information. In effect, Conventionalism is self-supporting!

Let us illustrate the economics of information with another diagram. Consider Figure 4.3, in which the cost of information is represented by a fixed dollar multiple of the quantity of information collected, and the benefit of information is represented by a fixed dollar multiple of the probability. The economics of information is simply that the optimum amount of information will be obtained when the marginal benefits (the slope of the benefits curve) just equal the marginal cost (the slope of the cost curve). That is, the optimum amount of information collected means only that quantity of information for which the net benefits have been maximized. This also means that as long as there are positive costs for each bit of information collected, the optimum amount of information will not support a probability of 1.00. Economists might argue that even if induction were logically possible it might not be economical!

It should be noted that it is quite easy to make this Conventionalist theory of knowledge part of a psychologistic individualist program. All that we would have to do is to add the additional interpretation that the probability in question is a 'subjective probability' and then the analogy between probability and utility would be almost redundant. It must be added, though, that this additional interpretation is an unnecessary frill. It only helps some theorists feel that they are not far from fulfilling the requirement of a psychologistic individualist research program.

The Role of the Rational Expectations Hypothesis

The point of all this is that expectations are rational if they are inductively based on the 'best' available information set. The expectations will not usually be absolutely true for the simple reason that to make them so, even if it were logically possible, would cost far too much. We can now state the Rational Expectations Hypothesis that has been receiving so much attention in recent years. Those models employing the Rational Expectations Hypothesis assume merely that every decision-maker has acquired information only to the point that its acquisition is economical. In effect the Rational Expectations Hypothesis is a straightforward application of the maximization hypothesis to knowledge acquisition in a real-world setting where opportunity costs matter - along the lines of Figure 4.3.

Now, let us consider how the Rational Expectations Hypothesis is used in neoclassical research programs based on the hidden agenda of the Problem of Induction (or of Conventions) and psychologistic individualism. For our purposes, we only need to show how the agenda items are served by the Rational Expectations Hypothesis.

Rational expectations and the Problem of Conventions
Whether any given assumption serves as one of the main items on the hidden agenda is only a matter of logical consistency and adequacy. Consider the first item on the agenda - either the Problem of Induction itself or some variant in the form of the Problem of Conventions. On

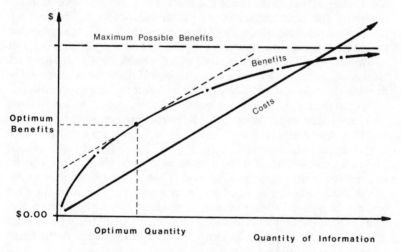

Figure 4.3 *Rational knowledge acquisition*

the basis of what we have been saying here, it is relatively easy to see that the Rational Expectations Hypothesis is quite compatible with the Problem of Induction, although no solution is offered. It is the Problem of Conventions that is solved. In one sense, the Rational Expectations Hypothesis is the only logically adequate solution to the Problem of Conventions (although the solution appears to border on the realm of Instrumentalism [see Boland, 1979a]).

The Rational Expectations Hypothesis solves the Problem of Conventions by saying that one should choose the model or theory which maximizes the net benefits of the present information set. This is analogous to maximizing short-run profits given the current capital. Furthermore, rather than providing a solution to the Problem of Induction, it provides a good reason for not requiring inductive proofs, since, even if logically possible, they would be too expensive. The basis of the rational expectations version of Conventionalism might thus be called 'partial' induction. And in this sense it could be argued that traditional Inductivism is a special case based on what might be called 'extreme' induction - which assumes that successful induction implies an absolute proof. A more moderate view of induction might be satisfied with a large quantity of supporting facts even though they do not constitute an absolute proof [e.g., Rotwein, 1980].

Rational expectations and individualism
The major beneficiary of the Rational Expectations Hypothesis is the other main item on the neoclassical hidden agenda, psychologistic individualism. To the extent that individual decision-makers must form some expectations about the market in order to make ordinary decisions, the maintenance of any stable balance or equilibrium necessitates a minimal adequacy of those expectations - in the sense that the benefits of better expectations would not outweigh their cost. For any model which is to be consistent with the hidden agenda of neoclassical economics, the Rational Expectations Hypothesis is supposed to provide the minimal adequacy of the decision-makers expectations.

Although the individual decision-maker is not assumed to hold absolutely true expectations, the Rational Expectations Hypothesis would at least provide that the actual expectations are consistent with any state of equilibrium. Specifically, if the Rational Expectations Hypothesis holds, then there cannot be a possibility of gains to be made by collecting more information. Thus, as long as the remainder of the model implies an equilibrium, the state of the information set will not be a destabilizing influence. In effect, the Rational Expectations Hypothesis repairs the older versions of neoclassical economics which had to presume perfect knowledge in order to assure the existence of an equilibrium.

If everyone is created equal when it comes to knowledge acquisition, then for general equilibrium the Rational Expectations Hypothesis presumes that everyone has gathered the optimum amount of information. Furthermore, if all actions depend on available knowledge, then the decision-makers' knowledge can be revealed by their actions in the same sense that their preferences are revealed by their choices. We note further that such an assumption of equilibrium precludes privileged (or 'insider') information, as any attempt to benefit from secret information must reveal that information in the market for everyone else to see (or infer). This is the basis for some versions of the so-called 'efficient markets hypothesis' which in this sense is closely related to the Rational Expectations Hypothesis. In either case, the idea of an equilibrium - the absence of any affordable further gains - also precludes any gains from the further collection of information.

In terms of our discussion of psychologistic individualism, what the Rational Expectations Hypothesis provides is a 'naturalization' of a potential source of non-individualist or non-natural exogenous variables. It does this by presuming the existence of a natural given which we have labeled the 'inductive learning possibilities function'. We illustrated this in Figures 4.1, 2 and 3. It has the natural property of being everywhere monotonically increasing. Even in those versions of the Rational Expectations Hypothesis which identify subjective probabilities as the end result of learning, the process of learning is constrained by the Nature-given inductive learning possibilities function. The only endogenous variable introduced is the extent of the information collection and that variable is made a matter of choice, like everything else which is not Nature-given.

A Critique of the Critics of Rational Expectations

It is interesting that although there are many critics of the Rational Expectations Hypothesis, none of the leading critics has noted its dependence on induction or inductive learning. Instead, the critics are concerned with the fact that the Rational Expectations Hypothesis is employed in models which deny any effective governmental intervention such as that implied by Keynesian stabilization policies. What is alleged is that the use of the Rational Expectations Hypothesis yields models of the economy in which it is always possible for individuals to gain by 'outguessing' the government. That is, by including the information collected by observing the government's behavior over time, any individuals can induce the true (*ceteris paribus*) outcome of the governmental policy and, if it is in their interest, alter their behavior to change the final outcome in their favor.

The rational expectations learning theory

Given that the critics do not deny the Inductivist underpinnings of all current versions of neoclassical economics, it is difficult to see how they can argue that there is anything logically wrong with equilibrium models which employ the Rational Expectations Hypothesis. Even Benjamin Friedman's criticism [1979] (and Herbert Simon's [1979]) that there is no discussion of an explicit learning theory to back up the acquisition of the expectations falls short of the mark because, as we noted above, there is a learning theory built into the hidden agenda. Thus, no additional learning theory is logically necessary.

Comparative advantage of individualism

Those critics who favor governmental interventions, such as stabilization policies, imply that such policies are necessary because individuals' expectations are often wrong. But does this mean that somehow the government can know more than any individual? On what basis can the critic argue that the government can form better expectations? We suspect that the answer to the latter question is that the government in these modern days of the computer and high-speed communications can gather and process much more information. This is an effective argument if one believes in induction. If there is no inductive logic, then it is just as easy for governments to make mistakes in forming expectations as it is for any individual. If induction is denied, then arguments for stabilization policies are just as weak as the typical Rational Expectations model.

Adaptive learning vs. rational expectations

Some critics of Rational Expectations models argue that in the long-run the Rational Expectations Hypothesis is equivalent to the more elementary 'adaptive expectations hypothesis' [B. Friedman, 1979]. That this claim is supposed to be a criticism suggests that there is something wrong with adaptive expectations. What is wrong is that adaptive expectations explanations are *ad hoc*. Adaptive expectations are formed merely by trial and error; each subsequent prediction (expectation) is adjusted as indicated by the sign and magnitude of the previous error. For example, to predict the price, P, one could adjust the prediction according to the difference between the previous prediction (P_E) and the observed price (P_O) as follows:

$$dP_t/dt = h(P_O - P_E) \qquad [1]$$

The usual version of adaptive expectations simply assumes that the parameter h is a fixed constant. In effect, Benjamin Friedman argued that if h is appropriately adjusted, then, in the long-run, rational expectations are the same as adaptive expectations. But, if that is the case, what is wrong with adaptive expectations?

Let us offer a different view. Rather than assuming that h adjusts, the equivalence can be obtained by assuming that the 'true model' being estimated is constant. In these circumstances and given Conventionalism, learning by trial and error is constrained by the inductive learning possibilities functions, as illustrated in Figure 4.4. The parameter h determines the speed of adjustment, but as long as the number of trials is not infinite the probability will still not be 1.00. Trials continue until the probability of one's estimate is 'sufficiently close' to 1.00. That is, referring to Figure 4.4, once the probability is within the distance e of the maximum, the estimate is considered a sufficient approximation.

We argued above that the only question of learning in such models is about how to determine the quantity of information (or trials) needed. Rational expectations are determined economically. Adaptive expectations are formed arbitrarily in the following sense. The determining factor in this Conventionalist version of adaptive expectations is the 'arbitrary' error factor, e. If e is chosen to conform to standard statistical test criteria, is the number of trials necessarily arbitrary? A proponent of Rational Expectations models could argue that unless e is chosen so as to indicate the same optimum number of trials as would be determined on the basis of recognizing the cost of the trials, the adaptive learning model will not be the same in the long run.

What is more significant for our purposes is the recognition that the adaptive learning model illustrated here may accurately portray a Conventionalist theory of learning. Yet, *if* one accepts Conventionalism, the rational expectations approach is definitely superior, since it is not arbitrary.

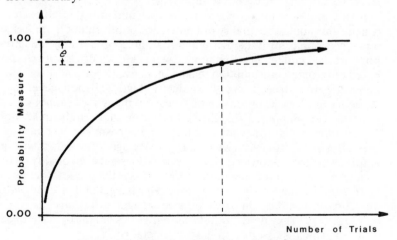

Figure 4.4 *Adaptive Conventionalist learning*

A Critique of Theories of Imperfect Knowledge

The epistemological basis of the Rational Expectations Hypothesis is the same theory of knowledge which underlies virtually all neoclassical models which deal with uncertainty and information. It is the view that presumes (1) that true knowledge requires inductive proofs, and (2) that the acquisition of knowledge is constrained by what we called the 'inductive learning possibilities function', which itself is constrained by the currently accepted information set. The standard view of information and uncertainty is that it would be unrealistic to assume 'perfect knowledge'. Of course, it is unrealistic. It would take an unrealistic amount of information or time to provide the presumed necessary (inductive) proof of 'perfect knowledge'. A realistic neoclassical model would have to presume some form of 'imperfect knowledge' or equivalently be based on 'imperfect information'.

We wish to close this chapter with a simple, but fundamental, criticism of all models which employ some form of 'imperfect' knowledge or 'imperfect' information. Our critique is rather straightforward. How would one ever *know* his or her knowledge is imperfect? If one knows what is imperfect, then one must know what is perfect. For example, how would one know that his or her expectations are not true (perfect)? The answer to this question is rather simple. Those economists who assert that anyone's knowledge is 'imperfect' are merely stating a form of Conventionalism which demands the attainment of an inductive proof before anyone's knowledge is to be considered perfect. Since induction is impossible, perfect knowledge is declared impossible.

It should be obvious by now that our argument is that all current conclusions about the quality of knowledge or information are based on an acceptance of Inductivism and that the acceptance of Inductivism is not warranted. The common view that knowledge is imperfect is based only on the presumption that an inductive proof is necessary for knowledge to be true. There is no inductive logic, and there never was. A theory or an expectation can be true even though we cannot prove that it is true [Popper, 1972, ch. 3]. Furthermore, even the quality of the information is irrelevant whenever Inductivism is rejected.

As Bertrand Russell argued many years ago, the Inductivist or empiricist view of knowledge is a view that does not even qualify on its own terms. There is no inductive proof that says that for knowledge to be true it must have an inductive proof! This is a general problem with all Conventionalist theories of knowledge - they are all self-contradictory. They deny truth status to theories but the denial is itself a theory which is asserted to have truth status!

5

On the 'Necessity' of Microfoundations for Macroeconomics

The centerpiece of microeconomics is the purely competitive auction market in which buyers and sellers participate atomistically as price takers and where supply and demand are equated continuously by variations in price. These individual markets aggregate into a Walrasian general equilibrium model.... In that aggregation of perfect markets, shifts in nominal aggregate demand affect only prices and never quantities.

Macroeconomics contrasts sharply with these implications of aggregated microeconomics. It begins with the observation that output and employment display significant deviations around their supply-determined trends.... These fluctuations around the trend of real activity are the 'business cycle'.... Clearly, the business cycle could not happen in aggregated classical microeconomics. Thus any macroeconomics that is connected to microeconomics by a solid bridge must explain how it departs from the classical micro model in its conception of the operation of markets.

...Keynes... departed from classical microeconomics *only* by modifying the labor supply function to include a wage floor.... But his bridge was defective; none of the explanations flowed directly from the implications of optimization by economic agents or from a specific institutional constraint. Many of [his] followers ...operated with no bridge to microeconomics. Instead, they adopted the 'fixprice method'....

The fixprice finesse may have helped economists develop a sharper focus and a better understanding of real relationships.... But it had important costs. One of these was a professionally disturbing gap between macroeconomics and microeconomics....

Arthur Okun [1980, pp. 817-19]

> the same highly special theoretical presuppositions
> which led to Keynes' original attack on orthodox
> economics continue to pervade contemporary price
> theory and ... the Keynesian Counterrevolution would
> collapse without them. ... Like us, Keynes does not in
> any way deny the generality of orthodox equilibrium
> analysis; he only denies that orthodox economics
> provides an adequate account of disequilibrium
> phenomena.
>
> Robert Clower [1965, pp. 104, 109]

There is virtually no discussion among economists of a need for macrofoundations for microeconomics, except, perhaps implicitly, in the writings of some institutionalists. In contrast, the demonstration of the existence of microfoundations for macrotheories is considered essential by many leading economists. The reason is the same for both and is easy to find. Demonstrating the dependence of all macroeconomics on microeconomic principles is essential for the fulfillment of the (methodological) individualist requirements of neoclassical economics. However - and this is not widely pointed out - this 'necessity' presumes that microeconomic theory, in the form of general equilibrium theory, is a successful individualist program. In some quarters, as we explained in the previous chapters, this is still an open question.

General Equilibrium vs. Macrotheory

Before going much further, we need to make sure that our use of the widely used terms 'general equilibrium', 'aggregation' and 'macroeconomics' is clearly defined. Historically, the concept of a general equilibrium is distinguished from that of a partial equilibrium. Specifically, much of microeconomics is concerned with the individual maximizer or an individual market. The use of the Marshallian strategy of *ceteris paribus* implies a temporary methodological disregard for other individuals or other markets. Thus, followers of Marshall's economics often speak of a partial equilibrium of one market so as to make clear that they have not yet assumed that all other markets are in equilibrium. However, as we noted before, any market is in equilibrium only if all participants are maximizing [see Hicks, 1939/46; Clower, 1965].

General equilibrium
It is unfortunate that in the effort to avoid discussing cardinal utility and to switch to the more general concept of ordinal utility or preferences, Hicks (and to a certain extent, Samuelson) caused an unneces-

sary confusion of the concepts of equilibrium and maximization. Specifically, in the mathematical appendix to his book [1939/46, appendix to ch. 1], Hicks refers to a maximizing individual as being someone in a personal equilibrium without also requiring that the rest of the markets be in equilibrium. Of course, maximization is a form of stable equilibrium, but by confusing an individual's maximization with an individual's equilibrium we ultimately lost the distinction between individual decision-making behavior and market price-determining behavior. For example, to the extent that the individual depends on a market, one individual may be maximizing, but only temporarily, unless the market, and every other individual, is in equilibrium as well. Without the assurance that everything else in the world is in equilibrium, an individual's actions toward planned maximization may not be consistent with what is usually meant by an equilibrium (which implies a minimum degree of stability or feasibility) - thus an individual can be in equilibrium *only if* the market is also in equilibrium.

Perhaps Hicks can be excused because he was interested in promoting a combination of Walras' and Pareto's approach to economic explanations - namely, general equilibrium theory [1939/46, pp. 1-25]. In this sense, the assumption of general equilibrium provides the necessary or required feasibility and market stability in a straightforward manner. It provides an assurance that nothing outside the purview of the individual will upset the planned maximization.

Contrary to Roy Weintraub's recently promoted non-Walrasian version of general equilibrium, we do not think it is easier to comprehend current research if that comprehension is not based on a distinction between Keynes' macrotheory and the traditional concept of general equilibrium. Weintraub's concept of general equilibrium is really a form of 'generalized' equilibrium that covers any 'questions of multimarket interactions' which allows for 'any level of aggregation' [1977, pp. 1-2]. When we refer to general equilibrium we will always mean the traditional view which presumes explicitly either that all markets are in equilibrium or that all individuals are maximizing.

It does not matter which way the concept of general equilibrium is stated, since there is no way one market could be in disequilibrium (i.e., at least one demander or one supplier is not realizing his or her planned actions) while everyone is still maximizing [Hicks, 1939/46, p. 58, fn. 1; Clower, 1965, p. 106]. Similarly, there is no way one individual could have realizable gains (i.e., not maximizing) when all markets are in *equilibrium*, since that individual will upset the equilibrium in order to make the changes necessary for maximization. Note that these conclusions are based entirely on what is meant by the term 'equilibrium' - namely, the continued existence of a stable balance in the absence of any changes in the *exogenous* variables.

With this view of the minimum conditions for equilibrium, in order for an individual to be in an 'equilibrium of the consumer' (to use Hicks' term), all givens - such as the prices of all goods - would have to be fixed or stable. Only when one or more of the markets are not in equilibrium would the given prices not be stable or fixed. Thus we see that Hicks, by identifying the individual's maximization (or optimization) with the individual's equilibrium, has in effect built in a presumption of general equilibrium in order to explain the behavior of any individual. We argue that this is a major source of the difficulties that have led to confusions concerning the differences between macroeconomics and general equilibrium analysis.

Macroeconomics: Keynes' 'departure'

In his 1937 *QJE* article, Keynes attempted to explain to his critics how his *General Theory* was a departure from 'previous theories'. He discussed two major points. First was the matter of uncertain expectations:

> recent writers like their predecessors were still dealing with a system in which the amount of the factors employed was given and the other relevant facts were known more or less for certain. This does not mean that they were dealing with a system in which change was ruled out, or even one in which the disappointment of expectations was ruled out. But at any given time facts and expectations were assumed to be given in a definite and calculable form; and risks, of which, tho admitted, not much notice was taken, were supposed to be capable of an exact actuarial computation. The calculus of probability, tho mention of it was kept in the background, was supposed to be capable of reducing uncertainty to the same calculable status as that of certainty itself....
>
> Actually, however, we have, as a rule, only the vaguest idea of any but the most direct consequences of our acts....
>
> By 'uncertain' knowledge ... I do not mean merely to distinguish what is known for certain from what is only probable.... Even the weather is only moderately uncertain. The sense in which I am using the term is that in which the prospect of a European war is uncertain, or the price of copper ... twenty years hence.... About these matters there is no *scientific basis* on which to form any calculable probability whatever. We simply do not know....
>
> I accuse the classical economic theory of being itself one of these pretty, polite techniques which tries to deal with the present by abstracting from the fact that we know very little about the future. [1937, pp. 212-15, emphasis added]

His second major departure, according to Keynes, was concerned with the absence of an adequate macrotheory, specifically with

> the traditional [theory's] ... apparent conviction that there is no necessity to work out a theory of the demand and supply of output *as a whole*. Will a fluctuation in investment ... have any effect on the demand for output as a whole, and consequently on the scale of output and employment? What answer can the traditional theory [which he noted above 'takes the amount of factors as given'] make to this question? I believe that it makes no answer at all, never having given the matter a single thought; the theory of effective demand, that is the demand for output as a whole, having been entirely neglected for more than a hundred years.
> My own answer to this question involves fresh considerations. I say that effective demand is made up of two items - investment-expenditure ... and consumption-expenditure. Now what governs the amount of consumption-expenditure? It depends mainly on the level of income. People's propensity to spend ... is influenced by many factors such as the distribution of income, their normal attitude to the future and ... by the interest rate. But in the main the prevailing psychological law seems to be that when aggregate income increases, consumption-expenditure will also increase but to a somewhat lesser extent.... This psychological law was of the utmost importance in the development of my own thought, and it is, I think, absolutely fundamental to the theory of effective demand as set forth in my book.... [1937, pp. 219-20]

It is easy to conclude from these fragments of Keynes' own view of his departure that he was not arguing that macroeconomics lacked micro-foundations. Rather, he was arguing that the traditional (micro) theory lacked necessary macrofoundations! We should also note, for future reference, that Keynes did not disagree with the hidden agenda of neoclassical microeconomics. First, when he referred to the lack of a 'scientific basis' for expectation formation he merely meant the lack of an *inductive proof* - that is, he still accepted the Problem of Induction. Second, to deal with the Problem of Induction in the 1937 article he specifically identified three different Conventionalist bases for the formation of expectations [1937, p. 214]. And third, his dependence on psychologism is openly admitted in the above quotation.

In effect, by denying the adequacy of the macrofoundations of traditional theory Keynes was simply arguing that microeconomic theory is *false*! Presumably, it is false because it is not logically consistent with all macrophenomena - such as persistent disequilibria - and thus, by *modus tollens*, at least one of the assumptions of microtheory is false and hence microtheory as a whole is false. If this is granted, why is there a concern for the microfoundations of macrotheory? One might argue that the reason is that many believers in the truth of traditional microeconomic theory think that by showing Keynes' macrotheory to be logically consistent with microtheory (by providing the microfoundations), the strength of Keynes' critique of microtheory would be defused by the embarrassment of an inconsistency in Keynes' position. But we do not think such an obscure reason could support all of the recent concern for microfoundations. Rather, we argue that it is the implicit recognition that Keynes accepts the neoclassical hidden agenda that has thereby led many to think that he accepts neoclassical microtheory and, in particular, general equilibrium theory. If one accepts microtheory, then it would be easy to argue that Keynes' macrotheory - namely, his theory of aggregate demand and supply - must have microfoundations.

Aggregative economics and microfoundations
In one sense the market, by textbook definition of the market functions, is an aggregation of the planned demands and supplies. That is, a minimum condition for a market equilibrium is that the *sum* of all planned quantities demanded must equal the *sum* of all planned quantities to be supplied. What if we extended the aggregation to an entire economy? This is just what was accomplished with the Hicksian grand synthesis in 'Mr. Keynes and the Classics' [1937]. We are led to believe that all we need are some big demand and supply curves in the sky which can be seen to imitate microanalysis of demand and supply. That is, what we need are curves representing a macro view of the economy. There are two ways to go in the direction leading to macroeconomics, although to be logically consistent they cannot be different. One is the direct aggregated demand and supply analysis which Keynes introduced. The other is the Hicksian IS-LM analysis. Either vision is difficult to keep in focus, since nobody can ever directly see the aggregated quantities.

Nevertheless, the basis of macroeconomics is the view that it is possible to keep the aggregated quantities in focus. But most important is the view that all of macroeconomic analysis is methodologically and perfectly analogous to microeconomic analysis. In this sense, one must be able to transfer all the microeconomic principles of market equilibria into a macro or aggregate context. Thus whenever aggregate demand exceeds aggregate supply, the price index of all goods aggregated must rise in the same way that the individual market price rises whenever the market's demand exceeds the market's supply. Of course, this analogy presumes that the microeconomic theory of individual prices is true.

The Problem of Microfoundations

In principle, *if* neoclassical microeconomic theory were successful in terms of methodological individualism, then any neoclassical macroeconomic theory must eventually be explicable in terms of the microtheory. Methodologically speaking, this means that neoclassical *macro*economic theory must not have exogenous variables which do not exist in neoclassical *micro*economic theory. If it does, then the completeness of microtheory would be in doubt. This is the problem of microfoundations. In these terms, the problem of providing microfoundations for macroeconomics becomes a purely technical matter. The problem of microfoundations is to show that necessarily the logical validity of any macroeconomic theory depends only on the logical validity of microeconomic principles. A corollary of this problem is that if there are problems with macroeconomic theory, as some have claimed [e.g., Weintraub, 1977], then there must be a problem with the (general) microeconomic theory underlying it.

We are saying that if microeconomic theory is true, then the nature of the macroview or the aggregated view of the economy cannot be inconsistent with the microview. Some critics of neoclassical theory thus have an alternative route to undermining neoclassical economics. They repeatedly demand a demonstration of the foundations - which, of course, must exist if the individualistic microtheory is true. But the failure to provide microfoundations today does not mean that they are impossible to provide. The critics would be better off taking the bull by the horns and trying to prove that it is impossible to provide them in the future. If the critics also fail, then the proponents of neoclassical economics are no worse off. If a successful microeconomic theory does exist, then the only uncertainty might be about how long it might take to solve the problem of microfoundations.

The key question underlying the dispute over microfoundations is: are there any limitations to the success of the neoclassical microtheory in terms of methodological individualism? For example, does the individual decision-maker require perfect knowledge? Similarly, do the knowledge requirements (what ever they are) presume induction? As we saw in Chapter 4, whenever induction is presumed it is possible to postpone consideration of perfect knowledge. Nevertheless, if equilibrium requires the absence of possible gains from further recontracting, then equilibrium is reached only if there are really no possible gains *and* every individual decision-maker knows that there are no further gains to be had. How does he or she know this?

Consider the possibility of disequilibrium. If there are possible gains, then it is possible for at least one individual to perceive them. This is the basis of the Rational Expectations Hypothesis. But does the absence of possible gains assure an equilibrium? If there really are no possible gains but someone *thinks* there are, the equilibrium will be upset. On what basis will individuals actually hold the correct view that there are no gains? What forces anyone to form the correct expectations? If induction works, then individuals may be forced to hold the correct expectations - although that may require a long time. But even if everyone currently thinks, erroneously, that there are no possible gains, we have no reason to think that even one person may change his or her mind. At the very minimum, the existence of an equilibrium in prices and quantities also presumes an equilibrium in knowledge acquisition along the lines of the Rational Expectations Hypothesis.

These considerations raise two problems. First, a logically consistent individualist theory of equilibrium must presume a general equilibrium, that is, an equilibrium for *all* individuals. Second, a 'stable' equilibrium presumes stable expectations or stable functional relationships [cf. Gordon, 1955]. We will examine the first problem in the present chapter and postpone consideration of the second until the next chapter.

General Equilibrium and Aggregation

If one has conceived of a world which is in general equilibrium as a result of free and independent choices (that is, one where the choices are consistent with methodological individualism), then, as we have said, in that world there cannot be any potential gains (e.g., total excess profits are zero for every firm) and everyone is a maximizer. Now let us consider one of the necessary features of that world. In such a world certain local properties of all production functions are the same for all firms and certain marginal properties of all utility functions are the same for all individual consumers. For example, since everyone faces the same prices (and hence the same relative prices), every individual is experiencing the same marginal rates of substitution as everyone else. But what is most important mathematically is that every production function must be locally linear-homogeneous [Baumol, 1977]. In effect, the world at the point of equilibrium is a linear world.

Linear worlds
Linear worlds have very special properties which are useful for the conception of a world of decentralized decision-makers - that is, for a truly methodological individualist world. There probably is no better representation of a linear world than the first essay in Tjalling Koopmans' *Three Essays on the State of Economic Science* [1957]. Let us further examine the nature of this world.

Based on the mathematical properties of linear functions defined on linear spaces (such as the typical coordinate system represented by quantifiable variables along the lines of typical textbook diagrams), Koopmans shows (his Proposition 1) that if any given number of independent maximizers are price-takers, then *the maximization of aggregate profit implies maximization of individual profits and the converse*. This proposition provides *sufficient* conditions for the solution to the problem of microfoundations.

There's no Santa Claus?

There is a related result which Koopmans does not pursue. If an individual or aggregate production function is linear and homogeneous (the latter condition only requires the absence of a 'Santa Claus', to use Samuelson's term - that is, the absence of any exogenous source to cover losses or eat the profits), then maximization is sufficient to provide zero excess profits. A corollary is that any non-zero profit implies non-maximization on the part of at least one individual. In other words, if linearity were exogenously given, behavioral competition is redundant! There are even more impressive implications. If there are no excess profits, then profit maximization yields an income distribution with no room for social disharmony. Every factor is paid its marginal product (which is directly implied by maximization) *and* there is nothing left over to distribute using non-economic means.

Few theorists would consider linearity to be exogenously given, so the question is: how are linearity and homogeneity provided? Well, as it turns out, both are direct consequences of the requirement of methodological individualism. Specifically, it is the result of the requirement that there be no exogenous variables constraining the variability of the chosen variables (such as the levels of production inputs), so that all choices are free. Add to this the assumption of maximization (i.e., individual 'rationality') and we can see the role of competition among individuals. Competition drives excess profits to zero, leaving all production functions with the property of linear-homogeneity. If any production function were not linear-homogeneous, then increasing the level of each input to the point where it is being paid its respective marginal product (in order to maximize profit) would yield either profits or losses. Profits and losses mean the existence of potential gains to be made, hence the equilibrium has not yet been reached or some inputs have not been recognized and thus they are not necessarily optimally utilized. Or even worse, the residual must be absorbed by some unrecognized exogenous variable (e.g., a Santa Claus) - but that explanation for non-linearity or non-homogeneity is against the methodological rules.

The situation, then, is the following. In a world of individualists guided only by their own interests, whenever they freely choose and all variables are really variable - that is, subject to free choice - all of the non-natural and non-psychological variables can be explained away because they can be shown to be matters of choice. Furthermore, no social phenomena - such as the prevailing income distribution - will be left unexplained. The question of social harmony is not often recognized. A side benefit of the assumption of linear-homogeneity is that, when combined with universal maximization, it yields the absence of excess profits and thus there is no difference between a 'labor theory of value' and a 'capital theory of value', as all prices will be proportional to the equivalent labor value of any good or its equivalent capital value. This is a direct result of the 'duality' provided by the implied linear system.

Needless to say, there is an abundance of 'ifs' in this macro view of the world. Nevertheless, one can see the methodological virtues of a linear world with respect to the individualist agenda item. For many model builders it is too tempting simply to assume a linear-homogeneous world or, what amounts to the same thing, a competitive equilibrium (viz., no exogenously fixed inputs, zero excess profits, universal maximization and thus general equilibrium). In any assumed linear world, everything adds up: the aggregates can never differ from their atomistic parts; nothing is left over to be accounted for by any forbidden exogenous means; and, most important, there is nothing *endogenous* to upset the general equilibrium.

Macroeconomics as a Conventionalist Construct

If, given a true neoclassical microtheory, all macroeconomics variables must be explainable as 'epiphenomena' - that is, by showing that they follow from the principles of microeconomics alone - why do we even have the sub-discipline we call macroeconomics? The answer is to be found in the combination of two factors. The first is that many, following Keynes, consider neoclassical *micro*economics to be false. Their reason may only be the claim that there are exogenous variables other than those allowed by the neoclassical methodological individualism. Or their reason may simply be that a neoclassical equilibrium world, although easy to define, is impossible to realize, hence could never be the basis of a true explanation of the state of a real economy. The second factor is more philosophical, as it is a consequence of the attempts to deal with the Problem of Conventions. Specifically, Conventionalism, which is today's primary item on the hidden agenda of neoclassical economics, does not allow theories to be considered true or false. If claims for truth or falsity were allowed, and Keynes was correct in claiming that neoclassical theory is false, then at the very minimum his version of economics would have to supplant neoclassical microeconomics completely. But since Conventionalism does not allow theories to be considered true or false and since there are no universally accepted or absolutely true criteria, there is always a danger that economics could be destroyed by a life-or-death struggle because it is still presumed that one theory must be chosen as 'best'.

One of the complaints against Inductivism was that it fostered such life-or-death struggles and outright dogmatism over whose theory was the one and only true theory [Agassi, 1963]. Conventionalism attempts to avoid such battles from breaking out in one, or a combination, of two ways. One way is to demonstrate that competing theories are merely two different ways of looking at the same thing - that is, the two competitors are logically equivalent. This way may take a long time. The other way is to compartmentalize the discipline, giving each competitor its own department. For example, in response to Keynes' 'departure' two new categories were created - micro to accommodate those who wish to retain individualist neoclassical 'value theory', and macro for those of all sorts who wish to consider aggregate variables. However, this second way is only a temporary measure whenever competitors deal with the same phenomena. Unless they are shown to be logically equivalent, there remains the possibility that the economics profession could be destroyed by a life-or-death struggle caused by those economists who think that neoclassical microtheory is applicable to all economic phenomena and thus think that there is no need for a separate macrotheory. For these economists macroeconomics can be accommodated only if it is shown that macrotheory is built upon a foundation of microeconomic principles.

Accommodating the macroeconomics of Keynes
The point here is that Conventionalism cannot tolerate disagreements over the truth or falsity of theories. The basic premise is that whenever any two individuals accept the same assumptions (i.e., microeconomics) they must agree about the conclusions reached by any logically valid argument. The Conventionalist position is that if any two individuals disagree, there must be some prior assumption which they do not both accept. Otherwise, at least one of them is crazy or 'irrational' [Pirsig, 1974]. This then provides the avenue for avoiding disagreements - we should search for assumptions which form a foundation for agreement.

With this view of the fundamentals of Conventionalist agreement in mind, let us now examine the way in which Keynesian macroeconomics has been accommodated. The following is a 'rational reconstruction' of the accommodation [cf. Lakatos, 1971; Wong, 1978]. The accommodation is founded on the following premises. It must be agreed, first, that (to be consistent with individualism) neoclassical macroeconomics must not be more than an aggregation of microeconomics. Second, equilibrium is the primary basis of macro behavior, that is, of observable non-individualist behavior. Third, general equilibrium assures the existence of a set of fixed prices which facilitate aggregation. Fourth, the nature of any general equilibrium prices can be explained by neoclassical microeconomics using only natural and (psychologistic) individualist exogenous variables.

Let us see the ways in which these principles allow for an accommodation. Since so much of Keynesian economics is about aggregates, the primary obstacle in the way of an accommodation is what used to be called the 'Problem of Aggregation' [e.g., Klein, 1946; Leontief, 1947; Blaug, 1978, p. 492] - the problem of constructing Keynes' aggregate demand and supply quantities from the demand and supply curves of individuals or other sub-macro entities. We can always calculate unambiguous aggregates if we assume prices are fixed. The Problem of Aggregation is about whether the fixed-price aggregate quantities correspond to the quantities that would have to hold if one viewed the aggregate economy from a general equilibrium perspective.

This problem can be solved if all production functions are linear (constant returns) or all prices are fixed at their long-run equilibrium values (where all production functions are locally linear). This is where general equilibrium comes to the rescue. It can be shown that for any given set of resource endowments (which are fully employed) it is always possible to define a set of Walrasian prices which would clear all markets [Dorfman, Samuelson and Solow, 1958] in a general equilibrium sense. The beauty of the general equilibrium sense is that the only exogenous givens are the individual utility or production functions and the naturally given resource endowments. All other variables can be calculated [cf. Boland, 1975]. Using the general equilibrium prices it is always possible to perform an aggregation, if one assumes that the economy is in competitive equilibrium (zero excess profits). The economy is in equilibrium only if all individuals are maximizing, given these prices, and the absence of profits guarantees that the aggregate value of the resources must equal the aggregate value of the outputs.

The Walrasian prices correspond to the Marshallian long-run equilibrium prices where every producer is making zero excess profits. Thus, the actual short-run prices cannot always be used for aggregation. From the macro perspective of Walrasian general equilibrium the *total* profits cannot be other than zero (no Santa Claus) but this does not preclude the possibility that the profits and losses of individual firms cancel each other out. In the short run the actual prices cannot be used for the aggregation except when one assumes that all production functions are linear-homogeneous. As we argued above, when all production functions are linear-homogeneous, if everone is maximizing, then everyone is making zero excess profits. If one assumes that the *aggregate* production function is linear-homogeneous (e.g., a Cobb-Douglas production function), then it might appear that, since the aggregate profits cannot be non-zero, the aggregate supply function must reflect profit maximizing outputs, just as the individual supply curves of microtheory are determined by the profit maximization of the individual producers. But it must be realized that unless all individual production functions are linear-homogeneous, the so-called Problem of Aggregation has not been solved, since the actual prices do not necessarily correspond to the Walrasian prices used to perform the aggregation.

For many economists the air around the mathematics of general equilibrium theory is much too thin and the assumption that all production functions are linear-homogeneous begs too many questions. While a general equilibrium over the relevant period of time is a sufficient condition for the fixity of prices, it is not always necessary. It is much easier merely to assume that prices are fixed over the period of time needed to calculate any aggregate quantity such as the GNP. In this sense the aggregate quantities can be calculated and thus 'observed' even if there is no way to show that they correspond to the logically consistent but unobservable Walrasian general equilibrium prices. For many this is the only viable and realistic way to accommodate Keynes' aggregative economics.

In order to be consistent with neoclassical theory, the disagreement between micro and macro theorists can always be explained away as mere pedagogical differences over whether prices are actually fixed. If the economy were in general equilibrium then as long as exogenous givens did not change over the relevant period, prices would be fixed. So neoclassical economics can tolerate Keynesian aggregate economics if the only difference is that macroeconomics presumes fixed prices [Okun, 1980]. That one or more markets may have 'sticky' (and non-equilibrium) prices can only help in the aggregation. Even when there exist one or more markets that are not cleared, as long as their prices are sticky, the fixity of prices is assured without recourse to an assumption of general equilibrium. This still begs the question as to whether the inflexibility of the prices is due to an implicit introduction of a non-individualist and non-natural exogenous variable.

Some neoclassical economists interested in explaining non-fixed price situations, such as inflation, obviously cannot accept accommodation on these terms. Instead, to the extent that macroeconomics involves changing macrovariables and to the extent that equilibrium theory is essentially an explanation of why prices could be fixed at particular levels, it is argued that, for macroeconomics to be consistent with microeconomics, prices must change only because a temporary disequilibrium exists. And as we saw above (e.g., Solow's comments), disequilibria are attributed to 'expectational errors'. The Rational Expectations Hypothesis can then be used to explain the 'expectational errors' away. In this way macroeconomics is accommodated as epiphenomena of the microeconomic decision problems which are caused by uncertainty. Either way, the accommodation, which Clower called the 'Keynesian Counterrevolution', tolerates the Keynesian 'revolution' only if Keynesian macroeconomics is concerned with temporary short-run phenomena.

The Keynesian challenge to neoclassical theory

Critics of this accommodation argue that it is completely against the thrust of Keynes' *General Theory* [e.g., Clower, 1965]. Keynes identifies 'classical theory' with the case of 'full employment'. What is wrong with the concept of full employment? First, full employment is a presumption of the orthodox Walrasian general equilibrium analysis which only attempts to identify the sufficient conditions for the existence of an equilibrium allocation of given supplies. Second, full employment is a necessary condition of any long-run equilibrium in a competitive world of price-takers. Again, if all production functions are linear-homogeneous, then profit maximization in the long run produces 'full employment' in the sense that further employment must not yield higher utilities for anyone without lowering the utility of others.

Now Keynes claimed to be opposed to all of these aspects of full employment. But if full employment is a logical consequence of any perfectly competitive, maximizing economy in the long run, how can Keynes' opposition to theories based on full employment be reconciled with classical theory? Is it only a matter of whether Keynes was speaking about a short-run world, or is it something more? Specifically, is it only a question of Keynes' macrotheory being a special case of classical theory? Is it that the short run has some temporary exogenous variables which in time can be made endogenous and that these temporary exogenous variables are the only cause of the deviations from full employment?

Can the so-called counterrevolutionaries safely explain away Keynes' opposition to classical theory in this manner? Keynes' specific indictment, according to Clower, is that Keynes only denies that orthodox economics provides an adequate account of disequilibrium phenomena [Clower, 1965, p. 109]. But can this interpretation of

Keynes' indictment be correct? All explanations are based on specifically recognized exogenous variables. If one can show that each of Keynes' disequilibrium conclusions follows only because of the intervening *temporary* exogenous variables, their existence *is* the basis of an explanation! It would appear that both Keynes and Clower were wrong.

This is the center of the whole matter. If the classical or the counterrevolutionary explanation is based on temporary exogenous variables which are neither natural nor individualist, then Keynes would be right all along. Keynes was right because the classical or counterrevolutionary position is nothing more than standard neoclassical theory and, as we have been arguing, neoclassical explanation allows only natural or (psychologistic) individualist exogenous variables. If the counterrevolutionaries must rely on the wrong type of exogenous variables to win their case against Keynes, they simultaneously violate their own requirements for a successful theory of economic phenomena. They can only win if the temporary exogenous variables are either naturally given or are aspects of individualism, such as psychological states.

Keynes' psychologism and Inductivism

Some of Keynes' defenders, notably Joan Robinson, argue that what Keynes was saying was that the results of past decisions are necessarily exogenous for current decisions and those results are not natural nor individualistic [Robinson, 1974]. That is, the individual decision-maker often makes mistakes which cannot be undone. Being mistakes, they cannot be explained as the outcomes of maximization, hence neoclassical explanations cannot be produced to explain away the temporal and temporary exogenous variables which supposedly yielded the short-run, disequilibrium situation.

On the surface Robinson's interpretation would appear to do the logical job that she intended. And it certainly appears to be consistent with the spirit of Keynes' argument in his *QJE* article of 1937. But if we allow this interpretation of Keynes' criticism of the classics, does his theory fare any better as an explanation of so-called disequilibria? We will argue that it does not.

In his 1937 *QJE* article Keynes took the opportunity to restate his objections to classical theory in more direct terms. But, unfortunately, he exposed his hand too much. As we noted above, when referring to his theory of the consumption function he said, 'This *psychological law* was of the utmost importance in the development of my own thought-....'(emphasis added). This is not an idle reference to psychological laws. Keynes was famous for his theories of *subjective* probability. And as also noted above, one of his primary arguments against classical theory was that the individual decision-maker must form subjective expectations concerning the future and those expectations cannot be inductively proven, hence decision-makers *must* make mistakes. This view has been admirably developed by George Shackle [e.g., 1972].

We see then that Keynes accepted both the psychologism and the Inductivism upon which neoclassical theory is founded. Some of his defenders may say that this is all the better because he was able to refute neoclassical theory on its own terms. But, to criticize neoclassical economics by basing the critique on the logical consequences of accepting psychologism and Inductivism *presumes* that psychologism and Inductivism are necessary for 'rational' decision-making. We will argue below that neither is necessary; hence the matter of the success of the Keynesian revolution is still an open question.

6

Time and Economic Theory

economic problems arise always and only in consequence of change.... [T]he economic problem of society is mainly one of rapid adaptation to changes in the particular circumstances of time and place....

Friedrich Hayek [1945/48, pp. 82-3]

Economics ... is concerned with decisions; decisions come in as the intermediate stage in most of its causal processes. The immediate cause of an economic effect is, nearly always, a decision by someone; or it may be the combination of decisions that were made by different people. But it is not enough, in economic analysis, to refer to the decision; we are also concerned with the reasons for the decision, the causes of the decision. ...All causative analysis ... depends on theory. If we think the decisions to be obvious, that can only mean that we are taking the theory for granted.

John Hicks [1979, pp. 88, 67]

Often in the writings of economists the words 'dynamic' and 'static' are used as nothing more than synonyms for good and bad, realistic and unrealistic, simple and complex. We damn another man's theory by terming it static, and advertise our own by calling it dynamic....

Paul Samuelson [1947/65, p. 311]

Time in Economics vs. Economics in Time[1]

For many it must seem obvious that any discussion of the need to explain any disequilibrium must also entail the need to explain the dynamics of such an economy, since, by definition, disequilibrium implies changes over time. But not much progress has been made towards a development of a neoclassical theory of a dynamic economy. The reason, according to some critics of neoclassical economics, particularly those who reject the 'Counterrevolution' (such as Robinson [1974] and Shackle [1972]), is that, unlike Keynes' macroeconomics, neoclassical economics is 'timeless' or that it is not '*in*' time' [Hicks, 1976]. They may be correct about Keynes' macroeconomics, but, strictly speaking, neoclassical economics is not necessarily timeless.

There is growing concern among followers of Keynes' macroeconomics about the adequacy of any microeconomic model that is based on the hidden agenda ever to deal with decision-making in real time. What we should be asking is not whether neoclassical economics is timeless but whether its treatment of time is adequate. The same question can also be asked concerning Keynes' treatment of time. For any treatment of time to be adequate, it is necessary for the given model to be *in* time - that is, real time must matter in some fundamental way. The critics might thus argue that an adequate 'dynamic' model must include at least one dynamic process. But we will eventually have to ask: can such a model ever be consistent with the hidden agenda?

The Elements of Dynamic Models

Not much progress has been made in neoclassical theory towards an adequate approach which deals with endogenous dynamics. This is partly due to a failure to distinguish between dynamics and dynamic processes. To a great extent, Samuelson is to blame for this. He foisted a simplistic version of the physicist's distinction between 'statics' and 'dynamics' on us. This version of the distinction is not appropriate for economics problems. According to Samuelson, 'a dynamical system might be regarded as any set of functional equations which together with initial conditions ... determine as solutions certain unknowns in function of time', while 'timeless, statical systems are simply degenerate special cases in which the functional equations take on simple forms and determine as solutions functions of time which are identically constants' [1947/65, pp. 284-5].

The major difficulty with this simplistic distinction is that it confuses 'timeless' with 'static'. Whether or not a system is static is more properly a question of dynamics. Specifically, a system is static only if the given 'initial conditions' are constant over time. In this sense, the distinction between static and dynamic is no more informative than the assumption that the givens are constant over the relevant time period. We will adopt a distinction between static and dynamic that more accurately reflects the sense in which the critics claim that a static model is limited by comparison with a dynamic model. Our distinction involves the disposition of any model's exogenous variables.

Dynamic explanation vs. explanations of dynamics
The basis of all explanations in economics is the behavior of exogenous givens. Once one has explained all the values of endogenous variables in any given model, their values cannot change without a change in at least one exogenous given. To the extent that neoclassical models involve at least one exogenous given which is also dynamic (i.e., its value changes with the passage of time), then it can be argued that such models are dynamic explanations. There are two aspects to this observation about neoclassical models. One involves the necessity of exogenous variables; the other involves what constitutes an explanation of changes over time.

All explanations are essentially causal explanations - there is no other type of explanation [Hicks, 1979]. No one model can explain everything; there must be some givens. Every model which is not circular has at least one variable which is exogenous. The values of endogeous variables are, in this sense, 'caused' by the values of the exogenous variables. When there is more than one, we cannot consider the exogenous variables to be causes in the ordinary sense. That is, we cannot say, for example, the price is determined by demand, since it also depends on the supply possibilities. This has long been a source of confusion in economics but it would be easily cleared up in the case of multiple 'causes' by referring to them as influences.

We point all this out only because the arguments raised below are not those raised by multiple 'causes' but rather those raised by the logic of explaining dynamic processes. Typically, changes in endogenous variables are explained by showing that they have been caused by changes in one or more exogenous variables - this is a simple matter in the case of one exogenous variable but a little confusing in the case of more than one. Since 'change' usually implies the passage of time, one could go further and explain the history of the endogenous variables as being caused by the history of the exogenous variables. In either case most economists would call these dynamic explanations. What we wish to consider here is whether one can have a dynamic explanation of the dynamics of any dynamical model. We shall argue that any model involving *exogenous* dynamic processes that does not explain those processes is, at best, incomplete.

Time in neoclassical models
There are a limited number of ways in which time can be incorporated into any model. The number is limited by the logical types of statement usually included in the model [Boland, 1977a]. Specifically, time can be an element in the statements which define goods and prices and the behavioral functions relating them, in the statements which identify the constraints or givens, in the statements of the conditions of

'equilibrium', or, as we shall argue, in the statements concerning the *process* of knowing or learning the truth status of any of the above statements. We shall argue that although neoclassical models are not strictly timeless, they are still incapable of rendering explanations of dynamic processes.

For the purposes of illustrating how time has typically been included in neoclassical models, some readers might find it helpful if we consider a simple model of Walrasian general equilibrium - such as the one first presented by Abraham Wald [1936/51; Boland, 1975]. In this model the endogenous variables are the output prices (Ps), resource or input prices (Vs), and the quantities produced (Xs). Since every model must have at least one exogenous variable, Wald specifies exogenously given amounts of available inputs (Rs) and for them an exogenously fixed system of linear production coefficients (As) and a set of exogenously given demand functions (Ds). For each output he adds an equation which represents a necessary condition for a competitive equilibrium (i.e., price equals average cost).

We note that there is no explicit time in Wald's model at this stage. It is the lack of explicitness that misleads the critics who claim that neoclassical models are timeless. It is quite possible to give a temporal interpretation of every competitive equilibrium condition. We shall consider each condition to be a statement which asserts an implicit consistency between the truth of the statements about the givens (the observed values of the Rs, Ds and As) and the truth of the statements about endogenous variables (the observed Ps, Vs and Xs) at the *same point in time*. But we must concede that this is our interpretation and may not have been Wald's intention.

A minimum requirement for any model to be considered an explanation of its endogenous variables is that one can always solve for those variables as positive stable functions of the exogenous variables and parametric coefficients of the other givens. Since this is not always possible for some values of the givens, Wald provides a set of additional conditions for the givens which will assure the solvability of his model for the values of P, V and X at the same point in time as the givens are observed.

Traditional Models of Dynamic Processes

Models which include statements that are only assumed to be true at a specified point in time are static models by our strict definition. Although a model's logical validity is timeless, its (empirical) truth status is always an open question. Therefore, with respect to any given model, today's values of the endogenous variables may be shown to be consistent with today's values of the exogenous variables, but tomorrow their respective values may not be consistent. Since dynamic processes obviously refer to more than one point in time, the explanatory usefulness of a static model would indeed seem rather limited.

The 'time-based variables' approach to dynamics

Koopmans [1957] and Gerard Debreu [1959] offer a means of overcoming the temporal limitations of static models. Their approach (which implements Hicks' suggestions [1939/46]) is to date all variables with subscripts and build models which cover many points in time. In these models any good, say, a bottle of beer (B_t), at time $t = t_0$ is not the same as a bottle of beer (B_t) at time $t = t_1$. Of course, in such a model we have many more goods than one could observe at any one point in time. But formally, such a model is similar to Wald's except that we have multiplied the number of goods (the Xs) and equilibrium equations by the number of points in time under consideration. One must, however, be very careful in applying one of Wald's conditions for his existence proof, namely, the weak axiom of revealed preference. It is usually defined in terms of a comparison between two points ranked according to the individual's preferences. But here the comparison cannot be made between two points at different times, since the time difference itself could explain the choice between them.

This form of equilibrium model implies that the explanation of P, V and X is essentially static for the entire period of time over which the goods are defined. There are no dynamics to be explained here because nothing is changing [cf. Smale, 1976]. The values of the endogenous variables at any point can be shown to follow from the values of the exogenous variables statically given at the unique initial point in time. The individual makes his or her only decision at that one point in time.

The 'economics of time' approach

Another method of including time in a neoclassical model is to make time a 'commodity', such as leisure time or waiting time. Examples are Gary Becker's theory of allocating time [1965] and Eugene Böhm-Bawerk's period of production [1889]. In both cases, time is spent on production, and increasing the time spent implies increasing the costs. In the Becker model the costs are the opportunities lost. The amount of time allocated to produce household benefits (e.g., meals, shopping, etc.) is such that utility is maximized over all possible uses of the time endowment. Similarly, in the Böhm-Bawerk model the costs are the needed working capital, which increases with waiting time. Time is allocated to waiting until the product is considered finished. The optimum waiting time will maximize the profit rate.

The difficulty with this approach is that time is just another exogenously scarce resource which can be uniquely and optimally allocated; thus the time allocation is viewed as another *static* variable that has been uniquely determined when it is logically consistent with other static and exogenous givens. Again, nothing is changing during the period of time considered. Neither Becker's nor Böhm-Bawerk's approach can avoid the static nature of the givens (constraints, tastes, production functions, time available, etc.). As with the Wald model, the endogenous variables are statically fixed by the exogenous givens. There is no reason for historical change; hence it cannot be explained.

The 'variable givens' or 'lagged variables' approach
As an alternative to the above approaches one might attempt to determine the *time-path trajectory* of the endogenous variables. Given that the solution of a model represents its explanation, the only way the endogenous variables can change over time is either by one or more of the exogenous variables changing, or by some of the parameters of the logical relationships autonomously changing, or both. The population's growth rate in Kaldor's growth model [1957] is an example of the former, and what Hicks [1976] called an 'autonomous invention' or a non-neutral change in technology might be an example of the latter [cf. Boland, 1971b]. However, in neoclassical economics the relationships are usually assumed not to change over the relevant time-period [cf. Wong, 1978]. The entire explanation of historical change is usually invested in the exogenous changes of the givens. The changes in the givens may be represented by movements along their fixed trajectories. Thus if some of the static givens of Wald's model are replaced by time-path trajectories for a specified time period, the result will be derivable trajectories for the endogenous variables over the same time period. With this method of including time we have only replaced a point in time with a static sequence of corresponding points in a fixed period of time. The solution will be a fixed sequence of changing values.

Obviously one does not necessarily have to assume that the time period of the exogenous variables is the same as that of the endogenous variables. One could assert that some of today's exogenous variables may be yesterday's endogenous variables [Nerlove, 1972]. An example of this approach is the von Neumann [1937/45] balanced growth model. With this 'lagged variable' approach we are able to derive a time-path trajectory for the endogenous variables. However, the position of the trajectory over a given time period will depend only on the initial set of values for the exogenous givens. The initial values of the givens are essentially the only exogenous variables of the model over the whole time period.

On the surface, the direct approach of including an exogenous time-path for the givens, or the indirect approach using lagged variables, looks like a solution to the problem of explaining historical change. But a closer examination will show this to be an illusion. In the exogenous trajectory approach, the endogenous variables are changing *only* because the exogenous variables are changing. In the case of lagged variables, the position of an endogenous variable on its trajectory is uniquely determined merely by the length of time which has transpired since the initial givens were established. The position of the trajectory itself is uniquely determined only by the initial values of the exogenous givens. In both cases the trajectories of the endogenous variables are exogenously fixed. The only 'dynamics' of the model are exogenous. Since exogeneity of any model results from an explicit choice to not explain the givens or their behavior [Boland, 1975], we have not explained the dynamic changes within the model. In other words we still are relying on a statically given time-path trajectory which is fixed over the relevant time period. We have not explained why it is that trajectory rather than some other.

We could, for example, assume the given path was such that the exogenous variable grew at a constant rate. If we should be asked why we did not assume an increasing rate, we cannot justify our assumption solely on the grounds that it yields the observed time-path of the endogenous variables. The truth of our assumptions regarding exogenous givens must be independent of our conclusions regarding endogenous variables [Boland, 1975].

The 'flow variables' approach

The criticisms raised against the approaches that add time by appropriately defining certain variables can be extended to those approaches that add a time-differential equation to an otherwise static model. One of the problems in using equilibrium models to explain prices is that observed prices may not yet have reached their equilibrium values. Thus it is often argued that we need an explanation of the disequilibrium behavior of the endogenous variables [Barro and Grossman, 1971]. Typically, a theory of price adjustment is attached to neoclassical equilibrium models. The basic approach is to add a differential (or difference) equation which gives the rate of change of the price as a function of the amount by which the two sides of one of the equilibrium equations deviate from equality prior to reaching equilibrium [Samuelson, 1947/65; Arrow, 1959]. In market demand and supply analysis this usually is an equation of the following form:

$$(dp_t/dt) = f(S_t - D_t), \qquad [1]$$

where $df/d(S_t - D_t)$ is negative and $f(0) = 0$. But unless this additional equation is explained, the dynamics are purely improvised and arbitrary. A make-shift differential equation for the 'dynamics' of the market does not even say who changes the price or why it is being changed. Until we can say why the price has changed (rather than describing how much it should change), we have explained neither the process of disequilibrium change nor the dynamics of the market.

Real time vs. long run
Significant as some may consider such criticism to be [Gordon and Hynes, 1970; Boland, 1977b], matters are even worse for the determination of the equilibrium level of prices. Most models which include time-differential equations only guarantee a solution in the long run. Such models are incapable of yielding a determinant and non-arbitrary solution for the prices at points of real (calendar or clock) time where equilibrium has been reached. If by 'in the long run' we mean that it takes anything approaching an infinite amount of time to yield a determinant solution, we are in effect conceding that we do not have a real-time explanation of the observed behavior of the endogenous variables. To be specific, we assert the following methodological proposition:

> *To assert the existence of a long-run equilibrium when its attainment requires an infinite length of time is to imply either that time does not matter or that we have no explanation.*

Obviously, the usual Conventionalist argument that true knowledge is impossible, based on what we called the inductive learning possibilities function, is also based on this methodological principle.

Time, Logic and True Statements

Going much further than we have here, recent critics claim that all neoclassical models are essentially timeless because, they say, all economic analysis has comprised merely logical derivations of solutions to abstract mathematical problems [Georgescu-Roegen, 1971; Shackle, 1972]. We shall argue that this criticism stems from a misconception about the logical nature of a model.

The logical nature of any model is determined by the extent to which the model represents an argument, that is, an explanation of its endogenous variables. There are only two basic forms of valid logical arguments. Arguments for and arguments against: arguments for something are formally in favor of the truth of a specific statement. Such an argument consists of one or more given statements which are alleged to be true and from which one can logically derive the specific statement in question. Arguments thus have two contingent but essential parts: (1) the purported validity of logical relationships *between* all the given statements and the statement in question, and (2) the purported truth status of *each* of the given statements. Standard logic provides only the means of 'passing' along the truth of all the given statements to any statement which logically follows from them [Boland, 1979a]. However, the truth of any given statement must be established independently of the argument.

With all the above models we have relied on a temporal interpretation of the truth status of individual statements. Each equation of a model is alleged to be a true statement of a given relationship between the observed (or observable) true values of the included exogenous and endogenous variables. The observation of the values of the variables is presumed to be made at the same time (or, in the case of lagged variables, at specifically defined but different points). Such a time-based or static concept of a 'true' statement is easily accepted. Moreover, we shall argue that it is the basis for the usual applications of logic in any explanation or argument.

Applications of logical deductions in any direct argument in favor of some proposition always require that the given statements be known to be true (or at least not known to be false). The internal consistency of some non-compound (simple predicate) statements *may* assure their truth status (e.g., identities, definitions, etc.), but the consistency of a compound statement (e.g., a conjunction of two or more non-compound statements) does not generally assure its truth status [Quine, 1972, p. 10]. For example, a conjunction of three simple statements (say, 'The price is $100', 'The quantity sold is twenty', and 'The gross revenue is $2000') is true *only if all* of its parts are true. The truth of any of its parts may be time-based (thus possibly false), but the consistency of such a compound statement only requires consistency between its parts, that is, that it is not inconsistent when all of its parts are true at the same point in time.

Any model can be seen to be a compound statement [Boland, 1977a], and its general solution represents its explanation of the endogenous variables. Formally proving the solvability of an appropriate set of equations establishes the consistency of the explanation the model represents. But solvability does not establish the truth of its parts (such as the statements about the givens), because the logical consistency of the statically observed values of the endogenous and the exogenous variables is only a necessary condition for the truth of the model.

Our static concept of a statement's truth status presumes that equations (such as those representing competitive conditions) are capable of being false; hence they are not necessarily tautologies. But the static nature of the definition of a statement's truth status does not preclude the statement from being true at many points in time. Although by definition an allegedly true dynamic statement is supposed to be true at more than one point in time, it does not have to be logically true at all points in time, which means that conceivably it can be false [see Boland, 1977b]. Since static and dynamic statements can be false at some points in time, time will matter to their truth status. If any equation were meant to be a pure logical relation (e.g., a tautology), then it is assumed to be always true, that is, it is impossible to conceive of its being false. Its truth status is thus 'timeless'. Any statements that are logically true at all points in time are simply statements whose truth status is independent of time.

If one were only concerned with the known truth of a single (non-compound) statement, it would appear that a model-builder must choose between statically limited observations (i.e., descriptions) and timeless generalities (i.e., logically true statements for which time does not matter). Since neither alternative is very promising, this would seem to spell trouble for anyone trying to build dynamic neoclassical models which are true at all points in time yet in which real time matters. It is along these lines that the critics have charged that neoclassical economics is timeless. However, even though we think the critics are wrong, we are not suggesting that one must accept static descriptions in place of (possibly false) dynamic explanations.

What we suggest is that the charge of 'timeless' neoclassical models should be rejected because the critics' arguments are based on two fundamental mistakes. They confuse conceivably false (dynamic) statements which may happen to be true at all points in time with tautological statements which are true at all points in time only because they cannot conceivably be false. Also they fail to distinguish between a single statement (e.g., a model's solution) which may be a timeless logical relation, and the logical consistency of a specific joint logical relationship such as the one between the values of all the endogenous variables and the time-based truth of the statements of the values of the exogenous variables. This latter mistake has probably been the major source of misunderstanding about the alleged timelessness of neoclassical models. That a model or any explanation can be shown to be logically valid does not say that its truth status (as a compound statement) is timeless. This, we are arguing, is simply because *a model is not timeless if any of its parts is not a tautology*. All models must have at least one such non-tautological statement, namely, the statement representing the values of the exogenous variables.

Time and Knowledge

Our previous discussion of the usual ways of including time seems to suggest that any reliance on neoclassical general equilibrium theory alone precludes an explanation of historical change. All the causes, motivations, or reasons for change are beyond explanation because they are being considered to be exogenous to the models. In other words, we always face the problem of having to choose between dynamic explanations and explanations of dynamics. Long before there was concern about the microfoundations or the Rational Expectations Hypothesis, this problem was recognized by Hayek [1937/48] and remains an essential consideration in most Austrian models [Hicks, 1973; Lachmann, 1976]. Hayek insisted that this methodological limitation of standard economic analysis only makes clear the importance of looking at the way in which individuals acquire and communicate their knowledge (of the givens). This, he argued (on the basis of an implicitly accepted Inductivism), is because the acquisition of the (true) knowledge of the givens or facts (constraints, etc.) is essential for any (stable) equilibrium.

Unfortunately, Hayek did not provide an explicit solution to the problem, although he implicitly outlined some acceptable requirements for a satisfactory solution. They were considered acceptable only because they were consistent with the hidden agenda of neoclassical economics. First, to be individualistic, he wanted the individual's knowledge (of the relevant givens) to be explicitly recognized. Secondly, to be consistent with inductivism, he claimed that the acquisition of one's knowledge must depend on objective facts, if the facts are to play an essential role in the *explanation* of the individual's behavior. For Hayek this was simply a matter of 'how experience creates knowledge' [1937/48, p. 46]. Supposedly, if one knew the individual's past experience, one could logically infer the individual's current knowledge. Given that there is no inductive logic, it is not surprising that Hayek was admittedly unable to offer an explanation for even one individual's acquisition process; thus the dilemma of having to choose between explaining dynamics and dynamic explanations remained unresolved [1937/48, p. 47].

Eliminating the dilemma would appear to be a simple matter of adding knowledge (or 'expectations'), say, to Wald's model. This approach seems to be what is now popular among avant-garde theorists, as we saw in the previous three chapters. But, we argue, if knowledge or its acquisition process is treated as another exogenous or statically given variable, then the problem of explaining dynamics remains. Similarly, no model that requires an individual to have the benefits of a correct economic theory (e.g., the Rational Expectations

Hypothesis presumes that the individual has correctly assessed the costs and benefits of collecting more information), thereby suppressing the role of the individual decision-maker's knowledge, solves the problem. Furthermore, if the individual's knowledge is suppressed only 'in the long run' we are brought back to the irrelevance of real time. To solve the problem of explaining dynamics, the individual's process of acquiring his or her knowledge must be endogenous; it must be something to be explained. In rational decision models in a dynamic context, the individual's process of learning and adapting must take place in real time.

Towards an essential role for time

In the previous chapters we observed that the reconciliation of Keynesian macrotheory has been founded on the view that since macroeconomists are most often concerned with immediate policy questions, it is reasonable to allow macrotheory to be centered on a theory of short-run disequilibria. To center macrotheory on the short run is to say that real time must matter. Furthermore, we noted, the primary means of explaining the existence of disequilibria is the recognition of 'expectational errors' which are in turn the result of dealing with real time. This is where the reconciliation rests - right where Hayek left it back in 1937.

Some progress towards incorporating real time in economics models would seem to have been made by some post-Keynesian theorists. For example, Shackle [1972] and Davidson [1972] have argued that the existence of money in an economy is a direct consequence of the importance of real time. Specifically, except in a barter economy where all transactions are direct and immediate, very many market transactions require placing an order at one point in time and acquiring the goods and sales revenue at another point in time. In many cases this involves a sales contract. A sales contract can specify the consequences of failure to deliver the goods. The penalty for failure is almost always expressed in monetary terms.

In this post-Keynesian view money makes real-time contracts possible. More important, contracts would be unnecessary without essential processes that involve the passage of time (e.g, growing corn, aging wine, etc.). But does recognizing money and contracts overcome the shortcomings of neoclassical models? If the only reason for the contracts is the exogenously given time-using processes, then we have not moved beyond the 'economics of time' approach of Becker and Bohm-Bawerk, which only makes the dynamics exogenous.

The only basis for the post-Keynesian view of the essential endogeneity of dynamics is the role of 'expectations'. Specifically, what is recognized in Shackle's view is 'uncertainty'. The fact that we cannot know for certain that our expectations are true makes contracts (and money) an essential part of an explanation of 'rational' decision-making. It would be all too easy for a clever neoclassical theorist to argue that the recognition of uncertainty, expectations and contracts is to explain why certain contracts are better than others and thereby to bring the contracts and uncertainty into the neoclassical research program.

What is the basis for the post-Keynesian view that expectations necessitate contracts and the use of money? Unfortunately, it is our old friend the inductive learning possibilities function (from Chapter 4). On its basis one's views of the future could never be true, since proof of their truth would require an infinite amount of time. But, we argue, relying on an exogenous learning function is no different than relying on exogenous trajectories of the exogenous variables. There are no endogenous dynamics in these post-Keynesian models.

Time and liquidity preference
The most recent attempt to deal with the problem of time in economics is Hicks' book *Causality in Economics* [1979]. There are some very promising aspects of dynamic processes in his approach that warrant close examination. It is interesting that although Hicks has criticized neoclassical economics for not being *in* time [1976], in this book he does not reject the formal (timeless) 'Keynesian' models which he helped to create; he wishes only that they be put into perspective by considering three types of causal explanations which he calls 'static', 'contemporaneous', and 'sequential'. Static causality corresponds to timeless physical theories. Contemporaneous causality corresponds to Book V of Marshall's *Principles* (e.g., relative to a given time period such as the short run) and to Keynesian models of period equilibria. Sequential causality corresponds to the theory of decision-making and liquidity which was Keynes' major departure from orthodox (textbook *laissez-faire*) economics. Hicks argues that (1) formal 'Keynesian' models are appropriate only for situations of contemporaneous causality, and (2) any improvement over orthodox explanations must be seen in terms of the sequential causality of realistic decision-making.

The primary methodological thrust of his book is that the methodology and causal precepts of physics are inappropriate for economics. The methodology of physics presumes the existence of natural constants which are to be discovered or proven. There are no *natural* constants in economics. Experimental sciences presume timeless (i.e., universal) facts from which one can argue by 'induction' [Hicks, 1979, pp. 28ff.]. There are no timeless facts in economics. All data collected in economics are historical - that is, *in* time. The use of the methodology of physics in economics must presume the existence of stable constants; hence the applicability of such methodology is limited to very short periods of time over which the 'constants' can be considered constant. Actually, Hicks argues, the constants of physics are limited to a finite amount of time (e.g., the life of the sun); however, the amount always can be considered to exceed the range of practical problems. But the problems of economics are in real time - the short run - and thus constancy is an open question.

Hicks' rejection of physics methodology presents a problem for his argument that the most important improvement over Keynes would be an emphasis on sequential causality. Since the time of Hume, sequential causality has usually been associated with physics - that is, with mechanics. If an object is in a state of (stable) equilibrium, it will remain in equilibrium unless caused by an outside force to change its position to another equilibrium. In physics there is no effect (change in position) without a prior cause (an outside force). The problem is that Hume's sequential causality must be instantaneous or constrained to a mechanical trajectory which is fixed by stable constants or coefficients. On the other hand, in economics there may be a considerable time lag between cause and effect. In economics, Hicks argues, whenever one explains the effect as a result of a *prior* cause, one must also explain why it takes so long - that is, what *causes* the delay - without the benefit of a fixed trajectory.

In the case of contemporaneous causality, where the cause and effect occur, or are *perceived* to occur, in the same period of time (e.g., a year of a production period), the lag is either irrelevant or not perceived. This is clearest in the case of the relation between stocks and flows [Hicks, 1979, ch. 5]. Stocks are perceived at the beginnings and ends of 'accounting periods'. Flows are the accumulated effect over the period (e.g., sales). If the flows are caused by changes in the stocks, both will be perceived to have occurred contemporaneously.

Contemporaneous causality (the 'equilibrium method') presents no problem for two of the major elements of formal Keynesian models - namely, the consumption function (or the multiplier) and the marginal efficiency of capital. But, as Hicks argues, when it comes to the element of liquidity, contemporaneous causality fails to deal with what Keynes intended; we need to use sequential causality.

According to Hicks, the necessary existence of a lag between cause and effect explains the need and purpose of liquidity. The key to the explanation, he says, is the recognition that 'Economics is specifically concerned with the making of decisions, and with the consequences that follow from the decisions' [p. 5]. In this he seems to be giving the same view as Shackle. But, as Hicks says, 'it is not enough ... to refer the effect to the decision; we are also concerned with the reason for the decision, the causes of the decision' [p. 88]. Hicks thus begins his theory of the relation between liquidity and sequential causality by noting that

> sequential causation in economics has two steps in it: a prior step, from the objective cause to the decisions that are based on it, or influenced by it, and a posterior step, from the decisions to their (objective) effects. With respect to the decision, the prior step is one of formation, the posterior of execution. Each of these steps may take time, so the total *lag* between cause and effect consists of two parts.... In order to explain the lag ... we have to explain the prior lag *and* the posterior lag. [p. 88]

Most analyses of economic history, dynamic models, or lagged cause and effect are concerned only with the posterior lag. The reason is simple: the posterior lag is rather mechanical. The analysis of Keynes was concerned with the importance of the problems of the prior lag [e.g., Keynes, 1937]. By considering those problems Hicks attempts to explain the decision-maker's need for liquidity.

For financial institutions, questions of liquidity may be treated as a matter of marginal adjustment and hence of contemporaneous causality. But outside the financial sphere, problems of liquidity cannot be so easily explained. For Hicks, 'Liquidity is freedom' [p. 94]. Marginal adjustments are made on the boundary of possibilities because there is no freedom except for the allowance of only marginal adjustments (this is what Latsis calls a 'single exit, or strait-jacket' view of rational decision-making [1972, p. 211]). Such adjustments are adequate whenever there are no surprises and are thus only mechanical changes. But the prior lag part of the decision's cause and effect always involves 'information and negotiation' [Hicks, 1979, p. 93], neither of which can be 'scientifically precise' or mechanical. There are no automatic responses (decisions) whenever new information appears. Liquidity *facilitates* a fast response but it does not require it. It also facilitates a slow response, as a little liquidity in the form of excess capacity permits some delaying of crucial decisions. Thus, it would seem, Hicks' emphasis on liquidity as a key endogenous variable opens the door to explaining the speed of adjustment that has been so elusive in the models discussed above.

We will argue in the Chapter 11 that the speed of the decision-maker's response is a matter of explaining the *methodology* of the decision-maker. But, more important, whenever there is liquidity, the usual (causal) explanations must break down in real time, because the economy is not operating on the boundary of its production possibilities. Hence not all of the usual necessary conditions of optimization (of what Hicks calls the Economic Principle and what Marshall called the

Principle of Substitution) will be operative. Thus, explanations which assume optimization (e.g., 'Keynesian' models) are, at best, inadequate for reality.

Has Hicks succeeded in overcoming the shortcomings of the usual neoclassical macroeconomic models of dynamics? Not completely. His Inductivist concept of a true science surely needs to be questioned. The same is true of his misleading concept of 'static' explanation, which suggests a timeless world; but as we explained above, a 'static' model is not timeless whenever it is considered to be an explanation. Nevertheless, we should applaud his attempt to develop his 'theory of liquidity' [pp. 94ff.] and raise the question of the adequacy of the microfoundations to deal with the deliberate efforts of some decision-makers to avoid being put into a position of making decisions only on the margins of production possibilities. We argue that not much progress will be made in this direction as long as the decision-maker is assumed to be forced to make only marginal moves along the inductive learning possibilities function. If the reconciliation of Keynes' macroeconomics with neoclassical microeconomics is founded on a common acceptance of the inductive learning possibilities function, then Keynes has won after all!

Our argument is straightforward. In real (calendar or clock) time, inductive learning cannot be a theory of successful decision-making but only a means of *explaining away* failures. Moreover, if neoclassical economists accept 'expectational errors' as the means of accommodating Keynes, the cost is an admission of the impossibility of the neoclassical research program of psychologistic individualism. Neoclassical economics can honestly survive the indictments of Keynes only by rejecting induction and psychologism.

With his little book about the methodology of macroeconomic theory Hicks is attempting to salvage something from his contribution to the foundations of 'Keynesian' economics (as distinguished from the economics of Keynes). He says that his interest in the methodological questions he examines grew out of his dissatisfaction with the profession's excessive concern for *micro*foundations of macroeconomics. He specifically argues that we should first be concerned with the foundations of macroeconomics 'without attention to "micro"' [1979, p. viii]. His first question then is, 'What is macro-economics for?' Although he recognizes many different answers, the one that interests him is that macroeconomics is used for the analysis of facts. For Hicks, this puts the methodological questions of the *adequacy* of macroeconomic theory (as a basis of explanation of facts) at center stage, in the spot-light. He does not go far enough.

We argued in Chapter 5, following Keynes [1937], that not only must we examine such methodological questions, but we must also question our views of methodology. Not only do economists hold views about their methodology, but they also attribute such views to the individual decision-maker who also must be assumed to have some methodology to deal with the available facts. Explaining how individuals deal with factual evidence should be the purview of methodology, so let us now turn to a consideration of the economists' views of methodology.

Notes to Chapter 6

1. Parts of this chapter have been drawn from [Boland 1978] and our review of Hicks [1979] in the November 1980 issue of the *Canadian Journal of Economics*.

PART III

CONVENTIONALIST METHODOLOGY IN ECONOMICS

7

Positive Economics as Optimistic Conventionalism

> The venerable admonition not to quarrel over tastes is commonly interpreted as advice to terminate a dispute when it has been resolved into a difference of taste, presumably because there is no further room for rational persuasion. Tastes are the unchallenged axioms of a man's behavior....
>
> ... On the traditional view, an explanation of economic phenomena that reaches a difference in tastes between people or times is the terminus of the argument.... On our preferred interpretation, one never reaches this impasse: the economist continues to search for differences in prices or incomes to explain any difference or changes in behavior.
>
> George Stigler and Gary Becker [1977, p. 76]

> Attacking any theory is easy enough, since none is perfect. But the wide class of empirical observation that *is* explained by economic theory should caution one against sweeping that theory aside and setting up new *ad hoc* theories to explain *only* or *primarily* those events the standard theory will not explain. What is wanted is a generalization of economic theory to obtain an expanded scope of validity without eliminating any (or 'too much') of the class of events for which it already is valid....
>
> Armen Alchian [1965]

> To abandon neoclassical theory is to abandon economics as a science....
>
> Douglass C. North [1978]

Our discussions in the previous six chapters have centered on the hidden agenda of neoclassical economic theory; our evidence was the nature of avant-garde neoclassical research programs. It is fair to question whether those considerations shed any light on the mainstream of neoclassical economics. By referring to them as 'avant-garde' we clearly indicate that they are not viewed as mainstream research programs. In this and the next two chapters we will examine the hidden agenda of mainstream neoclassical economics and show that in many ways the hidden agenda items are the same as those of the avant-garde programs but that the research programs of the mainstream are much more primitive.

The mainstream can be divided into two separate currents. One moves under the overt banner of 'positive economics', although not too many years ago it was merely called 'applied economics'; the other under the pretentious title of 'economic theory', although it is merely what was called 'mathematical economics' twenty or thirty years ago. Their differences are essentially analogous to the differences between optimistic (or 'naive') Conventionalism and pessimistic (or 'sophisticated') Conventionalism [Agassi, 1966a]. Optimism in matters of neoclassical economics tends in some circles to lead to anti-intellectualism. Pessimism too often leads to silliness. But we are getting ahead of ourselves. Let us begin this chapter with an examination of the available evidence.

Positive Evidence about Positive Economics

The salient feature of all the applied or 'positive' economic analyses is their conformity to just one format. Specifically, after the introductory section of a typical positive economics article there is a section titled 'The Model' or some variation of this. This is followed by a section titled 'Empirical Results' or something similar, and a final section summarizing the 'Conclusions'. The question we should consider is why do virtually all applied papers conform to this one format? As we shall explain, the reason is that this format satisfies the dictates of Conventionalism.

A 'model' of neoclassical empirical analysis
A trivial explanation for why a specific format is universally used is that all journal editors require that format, but they are only responding to what they think the market demands. Our concern here is not just why any particular individual might decide to organize a research paper according to the accepted format. We wish to examine why this particular format is so widely demanded.

One way to understand a methodological format is to emulate it - so let us attempt to build a 'model' of the format of a typical article in the literature of positive economics. Judging by what is often identified as a 'model' in positive economics, virtually every formal statement is considered a model. Nevertheless, there are some basic requirements.

In order to build our model of neoclassical empirical analysis, as with any model, the assumptions need to be explicitly stated. Let us begin by stating the obvious assumptions which form the 'visible agenda' of neoclassical economics. Our first assumption is that every neoclassical model must have behavioral assumptions regarding maximization or market equilibrium. Furthermore, the results of the model must depend crucially on these assumptions. Our second assumption is that every empirical model must yield at least one equation which can be 'tested' by statistically estimating its parametric coefficients.

Beyond these two explicit requirements almost anything goes when it comes to building the model. But there are two more requirements that are part of the first item on the hidden agenda of neoclassical research programs. Our third assumption is that every empirical paper must presume specific criteria of 'truthlikeness' - so-called testing conventions. For example, one must consider such statistical parameters as means and standard deviations, R^2s, t-statistics, etc. That is, every equation is a statement which is either true or false. However, when applying an equation to empirical data we know that the fit will not usually be perfect even if the statement (i.e., the equation) is true. So the question is: in what circumstances will the fitted equation be considered true? The use of the testing conventions implies that the investigator is not attempting to determine the absolute truth of his or her model. Rather, the objective is to establish its acceptability or unacceptability according to standard testing conventions.

Our last assumption is that in order to be published, every empirical paper must have contributed something to the advancement of 'scientific' knowledge. That is, it must establish some new 'facts' - that is, ones which were previously unknown - by providing either new data or new analysis of old data.

An 'empirical analysis' of neoclassical literature

In order to test our model of the methodology of neoclassical positive economics, we must consider the available data. First we must decide on where to look for mainstream 'positive economics'. Obviously, we should expect to find it in the pages of the leading economics journals.

So, let us sample one arbitrary year, say 1980, and examine the contents of a few issues of such journals for that year. Further, let us restrict our examination of the data to those articles intended to be positive analysis. That is, we are not interested in those articles considered to be avant-garde theories or concerned with the more technical (mathematical) aspects of 'economic theory'. We should also ignore topics such as 'history of thought' or 'methodology'. Let us examine the topics that remain:

- The Market for New Ph.D.s
- Family Size and the Distribution of Income
- Wages, Earnings and Hours of First, Second, and Third Generation American Males
- Foreign Trade and Domestic Competition
- Taxing Tar and Nicotine
- Murder Behavior and Criminal Justice System
- Optimal Order of Submitting Manuscripts
- Effect of Minimum Wage in Presence of Fringe Benefits
- Economics of Short-term Leasing
- Federal Taxes and Homeownership
- Decline in Male Labor Force Participation
- Open Market Operations
- Effects of State Maximum Hours Laws
- Job Queues and Layoffs
- Relative Capital Formation in the US
- Potential Gains from Economic Integration in Ghana
- Effects of the EEC's Variable Import Levies
- Unemployment, the Allocation of Labor, and Optimal Government Intervention

Our examination of the articles on these topics seems to indicate that all of them conform to the format specified by our model. The only empirical question implied by our positive model is whether there are any exceptions to what we have claimed will be found in the mainstream journals. We can report that there are none in the data considered. Our model of positive analysis does fit the data.

Some questions raised by this positive analysis

Now we do not wish to push this mockery of neoclassical positive analysis any further, as it is not clear what positive contribution it would make. Nevertheless, it does emphasize the point raised that there is an amazing empirical uniformity among positive neoclassical articles. Empirical uniformities beg to be explained.

There is apparently no discussion of why papers should be written according to the observed format. Of course, there is no need to discuss the standard format if everyone agrees that it presents no problem and it is doing its required job. But what is the purpose of the standard format? Our general theory is that the reason why the format is not discussed is that its purpose is simply taken for granted.

Taking things for granted is a major source of methodological problems and inconsistencies in economics, although the problems are not always appreciated. This is the case with the format of neoclassical empirical research papers. We are going to argue here that the purpose of the standard format is the facilitation of an inductive verification of neoclassical theory even though the format itself serves a more modest Conventionalist view of knowledge and method, a view which supposedly denies induction.

To understand the relationship between the standard format and the research program to verify neoclassical theory, we need to consider the following questions. What constitutes a successful empirical analysis? What would be a failure? What is presumed in the use of 'testing conventions'?

The Logic of Model-Building in Positive Economics

Every applied model in neoclassical economics is a specific attempt to model the essential idea of neoclassical theory - independent individual maximization with dependent market equilibria. In a fundamental way each model is a test of neoclassical theory's relevance or applicability to the phenomena of the real world. At the very minimum, each model is an attempt to make neoclassical *theory* testable.

Since our idea of applied models is still not universally accepted, perhaps we should be more specific about our view of the nature and purpose of model-building. While some economists use the term 'model' to specify the idea of a formal model as conceived by mathematical logicians, our use of the term reflects the more common usage in positive economics [e.g., Lucas, 1980]. Although we have discussed the nature of models elsewhere [Boland 1968, 1969, 1975, 1977a, 1977b], it would be useful to review the essentials here.

The role of models in testing theories
One way to determine if a theory will work in a given practical situation would be to build a 'model' of our theory much in the spirit of design engineering. Design engineers might build a small model of a new airplane wing design to test its aerodynamics in a wind tunnel. In other words, engineers commit themselves to specific models. Of course, many different models may be constructed (all based on the same new wing idea) by varying certain proportions, ingredients, etc. Unfortunately, such opportunities for testing in this manner (i.e., with scaled-down models in wind tunnels) seldom arise in economics.

Schematically, in model-building we traditionally start with a set of autonomous conjectures as to basic behavioral relationships which must include an indication of the relevant variables and which of them are exogenous and which are not. To these we add specifying or simplifying assumptions, the nature of which depends on what is being simplified or specified (i.e., on the behavioral assumptions). One reason why we must add these extra assumptions is that no one would want to make the behavioral assumptions of our neoclassical theory of the consumer (or producer) as specific as would be required in order to make it (or predictions deduced from it) *directly* observable. Applied models add another set of assumptions designed to deal with the values of the parameters either directly specifying them or indirectly providing criteria to measure them. This gives us the following schemata for any model (in our engineering sense):

(1) *A set of behavioral assumptions* about people and/or institutions. This set might include, for example, the behavioral proposition $Q = f(P)$, where dQ/dP is negative. The *conjunction* of all the behavioral assumptions is what traditionally constitutes a 'theory'.

(2) *A set of simplifying assumptions* about the relationships contained in the above set. For example, the demand function stated in the theory might be specified as a linear function, $Q = a + b P$, where 'a' is positive and 'b' is negative.

(3) *A set of assumed parametric specifications* about the values of those parameters created in the second set above. For example, the parameter 'b' above might be assumed to have the value $b = -4.2$; or the specification that the above model fit the available data according to certain statistical criteria.

Observing that any empirical model is a conjunction of these three sets of assumptions leads us to consider some problems concerning what constitutes a success or failure. Whenever it is shown that one of the predictions is false, then, by *modus tollens* (see below, p. 124), we can conclude that at least one of the assumptions (the constituent parts) must be false. Note, however, there is a certain ambiguity about which type of assumption is responsible for the false prediction. If any one of the assumptions is false, then some of the predictions are going to be false. But since any of them could be the false assumption, just noting that one of the predictions is false does not necessarily tell us anything about which assumption has 'caused' the false prediction [see further, Boland, 1981b]. We will call this the problem of the ambiguity of logical refutations. We shall see that this is particularly a problem for model-builders who are using models to refute neoclassical theory.

The logical problem of testing theories using models
To expect to refute a theory by showing that it is false by means of empirical testing means that we must expect to show that all possible models of the theory are false! In other words, to get at the basic behavioral assumptions themselves we must consider all possible ways of specifying them (however simple or complex). But there will always be an infinite number of ways. Assuming that there are no logical errors, if *every* one of them, when conjoined with the behavioral assumptions, can be shown to lead to *at least one* false prediction, then we *know* that at least one behavioral assumption is necessarily false. And if that were not the case, that is, if all the assumptions are (non-tautologically) true, then it is *possible* to specify the behavioral assumptions such that no false predictions could or would ever happen. Obviously, the requirement that we must show that *all* possible models are false is impossible for the same reason that it is impossible to verify a strictly universal statement [Popper, 1934/59]. We must therefore conclude that on this basis the empirical falsificaton of neoclassical theory using *models of the theory* is impossible. We will return to this question below.

Now what about building *specific* models of a theory intending to show that the theory is true? Well, this is the old logical problem which logic textbooks call 'the fallacy of affirming the consequent' [Boland, 1979a, p. 505]. In effect, every model of a theory is a special case and a confirmation of one model is good only for one given set of phenomena. Even though one may confirm a neoclassical model's application to one market during one period of time, one still has not proven that the same model can be applied to any other market or any other period of time. To say that a behavioral theory is true is to say that it applies to every situation to which it purports to be relevant. That is, *if* a theory is true, then it is *possible* to build at least one model that will fit the data in *any* given situation. If the theory is not a tautology (i.e., an argument which for logical reasons cannot be false), then to prove it true we would have to provide a potentially infinite series of models. That is, no finite set of confirmed models will do, since there will always be the logical possibility of a situation which cannot be modeled or fitted. It is easy to see that this is merely the Problem of Induction restated at a slightly different level of discussion.

The point of formalizing our view of models is to show that building models of a theory in effect insulates the theory from empirical testing if our purpose in testing is either refutation or verification. We can also conclude that neoclassical economists who are not prone to making logical errors, but are nevertheless building models to apply or to test neoclassical economics, must have some other objective in mind - otherwise there would be more concern for these logical problems.

The Problem with Stochastic Models

Some may argue that the logical problems discussed here are irrelevant for the neoclassical economist who is wedded to Conventionalism, since these problems concern only those cases in which someone is attempting to provide a proof of the absolute truth or falsity of any given theory. Instead, we should be concerned only with the problems of building models which fit the data with acceptable degrees of approximation [Simon, 1979]. But in response we might argue, if models are never refutations or verifications, what constitutes a successful model? When would a model-builder ever be forced to admit failure?

Virtually every applied neoclassical model today is a stochastic model. The reason for this is simple. Stochastic models are the primary means of accommodating the dictates of Conventionalism and at the same time solving the Problem of Conventions externally by appealing to universally accepted statistical testing conventions. One does not have to build stochastic models to satisfy Conventionalism, but it certainly helps.

The problem with the concept 'stochastic', or more generally, with the doctrine of 'stochasticism' - the view that realistic models must be stochastic models [Boland, 1977c] - is that it takes too much for granted. Some economists are fond of claiming that the world is 'a stochastic environment' [e.g., Smith, 1969]; thus technically no model is ever refuted or verified, and hence there could not be any chance of our construing one as a refutation or a verification of a theory. This concept of the world can be very misleading and thus requires a critical examination.

Our purpose here is to show that stochasticism involves model-building, as it requires an explicit assumption which is possibly false, and thus stochasticism should not be taken for granted, and, further, to argue that the retreat to stochasticism does not succeed in avoiding the logical problems of using models to test neoclassical economics.

The nature of stochasticism

The word 'stochastic' is based on the idea of a target and in particular on the pattern of hits around a target. The greater the distance a given unit of target area is from the center of the target, the less frequent or dense will be the hits on that area. It can also be said that there are two 'worlds': the 'real world' of observation and the 'ideal world' of the theory or mathematical model. Thus, we might look at a model as a shot at the 'real world' target. When we say the theory (or model) is 'true' we mean that there is an *exact* correspondence between the real and the ideal worlds. There are many reasons why we might miss the target, but they fall into two rough categories: (1) ours was a 'bad' shot, i.e., our model was false or logically invalid, or (2) the target moved unexpectedly, i.e., there are random, *unexplained* variations in the objects we are attempting to explain or use in our explanation. Some may thus say that a stochastic model is one which allows for movements of the target. However, it could also be said that stochastic models follow from a methodological decision *not* to attempt to explain anything *completely*.

Many will argue that even with true theories the *correspondence* between these two worlds will not be exact for many obvious reasons (e.g., errors of measurement, irrational mistakes, etc.). For these reasons neoclassical models are usually stochastic models which explicitly accommodate the stochastic nature *of the correspondence*. For example, we can assume that the measurement errors, etc., leave the observations in a normal, random distribution about the values of the ideal world. This means that it is the correspondence which is the stochastic element of the model. Note, however, we are saying that it is the model (or theory) which is stochastic rather than the world or the 'environment'. Any test of a stochastic model is a test as much of the assumed correspondence as of the theory itself.

One can see the world as being necessarily stochastic *only* if one assumes beyond question that it is one's model (the shot at the real world target) which is true (and fixed) and that the variability of the correspondence is due entirely to the movements of the target (the real world). Thus stochasticism can be seen to put the truth of our theories beyond question. There is a serious element of potential intellectual dishonesty in asserting that the environment is stochastic. We *assume* that the assumptions of our theory or model are true because we cannot prove them true. Thus there is no reason for any assumption to be beyond question, as stochasticism seems to presume.

The logical problems of stochastic models

If it is granted that it is the models or theories which are stochastic and not necessarily the real world, then stochastic models are still subject to the logical problems discussed above (see p. 121). Does this mean that we must give up any hope of testing neoclassical theories? We would argue that it does not; it just makes things a bit more complicated. The logical problems involved in any test of neoclassical economics are not insurmountable if it is recognized that it is the model rather than the environment which is stochastic. That is, we can overcome the logical problems outlined above if we explicitly recognize the specific assumptions which make the model stochastic.

Unfortunately, when we build stochastic models, the logical problems are not as apparent. So let us review the discussion with respect to non-stochastic models. We cannot refute a theory by first building a model of that theory and then refuting the model because of the problem of the ambiguity of logical refutation. We cannot logically identify the source of the refutation - is it the behavioral assumptions of the theory or is it only the 'simplifying' assumptions that we have added? This problem is solely the result of our having to add *extra* assumptions in order to build the model. Although stochasticism requires additional assumptions and thus suffers from this problem, it also adds an entirely different logical problem which is not widely recognized.

For now let us forget the problem caused by adding extra assumptions. Let us restrict our concerns to testing a model, not bothering about whether one can logically infer anything about the underlying theory. The logic of refutation is based on the three propositions. We refute a logically valid model (1) by arguing *modus ponens*: whenever all the assumptions are *true* then every prediction which logically follows from their conjunction *must be true*; or equivalently (2) by arguing *modus tollens*: whenever any prediction turns out to be *false* then we know that the conjunction of all of the assumptions cannot be *true*. If we actually observe a false prediction, does that guarantee that at least one of the assumptions is false? We are able to argue in favor of such a guarantee only because we accept (3) the logical condition of *the excluded middle*: 'A statement which is not *true* must be *false*.'

This is not a trivial word game about 'true' and 'false'. For example, if we adopt the stochastic-Conventionalist view that identifies absolute truth with a probability of 1.00 and absolute falsity with 0.00, then to say some given statement is not absolutely true does *not* imply that it is absolutely false. A stochastic statement with a probability of 0.60 is not absolutely true, nor is it absolutely false! This same ambiguity occurs when positive economists substitute 'confirmed' for the term 'true', and 'disconfirmed' for the term 'false' in the above logical propositions. Generally, 'not confirmed' does not mean 'disconfirmed'. In other words, when 'confirmed' and 'disconfirmed' are used in place of 'true' and 'false', proposition (3) is discarded. But when *the excluded middle* is discarded we sacrifice the logical force of any test. That is, we cannot construct an 'approximate *modus ponens*' such as (1) 'Whenever all assumptions are "confirmed" then every prediction which logically follows from their conjunction will be "confirmed"' because it does not imply (2) 'Whenever there is a "disconfirmed" prediction then all of the assumptions cannot be "confirmed"'. It is quite possible for all of the assumptions to be confirmed and, with the same data, for one or more of the predictions to be disconfirmed too.

This is probably not the place to argue this, so we will leave the analytical proof or disproof up to the reader. But in simple terms, what we are saying is that the conjunction of several assumptions, each with a probability of 0.60, does *not* imply that all predictions will have a probability of 0.60. One example should be sufficient. Consider the following four statements.

(a) Urn A has 100 red balls and no green balls.
(b) Urn B has 100 green balls and no red balls.
(c) I have withdrawn one ball from A or B.
(d) The ball is red.

Together these statements, if absolutely true, imply that the following statement is absolutely true:

(e) I have drawn a ball from urn A.

Now, if statements (a) through (d) are true 60 per cent of the time (that is, they have a probability of 0.60 of being true), then what is the probability of statement (e) being true? Surely its probability need not be 0.60, since it compounds the probabilities of the other statements and it must be false whenever (c) is false regardless of the probabilities of the other statements. In other words, given a logically valid argument which works for absolute truth, the same argument need not work for any given degree of approximate truth. If our argument here is correct, it has serious implications for the generally accepted view of the methods of testing stochastic models.

Testing with stochastic models
We have argued above that stochastic models are models which contain assumptions that detail the stochastic correspondence between the exact model and the observable real world. For example, a stochastic model might contain an assumption that observational errors will be normally distributed about the mean corresponding to zero error. But for the purposes of logical inferences we must specify in what circumstances such an assumption would be considered 'false' and in what circumstances it would be considered 'true'. Usually this assumption will be some sort of parametric limit applied to the observed distribution of the actual errors. There will be a range of possible statistically estimated means and standard deviations. The criteria are designed either to avoid Type I errors (rejecting the model as false when it is actually true) or Type II errors (the reverse acceptance) but not both. Remember that unless we are discussing absolute truth we need two different criteria because we can no longer rely on the proposition of the 'excluded middle'.

That statistical testing must choose between avoiding one or the other type of decision error is the key to the problem we wish to discuss now. If we build a model to test a theory by adding statistical decision criteria to the model (to specify when it applies to the available data) and then we deduce a test prediction (e.g., an equation to be estimated by linear regression), the results must be assessed by the same criteria. If the criteria specified minimum conditions for the assumptions of the models to be accepted as 'true' for the purposes of the logical deduction of the prediction, then it is logically consistent for us to apply the same criteria to assess the 'truth' of the prediction. For example, as above we could say if we accept the assumptions as 'true' when the fitted equation has a probability of at least 0.95, then we can accept the predictions as 'true' when they have a probability of at least 0.95. We still have not avoided the problems discussed above (pp. 123-5), but at least we can be logically consistent in our decision process. However, remember that this consistency is only for the purposes of deducing the confirming predictions. If all of the predictions pass the test, we can say without inconsistency that the theory is so far confirmed.

What can we say if a prediction fails according to the decision criteria? When we said that we would accept a statement (an assumption or a prediction) which has a probability of 0.95, we did not say that failure to have at least a 0.95 probability implied that the statement was false or 'disconfirmed'. On the contrary, a criterion of acceptance of a statement's falsity might be a probability of less than 0.05. Should our prediction fail the confirmation criterion by having a probability of say 0.80, it would still be a long way from being logically considered false. There is then a fundamental asymmetry between the criteria of confirmation and disconfirmation.

Since most stochastic model-building in positive economics is concerned with deducing stochastic predictions, the usual choice made is to use 'confirmation' criteria rather than 'disconfirmation' criteria for the purposes of defining a valid deduction [Friedman, 1953]. Such models cannot automatically be useful when we wish to test the model except for the purpose of finding confirmations. In order to test a theory by building stochastic models we must do much more.

We are arguing not just that whenever both criteria are employed there is a very large range of undecidable cases (e.g., where the probabilities are between 0.05 and 0.95 along the lines we have just illustrated) but also that even if one criterion is used, the results are often contradictory, leading to the conclusion that most statistical testing done in the neoclassical literature is more inconclusive than the reporting might indicate. Before we can show this we must consider what it would take statistically to refute a theory using a stochastic model. Remember that with exact models we can refute a model by showing that one of its predictions is false (*modus tollens*). In effect, a false prediction is a counter-example; that is, it is a statement which would be denied by the truth of the exact model. This is a clue for our design of a logically adequate test of any theory. Let us illustrate this with the exact model concerning the selection of red or green balls from two urns. Whenever we can show that statement (e) is false and that the statement

(f)   The ball was drawn from urn B.

is true, at least one of the statements (a) to (d) must be false. In other words, (f) is a counter-example to the conjunction of (a) to (d). If we really wished to test the conjunction, then the statistical question would have to concern how to decide when the counter-example is *confirmed*.

We know of only one case in which this form of statistical testing has been applied [Bennett, 1981]. In that one pioneering case the results were dramatic. It was shown that if one were to take some of the well-known reports of tests of models of post-Keynesian theories and extend them by performing a similar test of models of corresponding counter-examples, the results would show that *both* the theories and their counter-examples were confirmed *using the same statistical test criteria*! What this demonstrates is that testing models using confirmation criteria (i.e., a statement is considered true if its probability is at least 0.95) can lead to contradictory results and that thus the usual published tests are often very misleading. But it should also be noted that Bennett's demonstration shows that it is possible to have decisive tests subject to the acceptance of specific stochastic decision criteria. For example, relative to given confirmation criteria, a refutation is successful only if the predictions fail the confirmation test *and* the counter-example passes the same test. Not many reported 'disconfirmations' satisfy these requirements.

Positive Success or Positive Failure?

This now brings us back to the question we keep asking: what constitutes a successful model in positive neoclassical economics? And, more generally, to decide what constitutes success we need to ask: what is the objective of neoclassical model-building?

Let us now consider the available facts before we answer these questions. First, there are all the logical problems we have been discussing. Second, all the standard statistical parametric criteria have been designed or used to identify confirming predictions, even though some investigators have attempted to use them to establish 'disconfirmations'. Since there has been very little recognition of the logical problems, we can only assume that the positive economic model-builders are not attempting to deal with them. So it is the secondary evidence of the prevailing confirmation criteria and the recognition of the necessity to choose between Type I and Type II error avoidance that we must take into consideration.

We now argue that if the usual published positive neoclassical articles such as those noted at the beginning of this chapter are actually considered contributions to 'scientific knowledge', then it can only be the case that the hidden objective of such positive economics is a long-term *verification* of neoclassical economics. Specifically, each paper which offers a confirmation of the applicability of neoclassical economics to 'real world' problems must be viewed as one more positive contribution towards an ultimate inductive proof of the truth of neoclassical theory. Our reason for concluding this is merely that logically all that can be accomplished by the typical application of neoclassical theory to 'real world' phenomena is a proof that it is *possible* to fit at least one neoclassical model to the available data. Critics can always say that a model's fit may be successful in the reported case but it does not prove that it will be successful in every case. We argue that the agenda of positive neoclassical research programs presumes that if we can continue to contribute more confirming examples of the applicability of neoclassical economics, then eventually we will prove that it is the only true theory of the economy.

8

Analytical Theory as Defeatist Conventionalism

In recent years, mathematical tools of a more basic character have been introduced into economics, which permit us to perceive with greater clarity and express in simpler terms the logical structure of important parts of economic theory....

It may facilitate reference if we set out the basic assumptions of the model to be discussed in a number of postulates. This may be looked upon as a device for separating the reasoning within the model from the discussion of its relation to reality. The postulates set up a universe of logical discourse in which the only criterion of validity is that of implication by the postulates....Only the logical contents of the postulates matter....

Tjalling Koopmans [1957]

In all formal procedures involving statistical testing or estimation, there are explicitly stated but untested hypotheses.... In ... econometric studies ... the 'premises' [e.g., profit maximization, maximization of satisfaction] ... play that role. More in general, any statement resulting from such studies retains the form of an 'if...then...' statement....

The 'if ... then ...' statements are similar to those in the formal sciences. They read like logical or mathematical reasoning in the case of economic theory, and like applications of statistical methods in the case of econometric estimations or testing. The heart of substantive economics is what can be learned about the validity of the 'ifs' themselves, including the 'premises' discussed above. 'Thens' contradicted by observation call, as time goes on, for modification of the list of 'ifs' used. Absence of the contradiction gradually conveys survivor status to the 'ifs' in question. So, I do think a certain record of noncontradiction gradually becomes one of tentative confirmation. But the process of confirmation is slow and diffuse. Tjalling Koopmans [1979, p. 11]

Propositions and Proofs

In this chapter we shall examine the nature of the other mainstream research program in neoclassical economics which also conforms to a specific format but one unlike that of 'positive economics'. Again we shall describe the nature of the format and the problems involved in its application and then explain the hidden agenda implied by its widespread use. But first we must see why anyone might think there is a need for an alternative research program in neoclassical economics.

The problem of 'positive economics'

Those neoclassical economists who are pessimistic about the possibility of ever constructing an inductive proof for neoclassical theory based on observed 'facts' have slowly developed a research program which on the surface appears to depart significantly from that employed in 'positive economics'. They might argue either that induction is impossible or that inductive proofs are never final, as 'all facts are theory-laden' [Hanson, 1965; Samuelson and Scott, 1975]. But if one doubts 'facts', what is left? Is economic theory an arbitrary game? If there are no final inductive proofs, does this mean that all theories are circular or infinite regressions? Is there no solid foundation for a scientific economics? Such questions are seldom asked any more simply because economic theorists avoid making broad claims for economic theories. It might be interesting to consider why such questions are avoided. We think their avoidance is likely for the same reasons as those identified in earlier chapters for similar omissions - such questions do not need to be asked, since the answers are considered obvious.

We shall argue here that the reason why these questions need not be asked is that economic 'theorists' have found what may be considered a superior alternative to solid empirical 'facts'. The problem with empirical 'facts' or, more properly, with *reports* of observations is that they can easily be questioned. That is, they cannot be claimed to be absolutely true. For many mathematical logicians [e.g., see Hughes, 1981] *that* is the problem with induction. To begin any successful inductive argument what is needed are unquestionably true statements. It turns out that the only unquestionably true statements are those that are logically true.

Let us consider what constitutes a logically true statement [see also Quine, 1965]. Generally, many logicians argue that a statement is true if it cannot be false (e.g., truth tables). Thus a statement is true only if it is logically true. Logically true statements are to be distinguished from empirical truths, which are contingent truths - that is, an empirical statement is true only if it *logically follows* from other *true* empirical statements. The 'if' can be left unsatisfied by a failure to 'follow logically' or by the use of false supporting statements.

Now the importance of all this is not to argue that empirical theory cannot be true or that theories are empty tautologies. Such is simply not the case. The point is that empirical theories are concerned with *contingent truths*, that is, statements whose claimed truth depends on the truth of other statements whose truth in turn may be unproven.

Our argument is that today the research program of neoclassical economic 'theory' is one of seeking logical truths instead of empirical 'facts' so as to push on with an *ersatz* inductive science. That is, everything must be directed to establishing logically true facts - just as everyone once thought science established empirically true facts. However, there is a limit to all this, since we do not wish to end up with only pure logical truths (i.e., tautologies).

The format of 'economic theory'

The paraphernalia of the pursuit of logical truths include the following 'buzz-words': 'proposition', 'theorem', 'lemma', 'proof', 'corollary', 'hypothesis', 'condition', and 'definition'. These words play a prominent role in the format of recent theory articles. Usually they are printed in capital letters to highlight the format.

The topics of typical theory articles cover a wide range but most are concerned with the theoretical problems we discussed in Chapters 3 and 4 above. The standard format seems to yield an article with several numbered propositions or theorems, each followed by a proof. The standard format follows quite closely the format of Koopmans' first essay [1957], which in turn merely copied the format of many mathematics textbooks of its day. Procedurally, the standard theory article begins by setting up a 'universe of logical discourse' or a 'model', as it is sometimes called. The rules of the game do not permit any new terms to be introduced after this step, as the object of the game is to show that some particular given theorem or situation of concern can be handled using only the stated model.

Unlike 'positive' analysis, which attempts to show that a particular theoretical proposition is logically supported by available data, the 'theory' article attempts to show that a particular theoretical proposition is logically supported by available mathematical theorems. Where 'positive' economics seeks objectivity in repeatable or observable data, 'theoretical' or, more properly, 'analytical' economics seeks objectivity in the autonomy of the discipline of mathematics. And this, we shall argue, is the problem with this neoclassical research program. While it may be easy to dispute empirical 'facts', surely it is not supposed to be easy to dispute the veracity of the mathematics profes-

sion. But we shall ask a more fundamental question: what is the cost of
our reliance on these given mathematical theorems?

Analytical Model-Building

Acceptable givens

In order to assess the methodology of economic 'theory' we need only
begin with an examination of what are considered acceptable givens.
That is, if one is going to prove some given proposition, one still needs
some assumptions, some premises, which are beyond question. One is
successful at proving one's chosen proposition when one shows that
the proposition logically follows from the conjunction of one or more
acceptable premises. Years ago, there was a small set of mathematical
theorems which would be invoked in almost every book devoted to the
mathematical structure of neoclassical economics. The most frequent-
ly used theorems had names such as Kakutani, Lyapunov, Brouwer,
and Frobenius. For a while, until quite recently, this game had been
transformed into one of referring to theorems named after economists,
such as Arrow's possibility theorem, Sheppard's Lemma, Stolper-
Samuelson theorem, etc. Today, it is somewhat curious that theorists
refer to very few named theorems. So what is the set of acceptable
givens now?

It would appear that one item on the portion of the hidden agenda
devoted to the objectives of economic 'theory' is that we must appear
to be self-reliant - that is, we must no longer appear to be dependent on
the mathematics profession for our fundamental theorems. Nevertheless, the proofs do depend on established principles of algebra or set
theory. But since students of algebra or set theory are required to
duplicate the proofs of established principles, all major principles are
in the 'public domain' by demonstration. Thus the current fashion in
economic 'theory' methodology is to incorporate all givens in the
'universe of discourse' and provide a proof for anything else that is
introduced. This means that apart from the terms introduced in the
'universe of discourse' the only things we are allowed to take for
granted are the rules of logic, since everything else will be proven by
the economic 'theorist' within the 'universe of discourse'.

One of the consequences of this admirable show of self-reliance is
that many of the stated theorems and propositions for which proofs are
published yield trivial results. Usually they are nothing but some
familiar theorem from standard neoclassical theory. The contribution
provided by the given article is a 'new' proof or an 'alternative' proof
demonstrating that the theorem or proposition can be proven using
only the specified 'universe of discourse'. Anything novel or informative will have to be provided in the 'universe of discourse'. What we are

saying here is simply that economic 'theory' today is nothing but exercises in puzzle-solving - along the lines described by Thomas Kuhn [1962/70].

Avoiding pure analytical results: tautologies
If the only givens allowed, beyond the definition of the terms to be included in the model, are the rules of logic, what constitutes successful model-building? As we noted above, unless a reference is made to some contingent proposition, the only outcome can be a tautology. This is because, for the purposes of logic, to prove a statement true means to prove that it is always true in the given circumstances (i.e., the given 'universe of discourse'). If no contingent propositions are introduced, then the only possible true statement is a tautology. (To reiterate, a tautology is any statement which is true by virtue of its logical form alone.) Since a tautology is true regardless of our 'interpretations' of its terms, then the 'interpretations' are irrelevant to the truth of the proven proposition. Critics of neoclassical 'theory' are free to argue in this case that there is nothing empirical or 'scientific' about such neoclassical model-building.

Unfortunately, the critics are often a bit confused about the nature of tautologies. They tend to think that any argument involving definitions and logic must be purely analytical, resulting only in tautologies. Although by their nature tautologies make the meaning of non-logical terms irrelevant, tautologies are not just a matter of definitions [see Boland, 1981b]. To illustrate let us take an example from elementary neoclassical theory. We might say that every demand curve is downward-sloping, and if it is not downward-sloping, it cannot be a genuine demand curve. Such a statement is in effect a tautology, since all possibilities are covered - by the implied definition of a 'genuine' demand curve. As the previous example shows, not all tautologies involve peculiar definitions (apart from the accepted definitions of fundamental logical terms such as 'and' or 'or'). But considering how complex a theory can be, it is quite easy inadvertently to construct a tautology by defining the terms in a manner which indirectly covers all cases and thereby leaves no conceivable counter-example.

We are not facing up to a fundamental question: why not seek tautologies, since they are always true statements? In other words, why are tautologies unacceptable as explanations? This is a delicate question and it is more difficult to discuss than might be expected. Consider, for example, a common explanation offered by neoclassical demand theory. When we offer any explanation, we put the truth of our assumptions at stake. In this case, when we explain someone's consumption choice as a consequence of the maximization of his or her utility, we put our assumption of utility maximization at stake. If it matters whether our explanations are true, it is because we want our theories to be true while at the same time allowing the possibility that our theories might be false. If they cannot be false (for purely logical reasons), not much will ever be at stake and thus nothing much can be gained.

All this may seem perverse, but it is really rather simple. An explanation is interesting because, while it is claimed to be true, it could be at the same time false (hence, it is not a tautology). If someone offers us an explanation which is true purely as a matter of logical form alone (i.e., all cases have been covered and thus all possible counter-examples are rendered inconceivable), we are not going to be very impressed, except perhaps with his or her cleverness. What makes the theory that all consumers are utility maximizers interesting is merely that someone might think there is a possibility for consumers being otherwise motivated.

We thus have to be careful to distinguish between the logical impossibility of counter-examples to our theory (due to the logical form of our theory) and the empirical impossibility of the existence of counter-examples (because our theory happens to be true). This distinction is difficult to see when we use only elementary examples. So let us consider a different example, one which is a bit more complex.

Many years ago, economic theorists accepted as true what they called the Law of Demand. This allegedly true statement considers the question (identified above) of whether demand curves are always downward-sloping. Immediately, given the above considerations, we might suspect that such an allegedly true statement may only be a tautology, but let us suspend our judgement for a while.

Empirically it may be true that all demand curves are downward-sloping, but it may also be true that a good with an upward sloping demand curve is still a possibility. For instance, consider the allegation that a good with an upward sloping demand curve was observed many years ago by the statistician named Giffen. Such an observation is not logically ruled out by maximizing behavior [Samuelson, 1953]. The good demanded may have been an inferior good. For a good to have an upward-sloping demand curve the good must be an inferior good (a good for which the demand falls when income rises). Even inferior goods may still have downward-sloping demand curves as long as they are not too inferior (that is, their positive income effect does not overwhelm the negative substitution effect of increasing their price). However, if one restricts consumer theory to the question of the demand for non-inferior (i.e., 'normal') goods, then as a matter of logic it is possible to show that all such goods will have downward-sloping demand curves whenever the only reason for demanding them is to maximize utility.

In a 'universe of discourse' consisting only of non-inferior (i.e., 'normal') goods and utility-maximizing consumers, upwardly-sloping demand curves are logically impossible. In such a hypothetical world, Giffen's observations would not be empirically possible, since they are logically impossible. But this question of possibility depends on the special characteristics of our invented hypothetical world. There is no reason why the real world has to correspond to this restricted hypothetical world. In other conceivable worlds it is quite possible for there to be upward-sloping demand curves (i.e., Giffen goods).

The point of all this complexity and perversity is that a statement which some might consider to be a tautology may only be a statement for which the hypothetical world has been designed logically to rule out all counter-examples. In fact, in economics there are very few pure tautologies (statements which are true regardless of definitions). But there are many theories and models which invent hypothetical worlds that provide what we might call 'pseudo-tautologies'. What is important at this stage is the recognition that when we want to provide a true explanation or theory for something, we do not want our explanation or theory to be true merely because it is a tautology. A tautology is a true statement but its truth is, in a sense, too easy.

A Critique of 'Pure' Theory

The methodology of tautology avoidance
Although it is not widely recognized, it is interesting to note that Paul Samuelson's monumental Ph.D. thesis [1947/65] was, among other things, concerned specifically with methodology. Its subtitle was 'The Operational Significance of Economic Theory'. One of his stated purposes for writing the book was to derive 'operationally meaningful theorems' from economic theory. By 'operationally meaningful theorems' he meant hypotheses 'about empirical data which could conceivably be refuted, if only under ideal conditions' [p. 4]. As far as we are aware, Samuelson nowhere tells us why one would ever want to derive 'operationally meaningful theorems' or why anyone would ever think economics hypotheses should be falsifiable. But everyone knows why. If a statement or theory is falsifiable, it cannot be a tautology [cf. Boland, 1977a, 1977b].

To a certain extent requiring falsifiability is *ad hoc*, since falsifiability is not necessary for the avoidance of tautologies. All that is necessary for the avoidance of a tautology is that the statement in question be conceivably false. Some statements which are conceivably false are not falsifiable. For example, a 'strictly existential' statement such as

'There will be a revolution after 1984' can be false but we could never refute it.

Now the reason why Samuelson found it necessary to invoke the *ad hoc* requirement of falsifiability is that he wished to promote analytical models of neoclassical economics. Specifically, he 'wanted to find the common, core properties of diverse parts of economic theory' [1947/65, p. ix]. In short, he attempted to show that the foundations of economic analysis are nothing more than the analytics of maximization (or minimization). Not only did he show the logical equivalence of the theories of consumer behavior and of costs and production but he also demonstrated that they are equivalent to the theory of equilibrium stability. That is, they can all be reduced to the analytical properties of a maximizing system in which 'analytical properties' are merely provable theorems.

Samuelson's methodological contribution was to recognize that in order to avoid tautologies we must be concerned with the correspondence of the analytical model of an equilibrium to a dynamic process. That is, not only must our equilibrium explanation imply the existence of a potential balancing of demand and supply but we must also provide an explanation for *why* a market price or quantity converges to that balance point. He called this the *correspondence principle*. Unfortunately, it is too easy to transform his correspondence principle into another analytical issue and thus to defeat the effort to make economics refutable [see Boland, 1977b]. Specifically, this is the problem of explaining away disequilibrium which we discussed in Chapter 3.

Whenever someone attempts to satisfy the correspondence principle by adding a mathematically appropriate difference or differential equation for the rate of change of the price relative to the extent of disequilibrium (see pp. 101-2 above), the question concerning the testability of the original model of the nature of market clearing prices goes begging. That is to say, if one refuted the augmented model (which added a rate of change equation), one would not know whether the source of the failure was the added equation or the original model. This is merely the same problem of the ambiguity of logical refutations which we discussed concerning model building in positive economics in Chapter 7! This means that Samuelson's method for avoiding tautologies - requiring testability through a correspondence principle - can, in effect, make the original model untestable and thus is a self-defeating methodology.

Is falsifiability really necessary?

As our example above showed, if all we wish to accomplish is an avoidance of tautologies, then falsifiability is sufficient, but not necessary, since strictly existential statements can be false (hence not tautological), although they need not be falsifiable. An alternative way of avoiding tautologies is to consider the terms of the 'universe of discourse' to be contingent statements about the nature of the real world. That is, instead of the analytical model being defined by such statements as 'Suppose there are N goods, M people, constant returns, a competitive equilibrium....', some of those statements could be considered empirical statements about the nature of the real world (along the lines we suggested in Chapter 6). If this is allowed, then there is no necessary problem about the possibility of the model being conceivably false. Can the problem of tautologies be so easily solved?

The logical problem of analytical models
The question of the falsifiability or testability of economics is rather stale today. And, as we have just indicated, falsifiability is not really essential. Does this mean that analytical economics or 'pure' theory need not worry about the potential shortcomings of relying only on analytical proofs of (desirable) propositions? We hope to show that there is yet a more fundamental problem.

In order to discuss this new problem we will need to review some technical issues of formal logic. Our major concern will be the logical concept called the 'material conditional' - a concept which remains a skeleton in the closet of analytical philosophers who have fostered the format and methodology of 'pure' theory [cf. Hollis and Nell, 1975]. What we have to say here may not satisfy the tastes of fastidious analytical and linguistic philosophers but they will have to clean out their own closets.

Let us state our 'universe of discourse'. First, suppose that only statements can be true (or false). A theory is true or false only by virtue of its being a compound statement such as a conjunction of all its premises (or assumptions, as we would call them). Second, suppose that logical arguments (e.g., proofs) consist of one or more statements. An argument is sufficient only if it is logically valid - which only means that whenever all of its premises are true its conclusions (or predictions, to use our terms) are also true without exception. Third, suppose that there is no universal or general means of proving sufficiency. We have only minimum conditions for sufficiency. And fourth, suppose that an argument in favor of the truth of any particular proposition or statement has two essential parts. One asserts the *validity* of the argument connecting the truth of the assumptions to the truth of the proposition in question, and the other asserts the *truth* of all of the assumptions which form the conjunction representing the argument.

Since 'pure' economic theory takes formal logic as a given for the purpose of providing proofs of propositions, the only question of concern here is what constitutes a minimally acceptable statement to be included in the logical argument. This is a question which Aristotle addressed. He stated what amounted to three minimum conditions: (1) the *axiom of identity* - in the process of forming or stating an argument the definition of any term which appears in more than one statement cannot vary; (2) the *axiom of the excluded middle* (which we have already discussed) - admissible statements can be true or false (i.e., 'maybe' is not allowed), and, more important, if a statement is not-false, the only other possible status it may have is that it is true; (3) the *axiom of non-contradiction* - no admissible statement can be both true and false simultaneously in the same argument.

Most existential or universal statements would be admissible. For example, 'All consumers are utility maximizers', 'There is one equilibrium price', etc. are unambiguous candidates because we know what it means for them to be true or false, although we may not know how to prove their truth status. Now we ask the key critical question. Are conditionals, that is, statements of the form 'if ... then ....', always admissible? We offer the following argument for why they may not always be admissible and thus why the basis of analytical economic theory is not as secure as we are led to believe.

Consider the standard form of a conditional or 'if ... then' statement: 'If P then Q', where P and Q represent admissible statements. (Note that we are discussing conditionals and not necessarily 'implications' [Quine, 1965].) Some logic textbooks would have us believe in the material conditional, namely, that such a statement is false only when P is true while at the same time Q is false. In all other cases, we are supposed to accept the 'if ... then' statement as true because of the excluded middle. Now, we ask, why must we accept the material conditional?

There are two alternative answers to this question. Some logicians might say that the given 'if ... then' statement is logically equivalent to the statement 'It is not true that "P is true" and "Q is false".' In these terms the 'if ... then' statement appears equivalent to a conjunction and is thus admissible. As a conjunction, it is false whenever one or more of its constituent parts is false. But this argument might lead to circularity if we question what is meant by 'logically equivalent'.

We prefer a different explanation. We argue that the only reason for accepting the material conditional is that analytical philosophers want *all* compound statements which are not self-contradictory to be admissible into logical arguments. Specifically, let us consider the given statement 'If P, then Q' and grant that whenever P is false the statement 'If P, then Q' is *not false*.

Now we argue that whenever P is false the statement 'If P, then Q' can also be considered *not true*. Thus we argue that in these circumstances the statement 'If P, then Q' does not always satisfy the axiom of the excluded middle (since it is neither true nor false), hence it is not always admissible into a logically valid argument! The textbook argument accepts the material conditional, we conjecture, on the following basis. They claim that to say the statement 'If P, then Q' is not false means, on the basis of the excluded middle, that the statement is true. But we would claim that the invocation of the excluded middle presupposes that the statement is admissible - which is the moot point. That is, only if one presumes that the given statement is admissible can one infer that it satisfies the axiom of the excluded middle. If the question of its admissibility is still open, then we cannot infer that when it is not false it must be true.

If our argument here against the presumptions of the material conditional is accepted, then it deals a serious blow to the presumed universality of analytical proofs and propositions. It means that the 'if ... then' propositions that abound in analytical economics are actually much more limited in their logical force than is presumed. Specifically, the truth status of the compound statement 'If P, then Q' is decisive only in one of the four possible combinations of the states of P and Q. Whenever P is false we cannot determine what the truth status of 'If P, then Q' is. In particular, the statement is logically decisive only when it is false. Saying that the compound statement is not always logically decisive in no way questions the truth status of its parts.

Analytical Success or Analytical Failure?

We claim that either one or the other of the following propositions is true:

PROPOSITION 1: We are wrong about the problems of the universal applicability of 'if ... then' statements; thus analytical economics is a successful program to establish logical facts. Furthermore, the ultimate objective of this program is the 'generalization' of neoclassical economics - that is, an inductive proof of its universal truth.

PROPOSITION 2: We are correct and thus analytical economics cannot provide proofs of universal propositions. It can only provide analytical refutations of contingent propositions. A successful generalization of neoclassical economics is thus an impossibility for the same reason that inductive proofs of universal statements are an impossibility.

We will not try to prove either proposition, as that would be contrary to our stated argument. But analytically they cannot both be true. With regard to the first proposition, the second part follows from the conjunction of our previous argument that (dealing with) the Problem of Induction is a primary item on the neoclassical hidden agenda and our argument earlier in this chapter that analytical economics rejects 'positive economics' as an impossible means of establishing indisputable 'facts'. Instead only a valid logical argument could ever provide proof of a generalization, that is, could ever demonstrate the impossibility of counter-examples.

The basis of the second proposition was argued on pp. 137-9. Without the material conditional, analytical economics cannot establish any non-contingent or logical facts (i.e., proven propositions). Without universal propositions each proposition must be proven in each real-world case by proving that the givens are true. Without a logical proof any claimed generalization is always open to dispute since exceptions cannot be logically precluded.

9

Instrumentalism as a Rejection of Conventionalism

> The subject matter of economics is regarded by almost everyone as vitally important to himself and within the range of his own experience and competence; it is the source of continuous and extensive controversy and the occasion for frequent legislation. Self-proclaimed 'experts' speak with many voices and can hardly all be regarded as disinterested; in any event, on questions that matter so much, 'expert' opinion could hardly be accepted solely on faith even if the 'experts' were nearly unanimous and clearly disinterested....
>
> Milton Friedman [1953, pp. 3-4]

In the previous two chapters we have examined the revealed methodologies of the two leading currents in mainstream neoclassical economics. Both are Conventionalist research programs and thus are based on the presumed need to solve the Problem of Induction. 'Positive' economics is directly concerned, optimistically, with establishing empirical 'facts'. Although no claim is made for the absolute truth of the facts, it is presumed that they do make a positive contribution towards the ultimate verification of neoclassical theory. Analytical or 'theoretical' economics is more concerned with things that seem possible, the establishment of absolute logical facts. There is not much left for those who reject the concerns of Conventionalist methodology.

Popular Alternatives to Conventionalism

There is little new under the methodological sun. As we explained in Chapter 1, most methodological prescriptions can be traced to nineteenth-century reactions to Hume's recognition of the impossibility of providing a foolproof empirical basis for (scientific) knowledge. The most widely accepted prescription is the one suggested by John Neville Keynes: Thou shall not base positive economics on normative judgements. J. N. Keynes was attempting to devise methodological rules to implement an Inductivist philosophy of science in economics. His only problem was that he was a hundred years too late. Inductivism was on the way out as a result of Hume's arguments, and an alternative viewpoint was already being developed by Duhem, Poincaré, Eddington and others with respect to the philosophy of physics. Their view is what we have been calling Conventionalism. At about the same time another alternative was being developed by Dewey, Mach and others. This latter alternative is sometimes called Pragmatism and at other times called Instrumentalism, even though these two views are not equivalent. Where Conventionalism and Pragmatism are direct competitors, Conventionalism and Instrumentalism are not. This may seem confusing but it is the reason why there is much confusion about the differences between Conventionalism and Friedman's methodology which is merely a straightforward version of Instrumentalism [Boland, 1979a]. They both reject Pragmatism. Furthermore, if one gives up interest in the Problem of Induction, none of the popular alternatives seems worthwhile.

Conventionalism and Pragmatism
Modern Pragmatism, like Conventionalism, has its roots in our inability to solve the classic Problem of Induction, the alleged problem of providing a factual proof for every scientific statement. The old 'scientific method' - namely, systematic proof by induction - is no longer considered effective. Very many philosophers (but not all) think that the Problem of Induction still needs to be solved or dealt with in some other way; they think an alternative *must* be found.

Conventionalism and Pragmatism are the most common alternative ways of dealing with the Problem of Induction. They are both concerned with proofs of the truth of our scientific (or other) knowledge. Pragmatism, in effect, accepts practical success as a sufficient criterion of the truth of any theory. In short, if the theory works, it must be true, since that is all we ever want of a theory. Conventionalism takes a very different tack. It says that it is a mistake to think that scientific theories are true. Instead, any given theory is only 'better' or 'worse' than some other competing theory. In short, no theory is true, or provable by reference to facts. For adherents of Conventionalism, a theory is a convenient description of, or filing system for, the existing facts. Some filing systems are better than others. According to Samuelson's version of Conventionalism, 'explanation' is merely the name we give to a 'better description' [1965].

In order to distinguish Pragmatism let us restate the nature of Conventionalism. Conventionalism is designed to deal with the classic Problem of Induction but it does so by redefining the problem by changing it into a problem that can be solved. Conventionalism is designed to solve the revised problem of choosing the 'best' theory among several competitors. The 'best' is always relative (i.e. subject to conditions). That is, there is no claim that the 'best' theory is necessarily the one 'true' theory; this is the quintessence of Conventionalism. There are many different versions of Conventionalism which differ only to the extent that there are different criteria to be used to choose the 'best' theory.

All versions of Conventionalism require generous amounts of hand-waving and clever philosophical analyses to be convincing. Pragmatism is much more straightforward. Whatever 'works' is true. If a theory does not work, it cannot be true. If it is true, it will work. If it is false, then eventually we will find that there is something for which it does not work.

The important point we wish to stress here is that both Conventionalism and Pragmatism are based on the acceptance of the necessity of dealing with the Problem of Induction. The former deals with the problem by denying its original objective, which was to establish the truth of scientific theories. The latter deals with the problem by accepting a weak criterion of truth, namely, 'usefulness'. Friedman's 1953 essay is often mistaken for a version of Pragmatism. Some followers of Conventionalist methodology unfortunately think they are opponents of Friedman's methodology because the latter often invokes usefulness as its primary objective. They miss the point, however. Friedman's methodology also rejects Pragmatism!

Instrumentalism and the usefulness of logic

It is nevertheless true that once one recognizes 'usefulness' as a criterion of truth one is immediately reminded of the many methodological prescriptions emanating from the so-called Chicago School. The source is allegedly Friedman's 1953 essay which presents his version of Instrumentalism, the view that theories are only useful tools or instruments and they are not intended to be true. Many of the followers of Friedman's essay on methodology claim that the only criterion to use when it comes to assessing a given theory is the theory's usefulness. The question we should ask is whether by 'usefulness' they mean the same thing as do orthodox Pragmatists. To answer this we must look at what Friedman's essay contributes to the discussion, so let us now turn to a discussion of the philosophical basis of Friedman's methodology, drawing upon some of our previous examinations [Boland, 1979a, 1980, and 1981a].

For the purposes of discussing Friedman's methodology, one can consider any theory to be an argument in favor of certain given propositions or specific predictions. As such, a theory can be considered to consist only of a conjunction of assumption statements, each of which is *assumed* (or asserted) to be true. In order for the argument to be sufficient it must be a deductive argument, which means that at least some of the assumptions must be in the form of general statements [Popper, 1934/56]. But, without an inductive logic, this latter requirement seems to raise all the methodological problems we discussed in Chapters 1, 7 and 8. When can one assume a theory is true? It is such difficulties that Friedman's essay attempts to overcome.

As long as a theory does its intended job, there is no apparent need to argue in its favor, or in favor of any of its constituent parts. For some policy-oriented economists, the intended job is the generation of 'true' or successful predictions. In this case a theory's predictive success is always a sufficient argument in its favor. This view of the *role* of theories is called 'Instrumentalism'. It says that theories are convenient and useful ways of (logically) generating what have turned out to be true (or successful) predictions or conclusions. Instrumentalism is the primary methodological point of view expressed in Friedman's famous essay.

For those economists who see the object of science as finding the *one* true theory of the economy, the task cannot be simple. However, if the object of building or choosing theories (or models of theories) is only to have a theory or model that provides true predictions or conclusions, *a priori* truth of the assumptions is not required *if* it is already known that the conclusions are true or acceptable by some Conventionalist criterion. Thus, theories do not have to be considered true statements about the nature of the world, but only convenient ways of systematically generating the already known 'true' conclusions.

In this manner Instrumentalism offers an alternative to the Conventionalist response to the Problem of Induction. Instrumentalism considers the truth status of theories, hypotheses, or assumptions to be *irrelevant* to any practical purposes, as long as the conclusions logically derived from them are successful. Although Conventionalism may deny the possibility of determining the truth status of theories, Instrumentalism simply ignores the issue. Some followers of Instrumentalism may personally care about truth or falsity, or even believe in the powers of induction, but such concern or belief is considered to be separate from the Instrumentalist view of the role of theories in science.

There are only two useful ways of employing formal logic which we discussed in Chapter 7. There is *modus ponens*, which is valid only for arguments from the truth of one's assumptions to the truth of one's conclusions; and there is *modus tollens*, which is valid only for arguments from the falsity of one's conclusions to the falsity of one's assumptions. By the adherents of Instrumentalism, who think they have solved the Problem of Induction by ignoring truth, *modus ponens* will necessarily be seen to be irrelevant. This is because they do begin their analysis with a search not for the true assumptions but rather for true or useful (i.e., successful) conclusions. (Note that 'analytical theorists' start in the same way but they seek only logically valid conclusions!) *Modus tollens* is likewise irrelevant because its use can only begin with false conclusions.

Pragmatism vs. Instrumentalism

The point we wish to stress is that the criterion of 'usefulness' is not being applied to the same problem in each case. What Pragmatism desires is a truth substitute in order to provide what the old 'scientific method' was supposed to provide, a solution to the Problem of Induction. Instrumentalism, such as the view presented in Friedman's essay, does not seek a truth substitute. Instead, the Problem of Induction is dismissed. In fact, all such philosophical problems (and solutions such as Pragmatism) are dismissed. The only question at issue concerns which method is appropriate for success in choosing theories as guides for practical policies.

If followers of Instrumentalism reject Pragmatism, how do they assure the truth of the theories they wish to use? The answer is that they do not require such an assurance. When we take our television set to the repair man, we do not usually think it is necessary to quiz the repair man about his understanding of electromagnetics or quantum physics. For our purposes, it can be quite adequate for him to believe that, for example, there are little green men in those tubes or transistors and that the only problem is that one of the little green men is dead. As long as the tube or transistor with the dead little green man is replaced and our television set subsequently works, all is well.

This is the essence of Instrumentalism. If emphasis is being placed on success and there are no doubts about one's success - for example, the television set does, in fact, now function properly - there is no immediate need for a philosophical substitute for inductive science. However, it is also clear that since truth is not necessary, there is no need to confuse success with truth. Thus we see, while success-in-use is a criterion of truth for Pragmatism, for Instrumentalism it is not. Unlike Pragmatism or Conventionalism, which both offer a way to resolve the Problem of Induction, Instrumentalism does not attempt to deal with that philosophical problem. That is, Instrumentalism does not attempt to establish the truth of scientific theories, since truth is not necessary for practical success.

The Methodological Differences

This brings us to the alleged differences between Conventionalism and Friedman's Instrumentalism. Our argument here is simply that, contrary to popular opinion, the followers of Instrumentalism and Conventionalism do not necessarily disagree. Their differences are at cross-purposes. Conventionalism and Instrumentalism agree that there is no direct solution to the Problem of Induction; and that the Pragmatist solution may be rejected. They only disagree about what we should do about the Problem. While Conventionalism looks for some criterion to provide a truth substitute, Instrumentalism looks for short-run criteria which promise immediate success. There is no claim that Instrumentalist criteria are adequate truth substitutes. The classic dispute is between 'generality' and 'simplicity'. The former criterion is typical of Conventionalist objectives; the latter is typical of Instrumentalist objectives.

Conventionalist 'simplicity'

If one were to consider Friedman's methodology as a solution to the Problem of Induction (which would be an error), then one might see his methodological prescriptions as direct competitors with orthodox Conventionalist prescriptions, since all versions of Conventionalism seek criteria to use in the allegedly necessary task of choosing between competing theories. In this sense, analytical economists see Friedman's advocacy of simplicity as a rejection of generality.

Let us consider how simplicity might be desirable from a Conventionalist's standpoint. Simplicity is advocated by those Conventionalists who believe that Nature is essentially simple. Historically, simplicity was invoked because many philosophers would invent complexities in order to overcome the failure of their explanations. The historical details do not matter here, so let us illustrate this with a modern example. Let us say that someone might see the demand curve as a mathematical function relating the price to the quantity demanded. Supposedly, if we know the price, then we can calculate the quantity demanded. The demand function says that any time the price changes, the quantity changes in a predictable way. In some sense, then, the price is used to predict the demand. This would be the simplest possible explanation of the quantity demanded, as there is a minimum number of variables involved - two: the price and the quantity demanded. Now if it were observed that the price changed but the quantity demanded did not, how would we explain this? The only way is to introduce a third variable, say, income. Thus, it might be argued that although the price changed, so did the consumer's income, so that the effects of the price change alone were cancelled out by the income change. The obvious instance would be that whenever prices double and incomes double, the demand will not usually change.

This illustration is not intended as a criticism of demand theory. Rather, we are suggesting that no matter how many variables are involved or introduced, we can always explain away any insufficiency in our original theory by introducing a new explanatory variable. But is the introduction of additional variables an acceptable way of dealing with failures to explain? Surely such a method of dealing with explanatory failures could get out of hand. We could have so many variables that there would be one variable for every possible change. With so many variables things could get very complex.

Sometimes we have to admit that our explanations are wrong. But if we are allowed to invent new variables to explain away our failures, such admissions can be postponed for ever. This, historically, is the type of situation that fostered the desire for simplicity. The methodological prescription used to be that whenever facing the choice of two competing theories, always choose the one with fewer variables or conditions. This prescription would reduce the chance of opting for a complex theory which merely covers up an inherently false theory. Note that this prescription of simplicity can be misleading, since the true theory may actually be very complex!

Not all followers of Conventionalism advocate simplicity; some like Lucas and Samuelson advocate generality. Generality is the criterion invoked by those followers of Conventionalism who wish to explain much by little. The Conventionalist view that a theory is but a filing cabinet for systematically storing and describing available facts leads to the view that the more that can be stored, the better. This is the essence of the criterion of generality. The more the situations that can be described, the more general is the theory. In terms of the theory of demand, the ability to deal with various types of goods (e.g. normal, inferior, and Giffen, as well as complements and substitutes) is a definite plus for the generalized form of demand theory which Samuelson presented in his *Foundations* [1947/65].

This, then, would appear to be the difference between generality and simplicity. But is the difference so (sorry...) simple? Even when the number of variables is low, the relationship between them could be very complex. What one is looking for, given the Conventionalist penchant for choice-criteria, is a theory which is both simple and general. Thus, on purely Conventionalist grounds, there is no necessary choice between simplicity and generality, as it may only be a question of personal tastes.

Instrumental simplicity

Adherents of Instrumentalism do not usually advocate generality and they desire simplicity for entirely different reasons. For Instrumentalism the only criterion to be considered is the practical success of a theory; otherwise anything goes. General theories are all right if they work. The reason why Instrumentalism values simplicity is that simple theories are easier to implement. They require less information. If there are few relevant variables, then there are few calculations to be made in the predictions. There is not much more to say than that. The only caution is to note that a small number of variables does not always imply simplicity. Two variables could be related in a linear fashion, as with a straight-line demand function. On the other hand, two variables could be related by means of a very complex polynomial of a very high degree. Thus it is possible for the relationship between three variables to be less complex than the relationship between two variables.

From the perspective of Instrumentalism, there is no need to impose arbitrary criteria such as simplicity or generality. The only relevant criterion is whatever works. Simplicity arises only because it is related to the practical question of the amount of information needed to implement any given theory. But the difficulty of collecting information may not always be a problem. In such cases, it is possible for the more general theory to be more useful than the less complex. So be it. From the stand point of Instrumentalism, the only prescription is to choose the theory which is most useful.

Critiques of Freidman's Essay

Friedman's essay elicited a long series of critiques. The most popular of these were by Koopmans [1957], Eugene Rotwein [1959], Samuelson [1963] and, to some extent, Herbert Simon [1963]. All of these critiques fail because they misunderstand that Friedman is merely stating his version of Instrumentalism.

Most of the misunderstandings are the result of Friedman's 'Introduction', where he seems to be saying that he is about to make another contribution to the traditional discussion about the methodology of Inductivism and Conventionalism. Such a discussion would usually be about issues, such as the verifiability or refutability of truly scientific theories. What Friedman actually gives is an alternative to that type of discussion. Unfortunately, most critics miss this point. Consequently, the critiques are quite predictable.

Koopmans takes Friedman to task for dismissing the problem of clarifying the truth of the premises - the problem that Koopmans wishes to solve. The source of the disagreement is Koopmans' confusion of 'explanatory' with 'positive' [see 1957, p. 134]. Koopmans, adhering to Inductivism, would define *successful* explanation as being logically based on observably true premises, that is, ones that are in turn (inductively) based on observation. Friedman does not consider assumptions or theories to be the embodiment of truth but only instruments for the generation of useful (because successful) predictions. Thus, for Friedman 'positive' is not equivalent to 'explanatory' because he does not use *modus ponens*. Explanation in Koopmans' sense is irrelevant to Friedman's Instrumentalism. Followers of Friedman's methodology can easily escape from Koopmans' critique.

Rotwein merely asserts that everyone should adhere to optimistic Conventionalism, which he calls 'empiricism'. Specifically, empiricism prescribes that everyone must justify every claim they make for the truth of their conclusions or predictions. Amazingly, Rotwein as a follower of empiricism recognizes that Hume showed that 'there was no reasoning that could justify (inductively) expectations that past regularities would be repeated in the future' [1980, p. 1554]. But rather than drop the presumed need to justify one's empirical claims, Rotwein says: 'Hume, however, held that such expectations were to be accepted because, given the kinds of creatures we are, or the manner in which we form our beliefs, we had no alternative to their acceptance; and this view has been central to the empirical tradition ever since his time' [1980, p. 1555]. Somehow, in everyone's head there is supposedly a perfectly functioning inductive logic which does what we cannot do outside our heads. How do the empiricists who follow Hume 'know' that there is such a functioning induction? This form of empiricism is silly and Friedman is quite free to dismiss it as such.

Simon's critique of Friedman's essay is based on the acceptance of a surrogate inductive learning function which Simon calls 'the principle of continuity of approximation'. Simon says that 'it asserts [that] if the conditions of the real world approximate sufficiently well the assumptions of an ideal type, the derivations from these assumptions will be approximately correct' [1963, p. 230]. This principle is nothing more than a sophisticated version of the inductive principle often used by mathematicians to avoid the intractable complications caused by the absence of an inductive logic [see Boland, 1979a, pp. 506-7]. Formally, Simon's principle would appear to be a restatement of *modus ponens*, but, as we explained in Chapter 7, there is no valid *approximate modus ponens* [see also Haavelmo, 1944, p. 56]. It is to Friedman's credit that he did not opt for this sophisticated subterfuge which smuggles successful induction in through the approximate back door.

Samuelson's critique is easily the most popular. Many critics of Friedman's economics are eager to believe that here is a critique which works. And since Samuelson's is so obscure, it is easy to accept it as an adequate critique because it is not well understood. Samuelson tries to criticize Friedman's methodology by attempting to argue that it is self-contradictory. Specifically, he offers a false theory of the motivation for Friedman's methodology and applies the false theory to explain the behavior of Friedman's followers. By implication we are supposed to conclude from the alleged successful explanation that there is some merit in his deliberately false assumptions. This implication is supposed to be a criticism of Friedman's use of the 'as if' principle, but it is a misuse of that principle.

Perhaps Samuelson is correct in attributing a pattern of behavior to the followers of Friedman and in positing that such a pattern can be shown to follow logically from his assumption concerning their motivations, but the 'as if' principle still does not warrant the empirical claim that his assumption about Friedman's (or Friedman's followers') motivation is true. More important, the 'as if' principle is validly used only when explaining true conclusions [Boland, 1979a, pp. 512-13]. That is, one cannot validly use such an 'as if' argument as a *critical* device similar to *modus tollens*. If the *implications* of using Samuelson's false assumption are undesirable, then one cannot pass the undesirableness back to the assumption. Furthermore, there are infinitely many false arguments that can imply any given (true) conclusion. The question is whether Samuelson's assumption is *necessary* for his conclusion. Of course, it is not, and that is because Samuelson is imitating Friedman's mode of argument, which relies on sufficient conditions for success.

The irony of Samuelson's critique is that his followers accept it *as if* it were successful. Logically, there is no way Samuelson's criticism can be considered successful, since such a line of argument requires logically necessary assumptions. But worse than this, most critics of Friedman's essay object to its dismissal of the necessity of 'realistic' assumptions, yet Samuelson's criticism is based on deliberately 'unrealistic' assumptions! These critics are caught violating their own requirement in order to criticize Friedman's essay. In effect they employ 'as if' arguments while criticizing their use. By their own rules they should reject their own critiques.

Conventionalist Critiques of Instrumentalism

There have been many Conventionalist critiques of Instrumentalism [cf. Caldwell, 1980]. All of them have viewed Instrumentalism as just another alleged solution to the Problem of Induction. What is surprising about this is that Instrumentalism is a rejection of the philosophical questions addressed by Conventionalism.

In a previously published defense of Friedman's essay against what we considered to be unfair critiques [Boland, 1979a] we stressed the importance of distinguishing Friedman's Instrumentalism from the

Conventionalist philosopher's alternatives that are more concerned with methods of establishing the universal truth (or probable truth) of scientific theories. The key issue is the separation of purposes, that is, the separation of immediate practical problems from long-term philosophical questions. Although Instrumentalism may be appropriate only for the former, the view that Conventionalism is the superior alternative is at least open to question. It is time to examine critically the logic of Conventionalism and its relationship to Instrumentalism.

Realism of assumptions
The success of Instrumentalism is based on the following proposition: in the short run or for most practical problems, one's theories do not have to be true to be successful. Our story of the television repair man clearly illustrates this. As we argued [Boland, 1979a, pp. 512-13], logically the truth (or probable truth) of one's assumptions is not necessary. To say that it is necessary is the 'Fallacy of Affirming the Consequent'.

Instrumentalism through Conventionalist eyes
The common error of seeing the necessary superiority of Conventionalism over Instrumentalism is the result of falsely assuming that one's own objectives are shared by everyone. If Friedman's Instrumentalism were intended to be an all-encompassing philosophy of science, any modern philosopher could easily be dissatisfied. But we argued [Boland, 1979a, p. 510] that although Friedman gives an appropriate bow to J. N. Keynes, Friedman's approach is to drop the traditional problem posed by Keynes because its solution would require an inductive logic. Friedman's method of dealing with the question of a 'positive science' is to limit the domain of the question in the case of economics to only that which is appropriate for a practical policy science. Limiting the domain of applicability for any method or technique is a rather obvious Instrumentalist ploy - one which can easily be justified in Instrumentalist terms.

Philosophical comparisons of Instrumentalism with Conventionalism are not uncommon; but we think they can be misleading if presented only in Conventionalist terms. The late Imre Lakatos was noted for considering Instrumentalism to be 'a degenerate version of [Conventionalism], based on a mere philosophical muddle caused by a lack of elementary logical competence' [1971, p. 95]. But his judgement is based on whether Instrumentalism is a means of achieving the objectives of most Conventionalist philosophers of science, and not on whether it is a useful guide for dealing with practical problems. In terms of Instrumentalist objectives, any advocate of Instrumentalism could argue that Conventionalist philosophy of science is obviously useless. Moreover, as we have shown [Boland, 1979a], Lakatos is wrong; Instrumentalism on its own terms is devoid of the alleged elementary logical errors.

Some Words of Caution

Now before one jumps to the conclusion that the real choice is between Instrumentalism (i.e., Friedman's methodology) and Conventionalism (i.e., the methodology of Samuelson or Lucas) and, worse, that if one rejects Conventionalism, one must then embrace Instrumentalism for all of economics, let us add some further advice. Instrumentalism is always limited to short-run practical problems. If one is looking for a more universal, lasting understanding of the workings of the economy - that is, a true theory of economics - then Instrumentalism will never do, since it ignores the truth of theories. Of course, Conventionalism fails here too, since it denies any truth status to theories. If a true theory of the economy is our objective, then we will just have to look beyond the dispute over methodology between Friedman's Instrumentalism and the Conventionalism of Samuelson or Lucas.

PART IV

THE FOLLY OF AN ALL-PURPOSE METHODOLOGY

10

Contemporary Methodology vs.
Popper's Philosophy of Science

> No assumptions about economic behavior are absolutely
> true and no theoretical conclusions are valid for all times
> and places, but would anyone seriously deny that in the
> matter of techniques and analytical constructs there has
> been progress in economics?
>
> Mark Blaug [1978, p. 3]

> we look upon economic theory as a sequence of concep-
> tual *models* that seek to express in simplified form diffe-
> rent aspects of an always more complicated reality....
>
> Tjalling Koopmans [1957, p. 142]

> progress in a discipline is better described by a sequence
> of theories, or models, not by a study of individual
> theories. A 'research program' is the organizing concep-
> tion; to describe it is to characterize the various se-
> quences of models that have family resemblance....
>
> E. Roy Weintraub [1979, p. 15]

So far we have examined the effects of the hidden agenda on neoclassical theoretical problems and research programs; now we wish to
examine its effect on the neoclassical views of methodology. Generally
speaking, methodology is rarely discussed in the leading journals. We
need to examine this empirical fact before we examine the more subtle
questions of 'realism', 'usefulness' and the meaning of a 'sequence of
models'.

Methodology and the Hidden Agenda

Methodology is not considered an urgent topic for neoclassical research programs simply because methodology has historically been
concerned only with the nature of the items on the hidden agenda.

Being concerned with the items on the hidden agenda means that, to the extent that methodologists tend to question the adequacy of various views of the agenda items, the subject of methodology is paradoxically considered either a waste of time or too dangerous to handle. Consequently, novice economists are often advised to steer clear of methodology, as there is no way to establish a career based on methodology. It is claimed that no significant contributions can be made in that area. The question we shall consider is: does this orthodox attitude towards methodology merely reflect a deep-seated insecurity about the adequacy of the hidden agenda? If it does, then there can be no doubt that the advisors are correct!

A 'significant contribution' to neoclassical economics can be made in only two ways. One can either (1) provide a new application of neoclassical theory, or (2) provide a proof of a theoretical proposition which is relevant for applications of neoclassical theory. It is easy to see that with such a limited range of possibilities there is little room for the study of methodology as part of a neoclassical research program.

As long as the domain of methodology is limited to the study of the hidden agenda, the logic of the situation facing an aspiring methodologist is limited. Primarily, given the presumed need to deal with the Problem of Induction and the logical impossibility of providing inductive proofs, the only methodological questions of concern are those relating to acceptable ways of solving the Problem of Conventions. If one can provide a new theory-choice criterion which is in some way superior to previous criteria, then that would be considered a contribution to methodology. But since the purpose of any criterion is to provide a basis for justifying a given theory-choice, the givenness of the theory-choice precludes any methodological contribution. For example, in the methodological debates between the followers of Samuelson and the followers of Friedman's so-called Chicago School, or those between the 'Keynesians' and the 'Monetarists', the appropriate theory-choice criterion is dictated by the opposing theories that are given. Samuelson and the 'Keynesians' urge the dominance of a criterion of 'generality', while Friedman and the 'Monetarists' argue for 'simplicity' or for 'usefulness'.

Many economists consider such debates to be sterile. Although it might appear that questions of methodology matter, they really are not decisive, since each side is already committed to its respective theory. Methodology is only an afterthought. Those liberal methodologists who wish to defuse such extremist methodological debates try to confuse the methodological issues. Usually they recommend some *ad hoc* middle ground where both methodological views are represented and thus make methodological questions irrelevant. A recent example is the view expressed by Robert Lucas:

One of the functions of theoretical economics is to provide fully articulated, artificial economic systems that can serve as laboratories in which policies that would be prohibitively expensive to experiment with in actual economies can be tested out at much lower cost. To serve this function well, it is essential that the artificial 'model' economy be distinguished as sharply as possible in discussion from actual economies. Insofar as there is confusion between statements of opinion as to the way we believe actual economies would react to particular policies and statements of verifiable fact as to how the model will react, the theory is not being effectively used to help us to see which opinions about the behavior of actual economies are accurate and which are not. This is the sense in which insistence on the 'realism' of an economic model subverts its potential usefulness in thinking about reality. Any model that is well enough articulated to give clear answers to the questions we put to it will necessarily be artificial, abstract, patently 'unreal'.

At the same time, not all well-articulated models will be equally useful. Though we are interested in models because we believe they may help us to understand matters about which we are currently ignorant, we need to test them as useful imitations of reality by subjecting them to shocks for which we are fairly certain how actual economies, or parts of economies, would react. The more dimensions on which the model mimics the answers actual economies give to simple questions, the more we trust its answers to harder questions. This is the sense in which more 'realism' in a model is clearly preferred to less.

On this general view of the nature of economic theory then, a 'theory' is not a collection of assertions about the behavior of the actual economy but rather an explicit set of instructions for building a parallel or analogue system - a mechanical, imitation economy. A 'good' model, from this point of view, will not be exactly more 'real' than a poor one, but will provide better imitations. Of course, what one means by a 'better imitation' will depend on the particular questions to which one wishes answers. [1980, pp. 696-7]

A major factor determining the irrelevancy of contemporary methodology is the lack of a logical consistency of purpose. As we see in the comments of Lucas above, there is a little bit from Instrumentalism (e.g., 'usefulness') and another bit from Conventionalism (e.g., 'better imitation'). Of course, such a mixture is consistent with Instrumentalism. Perhaps that is all that is revealed by the liberal compromise methodologies.

No matter how much methodological discussion appears in neoclassical articles, as long as the theories presented are put beyond question, the methodology provided is irrelevant. But many neoclassical economists who do provide some mention of methodology would imply that methodology potentially matters in their choice of their theories; and this also implies that their theories are not beyond question. Nevertheless, there is little a methodologist can contribute, given the second item on the hidden agenda - the explanatory problem of methodological individualism. As long as psychologistic individualism is considered to be the only acceptable form of individualism for neoclassical economics, the Problem of Induction will not be considered questionable. The key to the apparent irrelevance of methodology is the implicit acceptance of psychologistic individualism.

Methodology and the History of Economic Thought

The area where methodology is supposed to matter most is the study of the history of economic thought. But if methodology (as we are led to believe) is not decisive in the choice of any particular theory, then how can methodology matter in the historical development of our theories? This contradiction is easily handled today. The common view is that the study of the history of thought does not matter either! Nevertheless, let us leave this controversial subject for a while and instead focus on the questions of methodology from the respectful host of the history of thought.

The study of methodology and the study of the history of economic thought go hand in hand. As the views of Koopmans and Weintraub (quoted above) indicate, a common methodological view says that we must see a research program as a 'sequence of models'. This immediately puts methodology into an historical context. What is probably not often appreciated is that putting methodology into an historical context is just a straightforward application of either Inductivism or Conventionalism.

Two views of the history of economic thought

Many historians of economic thought study methodology under the title of the 'Growth of Knowledge' [e.g., Latsis, 1976]. What is presumed by all such perspectives is that there is some sort of continuity. The continuity is established either by a logical relationship to some original theory or theorists or by a family and/or social relationship provided by the continuity of a specific community of scholars. The former view is usually in the tradition of Inductivist histories of science [see Agassi, 1963] and the latter in the tradition of Conventionalist histories of physics [e.g., Kuhn, 1962/70].

In the older, orthodox Inductivist tradition the history of any science is the history of the development of an inductive proof of some 'scientific law'. According to Inductivism, a 'scientific law' is established by the presentation of logically sufficient facts - facts which have been gathered by true scientists. A 'true scientist', so the tradition goes, avoids making mistakes by striving to be unbiased and open-minded, that is, by not jumping to conclusions until all the facts have been collected. This takes a great deal of patience and hard work (the similarity to the 'labor theory of value' is not accidental). One's patience and hard work will be rewarded in the end, perhaps by having one's work included in someone's history of science! Since the speed and veracity of one's inductive proof depend so much on the quality of one's collected facts, the real test of any science is the personal character of the scientists involved. For this reason, inductivist histories of science tended to dwell on the personal qualities of leading scientists.

Agassi [1963] argues that the older historians of particular sciences tended to see what they thought they should see. As he says, they were often unable to 'avoid being wise after the event'. That is, by taking Inductivism for granted, many historians of science would selectively portray a given scientist as if he were pure in heart and mind and unable to make mistakes. This is because whenever a 'scientific law' had been established (i.e., inductively proven), the facts must have been scientifically clean, and that is possible *only* when the scientist is unbiased, open-minded, etc. To those of us in economics these histories of science seem a bit silly, but that is because very few orthodox inductivist histories of economic thought have been written in recent times.

The other approach to writing histories of science is much more common in economics. More and more, the history of economic thought is considered to be the history of an impersonal enterprise. Today one can discuss the 'marginalist revolution in economic theory' without going into any detail about the lives of Jevons, Marshall, Walras, or Menger. What is recognized today is that although each of these men contributed to the body of economic thought, their contributions depended on acceptance by other economists. Of course, the idea that anyone's contribution depends on acceptance by others is the keystone of modern Conventionalism. Where Inductivist scientists strived to provide empirical, objective proofs, Conventionalist scientists provided acceptable arguments and propositions. Whether one's intended contribution is accepted depends on whether one has satisfied the currently approved criteria of acceptance for one's evidence and for one's mode of argument.

There are two essential elements in the Conventionalist view of the history of economic thought. First is the continuity of the enterprise; second is the tentativeness of the certification of one's contribution. In some sense there was a continuity involved in the Inductivist view of the history of science but it was due to the presumed durability of any alleged inductive proof. The Conventionalist view, which denies the existence of both inductive proofs and absolute truth, takes a broader historical view. Any body of knowledge is treated like a river flowing through time. We can all attempt to pour our contributions into the stream but their significance will be judged downstream.

Implicitly, the continuity of the growth of knowledge would seem to presume that whenever somebody is to have made a contribution, it remains a contribution forever. But this implication of continuity has not always fitted the facts. That is, 'contributiveness' itself must be judged downstream. What may be considered a contribution today might tomorrow be considered an illusion. The resulting tentativeness of the judgement concerning whether one has actually made a contribution leads to a breakdown in the continuity aspect of the history of the enterprise.

The best illustration of the tentativeness of contributions is the history of Samuelson's contribution to demand theory [see Wong, 1978]. In 1938 Samuelson said that he had solved the problem plaguing all psychologistic theories of behavior - namely, that the basis of such explanations of individuals' behavior is not 'operational', that is, is not observable. He offered a new way to explain an individual's demand. Instead of assuming the existence of a psychologically given utility function or preference ordering, we were to assume only that the individual was consistent in his or her choices. Consistent choices meant only that whenever one faced the same price-income situation one would make the same choices (i.e., if one could afford both bundle A and bundle B in two different situations, it would be inconsistent to buy A in one and B in the other). In effect, one was supposed to be a slave to one's past history. On the basis of this postulate of consistency (and a few minor postulates that provide that the consumer does make choices), Samuelson was able to prove what he thought was the essential purpose of the Hicks-Allen [1934] orthodox theory of the consumer - a theory that seemed to require the existence of psychologically given preferences.

Now, the success of Samuelson's research program is widely accepted and even hailed by many as a major contribution to economic knowledge. What is interesting about the history of Samuelson's contribution is that by 1950 he readily admitted that a complete version of his demand theory was logically equivalent to the 'ordinal demand theory' which Hicks and Allen had developed. Now, there is an inconsistency here. How can Samuelson's 'operational' theory of demand be both different from and logically equivalent to the Hicks-Allen theory? What appeared as a major contribution in 1938 disappears as a mirage in 1950. Probably more significant, what was hailed as a major breakthrough in economics methodology has disappeared in a puff of philosophical smoke. Such are the ways of Conventionalist histories of economic thought!

Methodology and continuity-based histories
The paradigm of continuity theories of the history of science is, of course, Thomas Kuhn's view, which he presented in his *Structure of Scientific Revolutions*. According to his view, we are to see a steady progress in everyday, 'normal science', with the steady accumulation of solutions to theoretical puzzles. What distinguishes a puzzle from a problem is that a puzzle is approached on the basis that there definitely is a way to solve it - if only we can find it. On the other hand, a problem may not always have a solution, no matter how long we look for one (e.g., the Problem of Induction). No one claims that the solution to the puzzle constitutes absolute proof. Nevertheless, each piece added to the puzzle warrants much the same reward as the discovery of each additional fact leading to an inductive proof.

It might be asked, if Kuhn's book is so concerned with puzzle-solving (i.e., normal science), why is the title concerned with 'revolutions'? The answer is that puzzle-solving is not very progressive and historians are more concerned with significant progress. Historians record the abandonment of one puzzle deemed to be a bit stale and its replacement by a new and more promising puzzle. He calls these puzzle-replacements 'revolutions', since each old puzzle is abandoned only after internal sociological developments within the scientific community. In particular, there are no devastating refutations, as might be suggested by Popper's view, but instead a steady evolution along Darwinian lines. A given puzzle is not abandoned until a 'better' puzzle comes along *and* is accepted.

The question of acceptance brings us right back to the Conventionalist basis of Kuhn's view. Although would-be revolutionaries are stimulated by Kuhn's book, it is really just an effort to explain so-called 'revolutions' away rather than to promote them. A 'revolution' is never a complete break but depends on the acceptance of an on-going community of scientists. The acceptance of a 'revolution' depends on the acceptance of any criteria used to assess the intended 'revolution'.

Methodologists could easily argue that a real revolution would require a revolution in criteria - but on what basis would the new criteria be assessed? Some may argue that such considerations show that Conventionalism is circular, but this is not the point we are making. What we wish to point out is that changes in any social enterprise require the stability of some frame of reference. In order to assess any change in methodological criteria we would still need some fixed basis from whence to assess the changes. We could appeal to some outside authority (such as philosophers of science) but this would only bring into question the basis of their authority. To assess methodology within an enterprise such as neoclassical economics requires the acceptance of neoclassical theory. Given this theory of social change, there could hardly ever be a genuine revolution.

Conventionalism and the 'growth of knowledge'
If it is difficult to specify a revolution within the context of a Conventionalist concept of the history of economic thought, can we at least identify unambiguous signs of 'progress'? If we no longer identify progress with establishing new 'scientific laws', then what is regarded as progress now? Consider Leijonhufvud's comments:

> Traditionally, the history of economic doctrines has for the most part been written as a 'straight' historical narrative - as a chronological story of 'progress' by accumulating analytical improvements in a field of inquiry of more or less stable demarcation and with a largely fixed set of questions.... [1976, p. 67]

The term 'stable demarcation' refers to what we are calling acceptance criteria. In this sense, given a criterion which specifies when a model or theory is 'better', we could simply say that progress is identified with finding a 'better' theory. But this reveals that there still is an element of the Problem of Conventions here, as long as there are judgements to be made about whether progress has been made.

So when Blaug asked, 'Has there been progress in economic theory?' his answer was a clear 'Yes' and his initial specification was a long list of Conventionalist criteria:

> analytical tools have been continuously improved and augmented; empirical data have been increasingly marshaled to verify economic hypotheses; metaeconomic biases have been repeatedly exposed and separated from the core of testable propositions which they enmesh; and the workings of the economic system are better understood than ever before. [1978, p. 7]

In more general terms he says:

> The development of economic thought has not taken the form of a linear progression toward present truths. While it has progressed, many have been the detours imposed by exigencies of time and place.... [p. 8]

Although Conventionalism and its presumption that there are standards of acceptance seems to dominate the historian's view of the methodology of economics, there does not seem to be as much agreement over what constitutes acceptable progress in economics as some historians might like us to think. For example, consider the views expressed at a recent meeting of the History of Economics Society:

> Jaffe expressed the opinion that there is a poverty of helpful economic ideas today and that future historians, though impressed by the technical progress of the discipline, may see a mismatch between means and ends....
>
> Bronfenbrenner, on the contrary, said that the last 50 years might be considered a golden age because of technical advances, the shift from statics to dynamics, and the shift from the exclusive emphasis on microeconomics to the inclusion of macro elements. Coase replied that the state of *today's* economics is near disaster, as evidenced by the concentration of interest in microeconomics, the sameness of treatment of all subjects, and the concentration on techniques rather than economic problems....
>
> In response to [a] question as to what of present-day economics will be remembered in 50 years, Bronfenbrenner listed (1) imperfect competition; (2) macroeconomics, including the *General Theory*, the new quantity theory, the theory of rational expectations, and the Phillips curve; (3) the rise of mathematical techniques; (4) the input-output table; and (5) growth models.... Coase believes that no book of the present will be remembered....
>
> [Dingle, 1980, pp. 18-19]

Conventionalism and the Sequence of Models

The view that a research program in economics should be seen as a sequence of models is an example of the Conventionalist continuity theory of the history of economic thought. Is there anything more that one can infer from such a view? Probably not, since the recognition of a sequence does not imply that each step represents unambiguous progress, although that may be what Koopmans and Weintraub have in mind. Today, few economics writers find it worth while to add some romantic comments about how far we have progressed beyond our primitive forefathers. This is simply because real progress was always the promise of those who believed in inductive sciences and, we might now say, in an inductive learning possibilities curve which reaches the probability of 1.00 in real time. Now, today, we are apparently more modest, as it is agreed that there is always room for improvement. Each subsequent model in the sequence may be *more* realistic but nobody will claim that it is *realistic* - that is, that it is true. Each model may be more useful but, as Lucas said, that depends on what you want to do. Given all this modesty, one might wonder why anyone bothers with neoclassical research programs.

Revealed Methodologies

We have now painted a rather bland picture of contemporary methodology in neoclassical economics. Perhaps we should say that we have constructed a collage. The unifying element is the predominance of Conventionalism which is only lightly colored by its Inductivist origins. Model-building is the primary focus of all recent studies of methodology. And we are led to believe that 'progress' is any movement along some continuum formed by the growing sequence of accepted models. No one model is ever claimed to be true. Successful model-building is only tentative; our final judgement is to be postponed.

So we ask again, why do so many economists strive to contribute to the body of knowledge if their success is to be considered so tentative? Our answer, which we have been developing in the previous chapters, is that although there is much talk that might indicate a belief in the postulates of Conventionalism (namely, since we do not have an *operational* inductive logic, theories are not true or false but only 'better' or 'worse'), the acceptance of Conventionalism is only a short-run measure. When philosophers tell us that we cannot conduct an inductive proof, neoclassical methodologists have interpreted this to mean that we cannot give an inductive proof in our lifetime, and this does not logically preclude an inductive proof in the *very* long run. What contemporary methodologists and historians of economic thought presume is that our short-run tolerance of acceptably false models will be rewarded with the one true model in the long run. Eventually the sequence of models has to lead somewhere. Each model added to the sequence is like one more fact in the process of providing an inductive proof. In effect, neoclassical methodologists accept Conventionalism in the short run but hold out for Inductivism in the long run - perhaps Blaug's methodological view of the history of economics [1978] can be considered the paradigm of this perspective.

Misappropriation of Popper's View of Science

Contrary to our view that contemporary methodology is dominated by Conventionalism, given all the popular references to falsifiability of economic theories some might think that Popper's view of science has been adopted by most methodologists today. For example, consider the following views:

Popper, more than any other philosopher of science, has had an enormous influence on modern economics. It is not that many economists read Popper. Instead, they read Friedman but Friedman is simply Popper-with-a-twist applied to economics.... [Blaug, 1978, p. 714]

I see no reason for denying to the study of the activities and institutions created by scarcity the title of science. It conforms fundamentally to our conception of science in general: that is to say the formation of hypotheses explaining and (possibly) predicting the outcome of the relationships concerned and the testing of such hypotheses by logic and by observation. This process of testing used to be called verification. But, since this way of putting things may involve an overtone of permanence and nonrefutability, it is probably better described, as Karl Popper has taught us, as a search for falsification - those hypotheses which survive the test being regarded as provisionally applicable.... [Robbins, 1981, p. 2]

Judging by Blaug's comments, one gets the impression that Karl Popper's philosophy of science has been adopted by most methodologists in economics. Judging by Robbins' comments, one gets the impression that Popper's role is only that of an elocution instructor. We shall argue here that Robbins' view is a better reflection of the state of affairs. So far, Popper's only real accomplishment in economics is the suppression of any open advocacy of Inductivism. Popper also claims to be opposed to both Conventionalism and Instrumentalism, yet both are openly promoted in mainstream neoclassical economics.

One reason why Popper has not had any significant impact on the nature of neoclassical methodology is that most economists have obtained their view of Popper by way of the writings of one of his students, Imre Lakatos. For many years most philosophers of science considered Popper to be in direct competition with Thomas Kuhn. As we noted above, Kuhn's view of science is quite compatible with that of most methodologists, as both are forms of Conventionalism. Lakatos endeavored to build a bridge between Kuhn and Popper; and to a great extent he has succeeded. But the cost of the reconciliation has been the abandonment of most of the more important aspects of Popper's philosophy of science.

The Foundations of Popper's Methodology

There are two essential and related considerations without which no clear appreciation of Popper's views can be reached. One is Popper's view of Plato's 'Socrates', the other is the observation that Popper has strong ties to what is usually called the Austrian School of economics.

Popper's anti-Justificationism

What makes Popper's view of methodology incompatible with Conventionalism is that he rejects the Problem of Induction [unfortunately, he calls his rejection a 'solution'; 1972, ch. 1]. What makes his view appear to be compatible with Conventionalism is that both deny the logical possibility of inductive proofs.

Popper's rejection of the Problem of Induction is based on a specific view which explicitly separates the process of knowing from the object we call knowledge. That is, for Popper we can examine 'knowledge' without the necessity of examining the 'knower' [1972, ch. 3]. All knowledge, in his view, must include one or more assertions which are of the form of 'strictly universal statements' [1934/59, ch. 3]. It is here that the impossibility of induction plays a crucial role. Where Conventionalism would say that these considerations would deny truth status for anyone's knowledge, Popper does not. For him, one's knowledge may very well be true, even though we cannot prove that it is true such as when it involves unverifiable universal statements.

A corollary of his separation of the question of what is the truth status of one's knowledge from the question of how one knows the truth status of one's knowledge is his separation of epistemology from methodology. Epistemology is about our theories of the nature of knowledge, and methodology is about our theories of learning or of the knowledge acquisition process [Agassi, 1969a]. Popper's epistemological position is that all knowledge is essentially theoretical conjecture [1972, ch. 1]. Any conjecture may be true or false - but even if it is true, there is no way we can ever prove that it is true. That is, even when we allow for specific observations to be considered true, there is no logic which can connect the truth of a finite number of observations to the necessary truth of any needed (strictly) universal statement. However, he observes that positive statements which are true are not completely useless - they can be used in refutations. In his terms, since strictly universal statements logically deny certain specified positive statements (i.e., observations), an observation of an instance of a logically denied statement constitutes a proof of the falsity of one's theory. Furthermore, since all theories involve universal statements, we can learn by proving that our knowledge is false if we continue to allow some observations to be considered true. But this is now a major departure from the traditional belief in what we have called the inductive learning possibilities function. More positive information does not increase the probability of one's model being true. If we are to learn from experience, it can only be that we learn that some of our theories are false. This, we shall argue, is the essence of Popper's Socratic theory of learning.

Now, for all we know, Socrates may have been a figment of Plato's imagination. There is a considerable difference between the Socrates of the early dialogues and the Socrates of the later dialogues [Popper, 1945/66, pp. 306-13]. In both versions Socrates spends much of his time asking questions. But there is a major difference. In the early dialogues Socrates is the student asking questions in the process of attempting to learn. In the later dialogues he is the teacher attempting to teach by asking critical and revealing questions. Popper identifies with the early Socrates - that is, with Socrates the student.

Socratic learning theory
The best illustration of Socrates the student is to be found in the one dialogue which everyone agrees is fictitious - 'Euthyphro'. Let us examine this dialogue, since it can provide an excellent basis for understanding Popper's theory of learning. The plot of the dialogue is quite simple. Socrates is on his way to the court, where he is to be tried for 'impiety'. Now, Socrates does not understand why he is being charged with impiety - that is to say, given Socrates' understanding of impiety, he does not understand the charges against him. He encounters his former student Euthyphro, who is also going to the same court. Euthyphro's business there is that he has charged his father with impiety for killing a servant.

It is immediately obvious to Socrates that Euthyphro is an expert on the question of the nature of impiety. Surely no man would take his own father to court for impiety unless he was absolutely sure that he understood what piety and impiety were. The dialogue between Socrates and Euthyphro is carefully staged to illustrate the Socratic approach to learning. In this case, Socrates attempts to determine where *his own* understanding of piety and impiety has obviously gone wrong. Cynics might say that Socrates was only using Euthyphro to prepare his own defense, but that misses the point, as Socrates is sure that Euthyphro is correct. So the dialogue consists of Socrates' attempt to reveal his own understanding of piety and impiety so that it can be *critically* examined by the expert.

Socrates puts his understanding of piety and impiety on the table for Euthyphro to examine in the same way that we approach a physician when we have an ailment. Piece by piece, each element in Socrates' understanding is put to the test of Euthyphro's expertise. Every time Socrates puts to Euthyphro the question 'Is this correct?' Socrates' understanding passes the test! In the end, nothing is accomplished, as Euthyphro is unable to help by showing where Socrates has gone wrong. But it is the supreme test - since if anyone were going to find something wrong with Socrates' understanding of piety and impiety, Euthyphro would.

For our purposes the point of this dialogue is that Socrates does not learn anything. The only thing that Socrates could learn with the help of his friend Euthyphro is that his understanding is faulty - that is, that there is an error in his understanding. For all of his agreement - that is, his verification of each of the elements in Socrates' understanding - Euthyphro is no help. He could only help by finding an error. Even though Socrates tries not to conceal any element in his understanding, the failure to find a flaw still does not prove that Socrates' understanding of piety and impiety is correct. Surely there is an error somewhere because the fact still stands that Socrates is being charged with impiety and Euthyphro is taking his father to court for impiety.

Now Popper's position is that science and the scientist are always in the same predicament as Socrates. We can never prove that our understanding is correct - even when it is. And the only thing we can ever really learn is that our understanding is false - if it actually happens to be false. For this reason, Popper sees science as a *learning* enterprise whose sole objective is to find errors in our understanding. This is why he puts such emphasis on testing, but it must be realized that the only successful test is the refutation of one's theory. This, then, is Popper's Socratic theory of learning: One's understanding is always conjectural but potentially true. The only way one can learn is to find a refutation - to find that one's understanding (i.e., one's theory) is false.

Learning as a process without end
There is a profound perversity in the Socratic learning theory. Given Popper's point that all explanatory theories involve unverifiable universal statements, learning in the more traditional, positive sense (verifying true explanations) is impossible. In this sense, one could never justify one's attempt to learn on the grounds that the ultimate end is possible. If one can never learn the true theory, why bother? This question is the essence of skepticism. But skepticism is merely an indirect expression of a belief in Justificationism - the view that we are not allowed to claim that our theories are true unless we can prove that they are true [Agassi, 1971a]. If one rejects Justificationism, then one is not necessarily led to skepticism. Although we may not be able to prove that our theory is true, it does not mean that our theory is not true. Even though we cannot learn in the more positive sense, we can still learn by correcting our errors. Discovering one's errors is definitely a positive step - as long as one does not reserve the idea of a positive step only for a step leading towards a justification or an inductive proof.

For Popper, science is a social institution that is pointing in the right direction even though it is readily admitted that it never reaches the goal at which we might think it is pointing. This is the same situation as that encountered when discussing Austrian economics. Economists from the Austrian School [see Blaug, 1980, pp. 92-3] do not recommend free-enterprise capitalism because it necessarily leads to Adam Smith's world of long-run equilibrium. On the contrary, as we saw with Hayek, to the extent that reaching any long-run equilibrium requires the acquisition of correct knowledge (or the correct expectations), reaching a long-run equilibrium is never possible. Besides that, what constitutes a long-run equilibrium depends on the exogenous givens, and we all know that they change faster than the process can ever get us to any long-run equilibrium.

If pushed to justify their faith in free-enterprise capitalism, the Austrians *cannot* say, 'We favor capitalism because, by following it, eventually we reach the 'best of all possible worlds' - that is, reach the long-run equilibrium where everyone is a maximizer and all resources are optimally allocated.' Instead, their justification must involve only an evaluation of the process at a specific point in real time. The fundamental Austrian position in this regard is that when individuals are free to choose they are able to exploit (and thereby unintentionally to eliminate) errors in resource allocation. Eliminating error in resource allocation is an improvement for society, just as the Smith-Schumpeter view saw attempting to get ahead as leading to improvements in the overall efficiency of the economic production process. However, unlike Smith's classical world, which begins with a long-run equilibrium in order to show how greed can thus be virtuous, the Austrians are satisfied with a short-run view.

If one took a survey among neoclassical economists, one would not find very many believers in Austrian economics, but that may only be because neoclassical economists require justifications based on the properties of the hypothetical long-run equilibrium. One of the major analytical tools used by neoclassical economists is 'comparative statics', which does nothing but compare alternative long-run equilibria that differ only because there is posited a difference in some of the exogenous givens. We can extend this difficulty one more step. As long as neoclassical economists accept only teleological (i.e., goal-directed) justifications, they will never understand Popper's Socratic philosophy of science!

False Problems Raised By Popper

The demarcation problem
Early in Popper's career he tried to impress the leaders of the Logical

Positivist school of analytical philosophy. His method of doing this was to offer challenging solutions to their problems [viz., 1934/59]. They were unimpressed. One of his tactics was to argue that they wanted to solve what he called the 'Demarcation Problem'. According to his story, the Logical Positivists claimed that science was distinguished from philosophy on the basis of the *verifiability* of scientific theories, which entails the view that empirical evidence is significant only when it contributes to verifications. Philosophy, supposedly, was not verifiable. Popper argued that the Logical Positivists had it all wrong: empirical evidence is significant only for refutations, thus if science were to be distinguished, (i.e., 'demarcated'), from philosophy, it would be only in terms of the *falsifiability* of scientific theories. For those of us who have approached methodology from the perspective of economics and without any prior commitment to analytical philosophy, all this seems rather silly. But perhaps we are being too wise after the fact.

If we do not get involved with the older Logical Positivist views of methodology, then the so-called Demarcation Problem is at best uninteresting. Popper misleads us when he seems to be saying merely that our choice is between falsifiable theories and metaphysics [cf. Bartley, 1968]. Metaphysics is a matter of choice and not a matter of logic [Agassi, 1971b]. Some theories which may appear to be tautologies may be transformed into non-tautological statements [Watkins, 1957]. As we have argued before, a circular argument need not be a tautology [Boland, 1974]. Theories which are falsifiable may still be false [Wisdom, 1963].

'Degrees of corroboration'

In another place Popper creates an intellectual fog with his 'degrees of corroboration'. Presumably this is his effort to accommodate some aspects of Conventionalism - namely, the well-established acceptance of degrees of confirmation. In Popper's view [1934/59, ch. 10], a theory is 'corroborated' whenever it passes a test by not being refuted. The greater the likelihood of being refuted, the greater the 'degree of corroboration'. In a sense, corroboration is just a fancy name for unintended confirmation - but this is Popper's point. We do not set out to corroborate a theory; we set out to refute it in order to test our understanding. To placate those who feel uncomfortable about not having a positive reason for testing theory (or their fear of looking for the hole instead of the donut), he offers them an unintended reward for their efforts. But if one really takes the Socratic theory of learning seriously, no such reward is necessary. What is worse, for Popper's purposes, is that it is too easy to incorporate 'degrees of corroboration' as just another (sophisticated) Conventionalist criterion of acceptability. Theories that are more corroborated are somehow superior to those which are less [see further, Hattiangadi, 1978].

The growth of knowledge

Another unnecessary dispute which Popper flames is the question of what constitutes the growth of knowledge. According to Popper's epistemology, knowledge consists exclusively of theories. Thus if knowledge is to grow, we must be able to compare theories on that basis. So Popper would have us believe that we are better off whenever (1) a new theory can explain everything that any rejected old theory explains, and (2) a new theory explains more and thus is capable of a higher degree of corroboration (because by explaining more it runs a higher risk of being refuted when tested). We are led to believe that when a new theory is offered that is better by these criteria we are supposed to drop the old, inferior theory. But if the old theory has never been refuted, why must it be dropped? The old theory may be true even though the new theory is considered superior by the criterion of the 'degrees of corroboration'. As long as we are comparing unrefuted theories, if they cannot be verified, then we are simply not in any position to choose! If we do, then the dreaded Conventionalism wins.

Friedman and Popper

According to Blaug, 'Friedman is not guilty of "instrumentalism"' [1978, p. 703] and, as the quotation above indicates, Blaug believes that Friedman's methodology is merely a version of Popper's philosophy of science. It is true, as we have previously argued, that Friedman rejects Conventionalism. However, we have argued that Friedman's alternative is a form of Instrumentalism [Boland, 1979] - and Friedman has stated that we were correct in this characterization of his essay [1978]. Added to this, Friedman claims to be closely aligned with Popper's views [see Boland and Frazer, 1982].

Now, this sets up an interesting triangular situation. Friedman identifies with Instrumentalism and Popper. Blaug identifies Friedman with Popper's views but denies the connection with Instrumentalism. Popper rejects Instrumentalism [1972, ch. 3], yet both Popper and Friedman reject Conventionalism [Boland, 1979]. There is no way all three positions can be correct. Given Friedman's statements to us, Blaug draws the short straw; his view cannot be true. But, given Popper's rejection of Instrumentalism, how can Friedman be correct?

We conjecture that the reason why Friedman thinks that he is in agreement with Popper is that Friedman sees only two options. Either one accepts the dominant Conventionalist view of methodology, or one does not. On this basis, since Popper supposedly rejects Conventionalism, it would seem to follow that as Friedman also rejects Conventionalism, he must agree with Popper's view. We think Friedman's position in this matter is rather weak. Nevertheless, when it comes to practical policy, Popper's 'piecemeal engineering' [1944/61, 1945/66] is difficult to distinguish from Instrumentalism - particularly since Popper seems to dwell on a problem-oriented methodology. By Popper's rules, if one defines one's problem as a purely practical one, then perhaps Instrumentalism is the only way to go.

Conventionalist Pseudo-Popper

According to Blaug:

> To the philosophical question 'How can we acquire apodictic [i.e., logically certain] knowledge of the world when all we can rely on is our own unique experience?' Popper replies that there is no certain empirical knowledge, whether grounded in our own personal experience or in that of mankind in general. And more than that: there is no sure method of guaranteeing that the fallible knowledge we do have of the real world is positively the best we can possess under the circumstances. A study of the philosophy of science can sharpen our appraisal of what constitutes *acceptable* empirical knowledge, but it remains a provisional appraisal nevertheless.
> [Blaug, 1980, pp. 27-8, emphasis added]

What is clear from such a comment by a well-meaning methodologist is that Conventionalism lives, no matter what Popper says. Why is acceptability so important? If one agrees with Popper that theories can be true or false and that even when they are true there still is no method to establish their truth, what does it mean for a theory to be 'acceptable'? It matters a great deal for the Conventionalist method of dealing with the Problem of Induction. But if we follow Popper's rejection of the Problem of Induction, why should anyone be concerned with the acceptability of empirical knowledge? Unfortunately, there is no way to answer these questions in a manner that would both satisfy a believer in Conventionalism and still be consistent with Popper's rejection of Conventionalism.

Falsifiability as a Conventionalist criterion
Despite Popper's intentions, his trumpeting of the falsifiability criterion to solve his Demarcation Problem is all too easily incorporated into the list of acceptable Conventionalist criteria. Again and again we

have to point out, no matter how well a theory fares by any Conventionalist criterion (which does not include truth or falsity), there is nothing to connect the success of the theory in those terms with the actual truth or falsity of the theory. So what is accomplished by requiring that all 'scientific' theories be falsifiable? It does preclude tautologies, but despite this criterion's origins, it does not preclude metaphysics [Agassi, 1971b].

The most important assumptions in neoclassical economics, such as the maximization hypothesis or the assumption of the variability of all factors, are unfalsifiable. Although the maximization hypothesis is not a tautology, it is usually unfalsifiable because it is put beyond question [see Boland, 1981b]. Similarly, the most important assumptions in Marxist theory are unfalsifiable. Almost every Marxist model presumes the existence of a class struggle or an exogenously given rate of capitalist accumulation. Neither of these assumptions is ever put to the test. Both are just assumed to be obviously true - just as the neoclassical maximization assumption is considered to be obviously true. If we believed in a Conventionalist implementation of the falsifiability criterion, there would virtually be no acceptable social theory, since all explanatory theories involve at least one key assumption which is put beyond refutation [Agassi, 1965].

Popper and the 'new heterodoxy'

Blaug identifies Popper's philosophy of science as the 'watershed between old and new views of the philosophy of science' [1980, p. 2]. The new view, according to Blaug, is the Conventionalism of Kuhn's or Lakatos' compromised version of Popper's view. How one conceives of a 'watershed' transition from the Conventionalism of the Logical Positivists to the Conventionalism of Kuhn which passes through Popper's anti-Conventionalism is difficult for us to understand.

The 'new heterodoxy' is nothing but the 'old heterodoxy' dressed up in clothes designed by Lakatos. The 'watershed' has yet to be crossed. Nowhere do we find Popper's Socratic view of learning represented in either neoclassical methodology or neoclassical theory. Without any doubt, Socrates did not submit to the conventional wisdom of authorities he faced in the court. Socrates considered his view of his situation to be true even though the votes were not in its favor. To the extent that Blaug's views represent the state of the methodology of mainstream neoclassical economics, Popper's impact on economics may be only cosmetic.

11

Putting Popper on the
Agenda

> L: Couldn't you have been more original?
> I: No, I didn't have enough time!
>
> > Anonymous

> When I was a boy, I had a clock with a pendulum which
> could be lifted off. I found that the clock went very much
> faster without the pendulum. If the main purpose of a
> clock is to go, the clock was the better for losing its
> pendulum. True, it could no longer tell the time, but that
> did not matter if one could teach oneself to be indifferent
> to the passage of time. The linguistic philosophy, which
> cares only about language, and not about the world, is
> like the boy who preferred the clock without the
> pendulum because, although it no longer told the time, it
> went more easily than before and at a more exhilarating
> pace.
>
> > Ernest Gellner [1959/68, p. 15]

We would be less than fair or honest if we let the issue end in such a
state of discordance. We think that if one drops one's interest in the
classical Problem of Induction, then Conventionalism ceases to be of
any interest whatsoever. No real problem is solved by Conventionalist
methodology. That is, there is no reason for our having to choose one
theory rather than another other than short-term practical
considerations. And, worse, if one turns to consider practical
problems, then Conventionalism is not appropriate, but instead
Instrumentalism should be the guide. But, far more important, if one is
concerned with the 'realism' of economic models, then
Conventionalism is totally inappropriate, as it eschews the models'
truth or falsity.

The only methodological perspective, other than the impossible

Inductivism, which is directly concerned with the realism or unrealism of economics models is Popper's so-called critical rationalism. Those neoclassical economists who are concerned with the realism of their models might now wish to consider Popper's methodological viewpoint. Let us explore what it would mean for an inclusion of Popper's methodology in the hidden agenda of neoclassical economics and its possible role in neoclassical theory.

Adjusting the Neoclassical Hidden Agenda

Eliminating the first item on the agenda
If one is so inclined, including Popper's methodological perspective is conceptually rather easy. The key to Popper's methodology is the rejection of the Problem of Induction. If we eliminate the need for authoritarianism, then there is no need to solve the classic Problem of Induction. This means that we can also cease taking such things as the inductive learning possibilities function for granted. For example, we might wish to recognize that some observations or additional bits of information actually refute our knowledge rather than increase its probability of being true. Instead we can focus on neoclassical model-building as a systematic attempt to learn by our theoretical mistakes and thereby emphasize the role of criticism and disagreement in the development of neoclassical economics. As long as one's contribution is criticizable, anything should be allowed to be considered. There is no theoretical reason why we should choose between competitors. What is more important, from the perspective of Popper's methodology, is our understanding of the problems that anyone's contribution is intended to solve, as well as the alternative ways the problems may be solved. For the purposes of learning, rather than looking for the one correct solution, it is more important that we continue to look for more and more alternative solutions.

Generalizing the second item on the agenda
Continuing along the lines of considering the implications of any attempt to include Popper's methodology among the items on the hidden agenda, let us now examine the second item, methodological individualism. If we reject the need either to deal with or to solve the Problem of Induction, then there is no need to adopt the extreme form of methodological individualism that is based on an unsupported presumption of psychologism. What this means for methodology is that individuals are not identified with their psychological states. Rather than taking individuals' psychological states as irreducible givens, we can attempt to explain their psychological states. This does not neces-

sarily rule out individualism. Individuals still make all of the decisions. We are concerned here only with the basis of their decision-making. What we will argue below is that a major ingredient in every decision is the theories held to be true by the decision-maker and that in the absence of an inductive logic such theories cannot be reduced to the given nature of the physical world. Why any individual may consider a particular theory to be true may or may not be at issue. It all depends on the problems that the individual is trying to solve.

Dealing with the knowledge basis of decision-making

By following Popper's rejection of the Problem of Induction - and with it, Inductivism and Conventionalism - the door is open for the neoclassical economist to attempt to explain the knowledge basis of decision-making. By dropping the presumption that permits only psychological states and natural givens, the way is clear for the recognition that in order to explain the process of decision-making, the methodology of the decision-maker needs to play an essential role. What a particular decision-maker's methodology actually is depends on the problem-situation facing the decision-maker. To a great extent the methodology of the decision-maker depends on the decision-maker's *theory* of that problem-situation. There is no reason why anyone should expect any decision-maker to hold a true theory of the problem-situation, nor is there any reason why all decision-makers should employ the same methodological perspectives. The focus of these considerations will ultimately be concerned with how individual decision-makers deal with the discovery of evidence that contradicts the theories which they thought were true in the process of making their decisions.

Real-Time Individualism in the Short Run

Combining Popper's methodology with neoclassical economics

Discussing arbitrary changes in the research agenda of neoclassical economics is really not very interesting unless we can see how the new agenda affects the nature of any neoclassical theory. The one research topic where Popper's methodology and epistemology can play a dramatic role concerns the appropriate short-run setting for neoclassical economics. As we explained in Chapter 6, the usual treatment of time in neoclassical explanatory models has been quite inadequate. Specifically, the dynamics of the usual neoclassical models based on Inductivism and Conventionalism are exogenous and hence unexplained. We wish to show here that by dropping Inductivism and Conventionalism and instead relying on Popper's views of knowledge and learning, the way is open to the development of real-time explanations in neoclassical theory. To be neoclassical all that is required is that we retain individualism - that is, the view that only individuals make decisions - as well as rational decision-making. However, it should be stressed that Popper's methodology focuses on rational decision-*making* and not on rational decision-*makers*.

As Hicks [1976, p. 136; 1979] observes, the general problem of explaining change (dynamics) in the context of rational decision-making is that the decision-maker's knowledge (of the givens) is hopelessly static. Although Hicks appreciates the problem, he has missed the source of the difficulty. It is not that our knowledge itself is static, but rather that the traditional *views of knowledge* assert that knowledge is static. We shall argue that there is not necessarily a problem with rational decision-making, except when its logical basis presumes that the individual's knowledge (of the givens), or its acquisition, is exogenously given.

Traditionally we are required to choose between the two views of knowledge that we have identified with the first item on the hidden agenda. On the one hand, there is Inductivism, which asserts that knowledge is only the facts collected up to a certain point in time. On the other hand, there is Conventionalism, which considers knowledge to be only the latest, accepted theory (of the facts) at a certain point in time. Both views make knowledge static because it is exogenously given at any point in time.

To emphasize our viewpoint of knowledge in the short-run setting, let us review the essentials of our discussion in Chapter 1 of these two views of knowledge. What is salient in both of the traditional views or theories of knowledge is that an empirical statement or a theory is considered knowledge only to the extent that it is supported by the facts. These traditional views differ only in regard to what is meant by 'supported by the facts', or what constitutes 'the facts'. With Inductivism, factual support is alleged to be direct and logically complete. However, with Conventionalism, all knowledge can be considered an accepted system of catalogues used to file or 'capture' the available facts and thus knowledge is only 'better' or 'worse' rather than 'true' or 'false'.

As we explained in Chapter 1, both views are based on the common belief in Justificationism, that is, the doctrine that a theory is not true knowledge unless it can be justified (i.e., proven true). A first step toward solving the problem of explaining dynamics in the short run is the recognition that Justificationism is false (not only because it is unjustified itself). We shall argue below that by rejecting Justificationism, that is, by separating the truth status of a statement from the proof or the provability of its truth status, the way is clear to resolving the dilemma discussed in Chapter 6 of having to choose between dynamic explanations and explanations of dynamics.

A basis for an individualist explanation of dynamics
To solve the problem of explaining dynamics we begin (closely following [Boland 1978]) by formulating a new, non-psychologistic, individualist research agenda based on the epistemology of Popper and a modified version of the methodological individualism of Hayek. We shall call this the Popper-Hayek program for explaining any rational dynamic process. For the purpose of discussion let us itemize the essential parts of this proposed agenda.

Anti-Justificationism. First, all knowledge is presumed to be essentially theoretical, hence conjectural; second, it is possibly true, although we cannot prove its truth status [Popper, 1972, ch. 3].

Anti-psychologism. It is presumed that everyone's knowledge is potentially objective [Popper, 1972, ch. 1].

Rational decision-making. It is presumed that what one does at any point in time depends on one's knowledge *at that time* and the logic of the situation in which that knowledge is used [Hayek, 1937/48; Hicks, 1973, 1979].

Situational dynamics. It is presumed that one's behavioral changes can result from changes in one's knowledge as well as from intended or unintended changes in one's situation [Hayek, 1937/48; Shackle, 1972].

It should be pointed out that this approach to solving the problem of explaining dynamics within a short-run individualist framework requires the rejection of Hayek's inductivist epistemology and its replacement with Popper's concept of objective knowledge. The latter requires the rejection of psychologism. The first step is to specify one or more actors, in the past or present, who have been causing or contributing to the change in question, and the *theories they held at the time of their actions.* Next, we must specify the unintended consequences of their actions, entailing conjectures about why their theories were *false.* Note that the falsity of the theories may be unknown to the actors at the time; in fact, it is by means of these unintended consequences that actors in question may learn that their knowledge is false. In short, this framework asserts that economics *in* time is a sequence of unintended consequences of acting on the basis of (unknowingly) false theories [cf. Hicks, 1965, p. 184; 1979]. (Note that this is not instrumentalism, since the truth status may still matter.)

Objective theoretical knowledge
Let us examine the elements of this Popper-Hayek individualist program. Discussing the nature of knowledge is quite difficult because knowledge itself is usually given a rather lofty status. Nevertheless, it

cannot be avoided. We propose to recognize a simple separation between the truth status of someone's knowledge (i.e., whether it is true or false) and the role that knowledge plays in his or her decision-making process - that is, to provide a sufficient and logically consistent explanation of the world he or she faces. Of course, at the very minimum, knowledge must be logically consistent if it is to be able to provide a true explanation of something. This is so even though the logical consistency of any explanation does not imply its truth. Nevertheless, it is the consistency of a decision-maker's knowledge which plays the major role in our explanation of his or her behavior. The truth of his or her knowledge is much more difficult to ascertain. But, more important, the truth of his or her knowledge is not always necessary for a successful action on his or her part. It should be noted that by separating the truth status from the role of knowledge we are not suggesting that theories or knowledge cannot be true; and we are definitely not agreeing with Solow's [1956] view that all theories are false, since that is a self-contradiction. On the contrary, we are asserting that a theory can be true even though its truth status is usually unknown to us.

By saying that knowledge is essentially theoretical we are emphasizing that the truth status of anyone's knowledge is always conjectural (i.e., not completely justified) and that it is potentially objective. By 'potentially objective' we mean only that by its logical nature it is capable of at least being stated in words or in other repeatable forms to the extent that it is the knowledge of the real world [Popper, 1972, pp. 106ff.]. It could be argued that the potential objectivity of any decision-maker's knowledge makes possible a so-called operationally meaningful explanation of his or her behavior.

In our view, since all knowledge is theoretical, anyone's knowledge can be put on the table for everyone to see. The view that knowledge is potentially objective stands in opposition to the implications of the more common view identified above as psychologism. Psychologism presumes that knowing is either a natural given, directly provable by induction, or a psychological process. While the former is precluded by rejecting induction, the latter makes one's knowledge private or subjective [Popper, 1972, pp. 1-7]. A corollary of psychologism is that one can never explain someone else's knowledge in the absence of induction. Either way, the proposed view requires at least a rejection of psychologism.

The common psychologistic view of knowledge may only be saying that one cannot guarantee a *true* explanation of someone else's knowledge. We propose this reading of psychologism to explain why anyone might think that it is impossible to explain someone else's knowledge. If this reading is correct, then psychologism is merely another variant of the Justificationism rejected earlier. In the remainder of this chapter when we speak of someone's knowledge we shall not be referring to his or her inherently private views but rather to his or her explanations or theories of the behavior and nature of the world around him or her.

The role of knowledge

Hayek and others have recognized that the individual decision-maker must have knowledge of the givens or constraints if these are to play an active role in the decision process. If this view is correct, the individual's knowledge must also play an active role in any explanation of his or her behavior. This prescription is not novel. Since late in the nineteenth century most social scientists have adopted a methodology in which the actor is presumed to be 'rational' concerning his or her given situation. This is evident in much of the formal sociology of the late nineteenth century, which often presumes a fixed frame of reference, an 'ideal type', whose behavior is based either on perfect knowledge or on a fool-proof method of acquiring perfect knowledge. In this old methodology the behavior of an actual individual is explained by noting to what extent, or why, his or her behavior is not ideal or perfectly rational.

In ideal-type methodology, one source of an individual's deviance from the ideal stems from the so-called imperfections in his or her knowledge of the givens. The imperfections of one's knowledge might result, as argued in previous chapters, from the fact that in real time an inductively rational acquisition of knowledge is always inadequate. With regard to explaining rational dynamic processes, we may wish to give the imperfections a systematic and prominent role, but this is possible only to the extent that knowledge itself plays a role. Perhaps the only complaint one might have regarding the ideal-type methodology is that it actually neutralizes the role of the actor's acquisition process by presuming that there is some ('scientific') method of acquisition which will always give him or her the true knowledge of the givens. Such a method is essential to the definition of the ideal type. If such a method is presumed to apply, any deviance from the ideal can only result from the actor's 'irrationality'. Note that the use of the Rational Expectations Hypothesis avoids this escape clause by arguing that apparent imperfections are actually quite rational! Except for a few 'a priorists' such as Ludwig von Mises, using the ideal-type methodology usually implies a reliance on inductive logic to provide the rational method of acquisition. With the prior rejection of inductivism, we thus have at least rejected any reliance on ideal-type methodology with regard to the knowledge of the individual decision-maker.

Here we argue that the question of the truth status of an actor's knowledge (i.e., whether it is actually true or actually false) is a separate question from why the actor thinks or believes his or her knowledge is true. In particular, the truth status of any actor's knowledge is usually independent of the method of its acquisition. An actor's theory of something can be true regardless of how he or she came to hold that theory to explain numerous observations; he or she could have dreamt it. Any method of acquisition may succeed or fail. In our view, this separation of status and method is important because the truth status of the actor's knowledge and the method of acquisition play different roles in any ongoing decision process.

Hayek's view of the essential role of knowledge seems to be widely accepted today [e.g., Hirshleifer and Riley, 1979] - but more care needs to be taken to avoid taking Inductivism for granted. For example, Hayek's use of the word 'acquisition' was consistent with an inductivist theory of learning, namely, one in which learning involves collecting facts (e.g., observing 'grey elephants') and then inductively leaping to the conclusion that some general proposition about them is true (e.g., the statement 'All elephants are grey') Such general propositions or theories are said to have been 'acquired'. We do not wish to limit the concepts of learning or acquiring to exercises in inductive logic, since, as argued above, such learning requires an unreal (infinite) amount of time. The actual (real-time) discovery of refuting evidence that shows one's current theory to be false is also a form of learning. This form of learning (i.e., having one's knowledge refuted) will be most important in our program for explaining dynamic processes in the short run. We shall argue that the status of an actor's knowledge may give a reason for change, but it does not tell us what the change will be. However, knowing the actor's learning methodology may provide a clue to what change he or she may attempt to effect [Boland and Newman, 1979].

An illustration

Let us consider an example from orthodox microeconomics. We traditionally say that the consumers know their preferences and their givens (i.e., what their budgets will be as well as what the 'given' prices will be). We explain their behavior, first, by assuming that their preferences are convex, transitive, etc., and that prices are given and, second, by assuming the consumers buy the 'best' bundles according to their preferences. Now, Hayek argued that the consumers in a competitive market economy cannot always 'know' *a priori* what prices, or availability, will be, or even what their incomes will be the next time they go to the market. In terms of the proposed epistemology, the consumers have theories of what their incomes and the prices will be, although those theories may not be provable by reference to the facts known at any point of time prior to going to the market. Nevertheless, we (and the consumers), on the basis of their theories, logically predict what they will buy. Their theories might be inferred from past experience or deduced from knowledge of some prior institutional controls or from the pronouncements of the local authorities, etc.

Even recognizing that our predictions might be wrong, this illustration has not gone far enough for our purposes because it is still taking psychologism for granted. So we argue that in addition to having theories about what their price-income situations are, the consumers may also have only theories of what their preferences are. Specifically, unless they have tried all conceivable 'bundles', they do not 'know' from experience what their preferences are or will be even if their preferences do not change over time. They may believe the orthodox demand theories, thus may assume that their preferences are 'convex', 'transitive', etc., and may thereby rationally choose their optimum bundles for their expected price-income situation. As long as they are able to buy what they *think* is their respective 'best' bundle, there is no reason for them to change to any other bundle. They would have to be willing to test their theories of their preferences before we could expect them rationally to try other bundles which, on the basis of their current knowledge, they think would be non-optimal.

If our orthodox theory of consumers' behavior is true, then they would find that they are not better off with the test bundles and may return to the predicted optimum. If our theory is not true, they may find that they are better off with their respective test bundles, and hence their prior knowledge about their own preferences will have been revealed to be false. Or they may still not be better off with those particular test bundles.

Consider an alternative situation. It is quite possible for the consumers' preferences to be concave somewhere, yet, for some unknown reason, for them to have picked their 'best' bundles. Most important, if their theories of their own preferences turn out, upon testing, to be wrong and if their preferences do play a significant role in their decision-making, they will at some point be led to change their behavior. Depending on their views concerning facts and knowledge, they may change immediately by buying their own 'better' test bundle if they have found one or may change at some future point when facing new price-income situations. Unless we can say something about the consumers' methodology, logically anything can happen.

In general, if one's theory of the world plays a decisive role but is false, accepting it as true must lead to errors in real time. How one responds to such errors depends on one's view of knowledge and how it is acquired. Furthermore, unless there is only one conceivable methodology, consumers can be clearly distinguished by their respective methodologies as well as by their preferences and their income situations.

Responses to the need for change

Our consideration of the role of knowledge offers two possible reasons for change. First, an actor may change his or her behavior because exogenous changes in the givens can cause the actor's knowledge to be 'out-of-date', i.e., *false*. A typical example of response to this type of false theory is a movement along the demand curve as a consequence of (disequilibrium) price changes. When the consumer learns that the price has gone up he or she adjusts to the new price by buying less.

Secondly, an actor's mistakes which result from acting on the basis of false knowledge, even when the givens have not changed, will directly and endogenously cause changes in the future givens. For example, consider how an imperfectly competitive firm decides on the quantity of its product to supply and its price, given its current financial situation. Let us say that in making a decision it estimates the demand curve incorrectly. Having supplied the wrong quantity, it soon discovers that it put the wrong price on its product - its actual sales do not correspond to the level it expected. This leads to unintended changes in its financial situation. The new givens will affect its future decisions even if it never learns anything about how to estimate future demand curves.

This example is not designed to suggest that an actor's situation changes only as a result of unintended consequences. It is quite conceivable that an actor might change his or her situation deliberately. The producer may decide to invest in new machines in order to reduce production costs or change the nature of his or her product. Such changes in the givens would be *intended* consequences. As long as the givens have changed, deliberately or not, the future behavior of the producer will usually change. New givens require new knowledge of the givens. Since there is no foolproof method of acquiring new knowledge, one's knowledge is very often false [Newman, 1976]. False new knowledge yields new errors and new unintended consequences.

The evidence of errors or mistakes could be considered a criticism of the 'realism' of one's assumptions and would thereby seem to bring about a change in one's theory of the world. However, this depends crucially on one's methodology and view of knowledge. By adopting a Conventionalist view of knowledge, decision-makers might find it possible to deflect such empirical criticism by some form of approximationism [Boland, 1970b]. For example, they might say that the evidence of a counter-example (an error) is not really contrary to their theory of the world, because that theory is probabilistic and thus allows a few counter-examples provided they are not 'too numerous' [cf. Rotwein, 1959, 1980; Shackle, 1972; Boland, 1977c]. Or it might be said that only when the errors continue to happen will one be pushed to consider changing one's view of the world. (Remember, one must not 'jump to conclusions'.) Thus adherents to Conventionalism may be slow to react to unintended consequences. On the other hand, adherents to instrumentalism such as the followers of Friedman's essay on methodology, who knowingly accept false assumptions may never change.

Alternatively, those actors with a 'skepticist' theory of knowledge may always be looking for indications that their knowledge is false and may always be ready to modify it. Their behavior, unlike that of typical adherents to Conventionalism, will appear very erratic and will certainly be more difficult to predict. More might be said about this; for now it is enough merely to conjecture that *the way one responds in a real-time short run to unintended consequences or counter-examples to one's assumptions reveals a great deal about one's theory of knowledge* [Boland and Newman, 1979].

Although we have used examples from microeconomics, these epistemological considerations are equally important to the usual conceptions of macroeconomics. Government policies today are based on the assumption that specific macro theories are true, and estimates are made of parameters of models of these theories, predictions are made, and so on. What would happen if these theories were false [Robinson, 1967]? How do governments respond to counter-examples?

A Neoclassical Program for a Real-Time Short Run

Having now presented all the ingredients for a non-psychologistic version of neoclassical economics, let us now present our program for explaining rational decision-making in the short run in a way in which real (i.e., irreversible) time matters. We should also point out at the outset that this research program is not limited to only questions of pure dynamics. As Samuelson pointed out with his famous 'Correspondence Principle' [1947/65], even the explanation of a static situation is not complete until we have also explained the dynamic path which led to the static situation.

We accept Hayek's view that all rational decision-making must depend on knowledge of the givens and any explanation of rational decision-making must include assumptions about the decision-makers' methodology (i.e., about how knowledge is acquired or changed). We argued that this depends on the decision-maker's *theory of knowledge*. Thus, in any explanation of an actor's behavior we must specify the actor's view of the nature of knowledge and how it is acquired or changed. Along the lines of Chapter 10, we should point out that the methodology that is adopted by the actor may depend on the actor's aims. A different aim may require a different methodology. For example, an actor may only have very short-run goals and thus it would be appropriate for us to assume that the actor adheres to an Instrumentalist methodology. Another actor may include long-term learning as a goal; thus this second actor may adhere to either Inductivism or the Popper-Socrates theory of learning.

Despite these examples, traditional explanations involving knowledge or information may be unsatisfactory in any a real-time short run. Similarly, any macroeconomic explanations which presume unanimity concerning the epistemology or methodology may not be considered adequate. Any static concept of the actor's knowledge or its acquisition - that is, a concept for which real time does not matter - renders Hayek's view incapable of explaining economic change. Furthermore, although it is well known that all models require at least one exogenous variable, any view which considers knowledge or its acquisition to be exogenous will not permit an explanation of the endogenous dynamics of a rational decision process.

Our program for explaining short-run dynamics consistent with neoclassical economics is based on a dynamic concept of knowledge where its acquisition is endogenous. In particular, the *process* of acquisition depends on the specific *view of knowledge* held by the actor. Primarily, all decisions are seen to be potentially part of the learning process. Learning, by definition, is irreversible; hence it is always a real-time process. The decision-maker can learn with every decision made. What he or she may learn at least is that his or her theory of the givens is false. *How* he or she responds depends on his or her theory of knowledge. Thus, an essential ingredient of the short-run neoclassical program presented here is the requirement of an explicit conjecture concerning the actor's objective theory of knowledge. Moreover, this solution specifically recognizes that even when facing the same facts (i.e., the same experience), two decision-makers who differ only with respect to their theories of knowledge will generally have different patterns of behavior *over time even in the short run*, patterns that may not be equally predictable.

Rational decision-making does not require rational decision-mak*ers* nor does it require proven true knowledge. It requires only the explicit assumption on the part of the decision-maker that some or all of his or her knowledge is true. Actions based on knowledge that is actually (but unknowingly) false will yield errors or other unintended consequences in the short run. These consequences are not evidence of the actor's so-called irrationality; rather, they are evidence that some of the actor's knowledge is false.

The view that one is irrational if one's knowledge is false presumes that there exists a rational process which yields guaranteed true knowledge. Unfortunately, such a process does not exist, so that the charge of 'irrationality' is misleading and perhaps unfair. Yet the actor's knowledge does play an *essential* role in his or her decision process. Not only is it not logically possible to assure that knowledge is true; it may also actually be false. Thus, our research program includes Popper's epistemological viewpoint which explicitly separates the truth status from the role that knowledge plays in the decision process. Primarily, this permits us to separate the static nature of the truth of knowledge from the dynamic nature of the learning process. However, this separation alone is not enough to solve the problem of explaining endogenous dynamics within an individualist framework. One must also assume that the learning process is not one of the exogenous givens of the explanatory model.

With traditional equilibrium dynamic models, as we explained in Chapter 6, explanations of changes rely on exogenous changes in the givens for the rational decision-maker. Every decision-maker would be expected to respond to the new givens, and the new equilibrium is reached at the point where everyone's behavior is consistent with the new givens. Thus traditionally there are two types of observable change: long-run moving equilibria and short-run movements towards a new equilibrium. In models where real time does not matter these two types of change are indistinguishable by simple observation. By definition, an unambiguous short-run change is identifiable only where there have been no changes in the givens. Long-run equilibrium change can occur only after the givens have changed. Once an equilibrium has been reached, no changes should occur without exogenous changes in the givens.

In Chapter 3 we discussed the limitations of the commonly accepted view that the explanation of macrodynamics should be based on the existence of disequilibria caused by the necessary uncertainties of the individual decision-makers. We argued that recognizing that false knowledge is a reason for change is not enough. A complete explanation of macrodynamics based on knowledge uncertainties must also explain *how* individuals respond to those uncertainties in real time - that is, individuals' views of methodology must be included in the short-run setting. However, in Chapter 4 we argued that current views of the individual's way of dealing with knowledge and learning are based on a false theory of knowledge - the inductive learning possibilities function - and thus can never be the basis of a realistic theory of economic behavior. We might add now that the common view is quite inconsistent with Popper's view of knowledge and learning. For Popper, learning occurs only when additional information forces a change in one's knowledge; thus learning cannot be characterized by the inductive learning function and thus the Rational Expectations Hypothesis is at best irrelevant for questions of endogenous dynamics.

Contrary to the views which base all dynamics on the existence of disequilibria, we argue that the absence of a disequilibrium does not imply the absence of change because any current equilibrium may not be compatible with existing knowledge. Any definition of long-run equilibrium which requires that existing knowledge (or 'expectations') be compatible with the given equilibrium is in effect presuming that there exists a solution to the Problem of Induction since every long-run equilibrium is merely a special short-run equilibrium (e.g., one where all markets are in a short-run equilibrium). Since there is no solution to this problem, knowledge incompatibility is always possible in real time. Depending on the actors' learning methodology, at least one of the givens (viz. their theories of the givens) may change. Such a change, which can be explained in terms of the actors' theories of knowledge, leads to a new disequilibrium. If the actors learn with each decision, their knowledge may always be changing. They will therefore always be in a state of disequilibrium. However, this state can be completely explained if we explain how the actors respond to knowledge incompatibility.

The evidence that one's knowledge is incompatible with the equilibrium values of the givens and the variables is one's unfulfilled expectations. Unfulfilled expectations are interpreted as unintended consequences. This means that in equilibrium models unintended consequences are the motivating reasons for *endogenous* change. Thus, if we are going to explain change in the short-run setting, we must focus on the sources of unintended consequences, namely, the actors' false theories and their methodologies, which together play a primary role in all learning and thus in all dynamic processes.

12

Problem-Dependent Methodology

> Do not presume, one of the thieves was damned; do not
> despair, one of the thieves was saved.
>
> St Augustine

Despite recent comments by methodologists indicating that Popper's
philosophy of science is a guiding light for economists, the fact is that
neoclassical economics is still founded on a methodology consisting of
Conventionalism mixed with bits of overt Instrumentalism and in-
advertent Inductivism. Popper's contribution so far has been limited to
only an improvement in the methodological jargon. Where Popper
sees science as an enterprise built upon systematic criticism, our profession's reliance on Conventionalism to deal with the Problem of
Induction has always put a high value on agreement, that is, on having
our views accepted by our colleagues. Given that there is no formal
inductive logic, everyone seems to think that a theory can be considered successful only if it has been included somewhere in the accepted
view of economics.

The opinion that there should be one accepted view is immediately
open to question. Yet it is an opinion that is at the core of virtually
every methodological dispute. The traditional view is that in order to
discover the true nature of the economy we must first have the one
correct method for analyzing the economy. As the tradition goes,
famous physicists such as Newton and Einstein were successful only
because they used the correct 'scientific method'. The companion
tradition says that anyone who is not successful must be using an
'unscientific method'.

These traditional views are so well entrenched that it may be difficult
for us to convince any reader that there may be something wrong here.
Nevertheless, that is our chosen task for this chapter. We shall argue
that the traditional view is misleading on two counts. First, it presumes
there is only one correct method for all of science; and second, it

reflects an even more fundamental item on the hidden agenda of every science that would require 'authoritative support' for anyone's explanation of anything of scientific interest.

Regardless of the wisdom or foolishness of anyone's concern for whether or not economics is a science, there is an overriding concern that whatever the outcome of an examination of our methods of analysis, we should at least agree on some general principles of analysis. The reason is simple. Economics is not a one-person affair these days. Improvements in our understanding of the workings of an economy usually depend on the combined efforts of many individuals. But we must be careful here. No matter how necessary common agreements may be, there are still some dangers of putting too much emphasis on them. (Remember how Hans Christian Andersen demonstrated those dangers in his story of 'The Emperor's New Clothes' in which the common, agreed upon view was definitely wrong.)

The primary reason for putting too much emphasis on common agreement is the frequent plea that the economic problems of society need urgent solutions. Sympathy with this urgency puts the academic economist in an awkward position. On the one hand, if we all could agree on general principles, less time would be wasted in arguing about fundamentals and more time would be available for finding good solutions to our pressing problems. On the other hand, good solutions may require new principles better suited to contemporary conditions. In effect, we always face a choice between immediate returns which may be limited by our current understanding and long-term benefits which follow from a new or improved understanding. The choice is never easy - and we, furthermore, deny the existence of universally acceptable criteria.

The Traditional View of Methods

Is there a method of analysis somewhere which, if we always used it, would ensure that we would never make a mistake? Indeed, it would be nice should there ever be such a method, but unfortunately there is not. We need not despair, though. Popper tells us that we learn by our mistakes; all we can hope is that our mistakes do not cause too much damage. As we discussed in Chapters 1 and 10, there was a time when many people thought there was a foolproof and objective method by which individuals could avoid mistakes by being extremely careful in the collection of 'facts' and, above all, by not passionately 'jumping to conclusions' before all the facts were collected.

Today, being a scientist is not such a personal matter. Rather, it is a matter of being part of a scientific community. Membership in a scientific community is governed by two factors: one's credentials and the acceptance of one's methods. The appropriate credentials are rather obvious - one needs a graduate degree or two. But one's education is not enough unless it involves being trained in the use of the accepted methods. Just what are the appropriate credentials or the accepted methods is not always obvious, since they can vary from one generation to the next or from one discipline to the next.

In many cases it is not easy to tell whether the latest accepted methods are not just the latest fad - but we will leave this critical note for now. It is important to recognize that what may be considered '*the* scientific method' today may tomorrow be considered very inadequate and thus may be replaced by another accepted method. The method supposedly followed in Newton's time would be considered rather silly or naive today by some scientists. Yet no one is willing to dismiss Newton's theories merely because his methods may be a bit suspect today. In retrospect, it would seem that the significance of one's theories may be judged separately from the acceptability of one's methods.

Notwithstanding this historical perspective, every scientific community operates day to day as if there were one and only one acceptable method of analysis. It is this fact that we must face. If you want to play an immediate role in the development of modern economics, you must learn how to use the currently accepted method. Paradoxically, even attempts to change the accepted method must proceed according to the currently accepted method.

Authoritarianism and the Hidden Agenda of Science

Apart from the obvious paradox, the problem of pulling oneself up by one's bootstraps that may trouble anyone who wishes to change the currently accepted method of analysis, there are other problems that should concern us. Although it is difficult for educated people to admit, the reliance on credentials and accepted methods as a means of discriminating significant from insignificant theories carries with it a more serious problem. It is the problem of inadvertently advocating authoritarianism.

The primary item on the hidden agenda (i.e., dealing with the Problem of Induction) is the view that if anyone wishes to be 'scientific', he or she must imitate the methods of physics or some other 'hard' science. It is as if physicists had a monopoly in clear thinking. Nevertheless, we must be careful to avoid overreacting. Economics and most of the natural sciences have many things in common. Logic, mathematics and statistics are the same regardless of where they are used. And many of the apparent differences turn out, upon close examination, to be merely terminological, reflecting only differences in professional jargon. But there is no reason why physics methodology should carry any authority in economics analysis.

The view that there is one and only one acceptable method of analysis implies that a theory created according to the accepted method has some authority over other possible theories. Despite our years of education, which were supposedly directed at teaching us to think for ourselves, we are supposed to surrender our judgement to the authority of the accepted scientific method or the current scientific community. It is unlikely that we could convince anyone that there is no authority implied by anyone's theory being deemed scientific because we will be asked to specify the authority upon which we have based such a claim. The best we can hope for is that we become aware of the hidden agenda involved in any enterprise. We shall not try to solve the problem of authoritarianism here. Instead, we shall just try to call attention to its role in the hidden agenda peculiar to methodology discussions in economics.

Methodological Agreement

Although there is considerable personal recognition given to individuals in science (for example, Nobel prizes), most of the everyday business of doing economic analysis relies on the cooperation and combined efforts of many people. The publication of articles and books would not be possible without some common intellectual framework, paradigm, or research program. All introductory textbooks are written to introduce students to that which is common to all members of the given scientific community. But apart from giving textbook writers a job, a common agreement is necessary for the coordination of a large community's research efforts. Those familiar with the current research program will know which problems are on the agenda, and most important, which research methods are considered acceptable.

The need for agreement
The necessity of commonly agreed upon research principles is most evident when the scientific community faces problems needing urgent solutions. Many of the current research tools were developed during the urgencies of World War II. Of course, the development of the tools was facilitated by large government grants. But what the grants did was to focus the research and to force a minimum amount of agreement on principles. When there is an agreement over research principles and

problems, it is possible for everyone to avoid endless arguments over which problems need solving and which tools should be used. Thus one expects research to be more productive when there is widespread agreement and very little disagreement. But such expectations can be misleading.

The dangers of forced agreement

Very often an argument in favor of the urgency of a problem may be only a disguised attempt to deflect a potential argument over basic principles. For obvious reasons, once one has spent many years of toil obtaining the necessary training in currently accepted research principles, one is not going to welcome a change to new and different techniques. This is very often the reason why methodology itself is not accorded priority on the research agenda, as it tends to focus criticism on currently accepted research principles.

One does not usually have to argue for the urgency of a problem when it is really urgent. Thus it is usually easy to spot such false arguments. Nevertheless, the dangers or costs of misrepresenting the urgency of a problem can be far-reaching. To the extent that any science progresses in Socratic learning terms, by improving its fundamental principles and theories, any diversion of research from fundamental theoretical problems in favor of short-term, immediate, practical problems may lead to extensive long-term costs.

Just as it is a mistake to think that there is one and only one scientific method for all problems and for all time, it is a mistake to think our understanding of the economy today will be adequate for everything in the future. It is thus in the scientific community's interest to allocate some research efforts or funds to the study of basic research methods.

The False Choice Problem

The primary source of disputes over criteria such as simplicity, generality, or falsifiability is the Conventionalist's choice problem itself. It is a false problem. That is to say, nothing much is accomplished by solving that problem. We realize that very many philosophers think it is an important problem, but we shall argue to the contrary. Specifically, we shall argue that when it comes to problems which require a choice between theories, those problems are usually the problems that involve Instrumentalism. But of course, we are going too fast. Let us take things one step at a time. Disputes over the choice of the best methodology (e.g., between Conventionalism, Pragmatism, or Instrumentalism) presuppose that there is one correct, all-purpose methodology. We will argue that this is wrong. The best methodology for today depends on the problems that concern us today. Different problems sometimes require different methods. This leads to a similar problem concerning choice criteria. There need not be an all-purpose criterion.

Is there an all-purpose criterion?

Our purpose here is to argue that there need not be one all-purpose methodology in the usual authoritarian sense, and that, instead, there are many different methodologies, each of which contains prescriptive or proscriptive criteria that are only appropriate for a specific set of problems. Every given methodology has its limitations and may not be appropriate for other problems.

Conventionalism is designed to deal with the shortcomings of our not having a direct solution to the Problem of Induction. Specifically, versions of Conventionalism can be used to provide a philosophical perspective when writing textbooks or when writing about the history of a given science. For example, Samuelson uses his form of Conventionalism to explain the history of Demand Theory. In his view, we can see how Demand Theory has changed over time, each change representing an improvement in generality. In his view the history of Demand Theory has culminated in the 'Generalized Law of Demand', which is a mathematical relationship between the slope of the demand curve and the nature of consumers' preferences [1953]. According to Samuelson's version of Conventionalism, then, the ultimate criterion for choosing among competitors is generality. Another follower of Conventionalism, Mark Blaug, in his history of economic thought utilizes a different criterion. For him progress is seen in terms of improvements in our ability to mathematize economic theories. Thus Samuelson's models are superior to, say, Marshall's because Samuelson's can be represented by mathematical functions, whereas Marshall's view is based on a rejection of mathematical models.

Judging by the current form of published articles [e.g., Lucas, 1980], many economists agree with both Samuelson and Blaug. The prescribed methodological objective of many writers is to increase the generality of economic analysis. Formal mathematics is recognized as the means of providing the most general form of any given theory. Surely there are some limitations to formal mathematical analysis? Open any leading economics journal and you will find rather complicated arguments concerning such questions as the mathematical stability of a given theory, the existence and uniqueness of its solution, its axiomatic basis, etc. It is all too easy to argue that little of the content of such journals has any direct relevance to practical questions of policy.

Few followers of Friedman's Instrumentalism would find anything useful in the leading analytical theory journals. Most of modern economic theory is so general that it is virtually impossible to apply it to practical situations. For example, the 'Generalized Law of Demand' basically says anything is possible. The old-fashioned 'Law of Demand' said that only downward-sloping demand curves were possible. This is not a trivial matter for those economists interested in making policy judgements based on a calculation of consumer surplus. Such a calculation requires a downward-sloping demand curve.

Generalized economic models have so many variables that it would take forever to collect all the information just to apply them to simple cases. For example, where a first-degree (i.e., linear) demand function between a single good's price (P) and the quantity demanded (Q) has only two parameters, its slope (b) and its intercept (a), as in the following equation:

$$Q = a + bP \qquad [1]$$

just raising its generality by saying it is a second-degree (i.e., quadratic) demand function between the two same variables adds another parameter (c):

$$Q = a + bP + cP^2 \qquad [2]$$

and increasing the degree increases the number of extra parameters that will have to be measured.

The linear model is very special and very simple. The non-linear model allows for the linear model as a special case (e.g., when $c = 0$) but it also allows for many other cases (i.e., when c is negative and when c is positive). In this sense the non-linear model is more general. But we can see why general models can easily get out of hand. We can allow for more and more types of cases but only by introducing more and more parameters.

These considerations show both sides. We can see why Instrumentalism puts a premium on simplicity rather than generality. And we can see why Conventionalism finds generality superior to simplicity. From the Conventionalist standpoint, increased generality allows for a larger filing cabinet; and the bigger the filing cabinet, the better the theory. For Instrumentalism, the benefits of increased generality may not always justify the extra costs.

Is there an all-purpose methodology?

These considerations also show us why Conventionalism and Instrumentalism can be at such odds whenever anyone thinks there is one and only one correct methodology. Except for very special occasions, both views cannot simultaneously be correct. Instrumentalism's desire for simplicity is appropriate whenever we are faced with immediate, short-run, practical problems which preclude measuring a large number of parameters. On the other hand, short-run practical success may not be very durable because parameters have a tendency to change quite often. For longer-run problems, perhaps Conventionalism's generality is more appropriate.

The Fundamental Choice Problem

Once one accepts that these two competing methodologies have their respective places, then one has reached the position where it seems that most of the methodological disputes in economics are rather empty on their own terms. If there is a dispute between adherents of Conventionalism (such as Samuelson, Solow, and Blaug) and adherents of Instrumentalism (such as Friedman and his followers), it is only about specifying what are the most important problems facing economists today.

Objectives come first
Before economists argue about what is the 'best' methodology (and note that the use of the term 'best' may have already predisposed the argument in favor of Conventionalism), they should reach some agreement about their objectives. If they do not, then their arguments will likely be at cross-purposes. But as we have just warned, one must be careful to avoid posing the choice problem so that only one method can win the debate.

Very often when economists think their methodology is the final word on the one true, all-purpose methodology they tend to search only for those problems that can be solved by their methods. Such an approach is not necessarily wrong, but from the perspective of the study of methodology it can be very misleading. When reading books or articles written by Conventionalist methodologists, one will find that the problems of 'scientific' interest are those problems for which one is supposed to choose the 'best' alternative theory (or model) from a list of competitors. Conversely, when reading Instrumentalist views of methodology, one will find that the truly scientific problems are those dealing with immediate practical problems and thus one should choose the most 'useful' method for dealing with those problems. Of course, the method that is most 'useful' is Instrumentalism itself. Thus one can see that in these cases, objectives do not come first. For these writers there is one fundamental choice problem in methodology: the arbitrary prior choice of one's all-purpose methodology.

Problem-dependent methodology

Once one accepts our argument here that there is no universal, all-purpose methodology, then most discussions of methodology become uninteresting because they are too biased. The celebrated dispute between Friedman and Samuelson is a case in point. Without some way of independently determining what are the really interesting problems, there will never be a way to resolve the dispute.

Instead of an all-purpose methodology there are really many possible methodologies. Each one is appropriate for a limited list of problems. If at present practical problems are most interesting, then Instrumentalism is appropriate. If catalogue choice problems are the most pressing, then perhaps Conventionalism is the appropriate methodology. If learning for learning's sake is an important consideration, then perhaps Popper's methodology, which emphasizes problems, criticism and, above all, disagreement, is a more appropriate perspective.

The Role of Methodology

As a final note, let us point out that throughout this book, we have been stressing a significant role for both the Popper-Socrates theory of learning of Chapter 10 and the related problem-dependent methodology of this chapter in any neoclassical program for explaining individual decision-making. We would welcome critics who may argue that in stressing one view of methodology we are in effect violating our own caution to avoid seeking an all-purpose methodology. We would argue that we are not, for the following reasons. (1) We are *not* arguing that a problem-dependent methodology is the 'best' methodology, but rather, that it is the only available methodology which is consistent with a realistic short-run neoclassical theory - that is, with one in which individuals are assumed to be making decisions in real time. (2) Conversely, not much will be gained by considering our Popper-Hayek program of explanation if one does not wish to consider such avant-garde research topics as real-time dynamic neoclassical models, 'expectational errors' or disequilibrium models of macroeconomics.

Bibliography

Agassi, J. [1960] 'Methodological individualism' *British Journal of Sociology* 11, 244-70

Agassi, J. [1963] *Towards an Historiography of Science, History and Theory, Beiheft* 2 (The Hague:Mouton)

Agassi, J. [1965] 'The nature of scientific problems and their roots in metaphysics' in M. Bunge (ed.) *The Critical Approach to Science and Philosophy* (New York: Collier-Macmillan)

Agassi, J. [1966a] 'Sensationalism' *Mind* 75(297), 1-24

Agassi, J. [1966b] 'The mystery of the ravens: discussion' *Philosophy of Science* 33(4), 395-402

Agassi, J. [1969a] 'The novelty of Popper's philosophy of science' *International Philosophical Quarterly* 8, 442-63

Agassi, J. [1969b] 'Unity and diversity in science' in R. S. Cohen and M. W. Wartofsky (eds.) *Boston Studies in the Philosophy of Science* 4 (New York: Humanities Press), 463-522

Agassi, J. [1971a] 'The standard misinterpretation of skepticism' *Philosophical Studies* 22, 49-50

Agassi, J. [1971b] 'Tautology and testability in economics' *Philosophy of Social Sciences* 1, 49-63

Agassi, J. [1975] 'Institutional individualism' *British Journal of Sociology* 26, 144-55

Agassi, J. [1977] *Towards a Rational Philosophical Anthropology* (The Hague: Martinus Nijhoff)

Albert, H. [1979] 'The economic tradition' in K. Brunner (ed.) *Economics and Social Institutions* (Boston: Martinus Nijhoff), 1-27

Alchian, A. [1950] 'Uncertainty, evolution and economic theory' *Journal of Political Economy* 58, 211-21

Alchian, A. [1965] 'The basis of some recent advances in the theory of management of the firm' *Journal of Industrial Economics* 14, 30-41

Archibald,G. [1961] 'Chamberlin versus Chicago' *Review of Economic Studies* 29, 1-28

Arrow, K. [1974] *The Limits of Organization* (New York: Norton)

Arrow, K. [1959] 'Towards a theory of price adjustment' in M. Abramovitz (ed.) *Allocation of Economic Resources* (Stanford: Stanford Univ. Press)

Barro, R. and H. Grossman [1971] 'A general disequilibrium model of income and employment' *American Economic Review* 61, 82-93

Bartley, W. [1968] 'Theories of demarcation between science and metaphysics' in I. Lakatos and A. Musgrave (eds.) *Problems in the Philosophy of Science* (Amsterdam: North Holland), 40-64

Baumol, W. [1977] *Economic Theory and Operations Analysis*, 4th ed. (Englewood Cliffs: Prentice-Hall)

Becker, G. [1965] 'A theory of the allocation of time' *Economic Journal* 75, 493-517

Bennett, R. [1981] *An Empirical Test of some Post-Keynesian Income Distribution Theories*, Ph.D. Thesis, Simon Fraser University

Blaug, M. [1978] *Economic Theory in Retrospect* 3rd. ed. (Cambridge: Cambridge Univ. Press)

Blaug, M. [1980] *The Methodology of Economics* (Cambridge: Cambridge Univ. Press)

Bohm-Bawerk, E. [1889] *Positive Theory of Capital*, trans. W. Smart (New York: Stechert)

Boland, L. [1968] 'The identification problem and the validity of economic models' *South African Journal of Economics* 36, 236-40

Boland, L. [1969] 'Economic understanding and understanding economics' *South African Journal of Economics* 37, 144-60

Boland, L. [1970a] 'Axiomatic analysis and economic understanding' *Australian Economic Papers* 9, 62-75

Boland, L. [1970b] 'Conventionalism and economic theory' *Philosophy of Science* 37, 239-48

Boland, L. [1971a] 'Methodology as an exercise in economic analysis' *Philosophy of Science* 38, 105-17

Boland, L. [1971b] 'An institutional theory of economic technology and change' *Philosophy of the Social Sciences* 1, 253-8

Boland, L. [1974] 'Lexicographic orderings, multiple criteria, and 'ad hocery'' *Australian Economic Papers* 13, 152-7

Boland, L. [1975] 'Uninformative economic models' *Atlantic Economic Journal* 3, 27-32

Boland, L. [1977a] 'Testability in economic science' *South African Journal of Economics* 45, 93-105

Boland, L. [1977b] 'Testability, time and equilibrium stability' *Atlantic Economic Journal* 5, 39-47

Boland, L. [1977c] 'Model specifications and stochasticism in economic methodology' *South African Journal of Economics* 45, 182-89

Boland, L. [1978] 'Time in economics vs. economics in time: the "Hayek Problem"' *Canadian Journal of Economics* 11, 240-62

Boland, L. [1979a] 'A critique of Friedman's critics' *Journal of Economic Literature* 17, 503-22

Boland, L. [1979b] 'Knowledge and the role of institutions in economic theory' *Journal of Economic Issues* 8, 957-72

Boland, L. [1980] 'Friedman's methodology vs. conventional empiricism: a reply to Rotwein' *Journal of Economic Literature* 18, 1555-7

Boland, L. [1981a] 'Satisficing in methodology: a reply to Rendigs Fels' *Journal of Economic Literature* 19, 84-6

Boland, L. [1981b] 'On the futility of criticizing the neoclassical maximization hypothesis' *American Economic Review* 71, 1031-6

Boland, L. and G. Newman [1979] 'On the role of knowledge in economic theory' *Australian Economic Papers* 18, 71-80

Boland, L. and W. Frazer [1982] 'An essay on the foundations of Friedman's methodology' (mimeo)

Buchanan, J. and G. Tullock [1962] *The Calculus of Consent* (Ann Arbor: Univ. of Michigan Press)

Caldwell, B. [1980] 'Positivist philosophy of science and the methodology of economics' *Journal of Economic Issues* 14, 53-76

Chamberlin, E. [1934] *The Theory of Monopolistic Competition* (Cambridge, Mass.: Harvard Univ. Press)

Chipman, J. *et al.* [1971] *Preferences, Utility and Demand* (New York: Harcourt Brace)

Clower, R. [1965] 'The Keynesian counterrevolution: a theoretical appraisal' in F. Hahn and F. Brechling (eds.) *The Theory of Interest Rates* (London: Macmillan) 103-25

Clower, R. and A. Leijonhufvud [1973] 'Say's principle, what it means and doesn't mean' *Intermountain Economic Review* 4, 1-16

Coase, R. [1960] 'Problem of social costs' *Journal of Law and Economics* 3, 1-44

Coddington, A. [1979] 'Friedman's contribution to methodological controversy' *British Review of Economic Issues*, 1-13

Davidson, P. [1972] *Money and the Real World* (New York: Wiley)

Davis, L. and D. North [1971] *Institutional Change and American Economic Growth* (Cambridge: Cambridge Univ. Press)

Debreu, G. [1959] *Theory of Value* (New York: Wiley)

DeVany, A. [1976] 'Uncertainty, waiting time and capacity utilization: a stochastic theory of product quality' *Journal of Political Economy* 84, 523-41

Dingle, M. [1980] 'Conversations' *HES Bulletin* 2, 18-19

Dorfman, R., P. Samuelson and R. Solow [1958] *Linear Programming and Economic Analysis* (New York: McGraw-Hill)

Duhem, P. [1906/62] *The Aim and Structure of Physical Theory* (New York: Atheneum)

Eddington, A. [1928] *The Nature of the Physical World* (Cambridge: Cambridge Univ. Press)

Einstein, A. [1936/50] 'Physics and reality' *Out of My Later Years* (New York: Wisdom Library) 58-94

Friedman, B. [1979] 'Optimal expectations and the extreme information assumptions of 'Rational Expectations' macromodels' *Journal of Monetary Economics* 5, 23-41

Friedman, M. [1953] 'Methodology of positive economics' in *Essays in Positive Economics* (Chicago: Univ. of Chicago Press) 3-43

Friedman, M. [1978] Correspondence dated 14 April

Gardiner, M. [1976] 'On the fabric of inductive logic, and some probability paradoxes' *Scientific American* 243 (3) 119-22 and 124

Gellner, E. [1959/68] *Words and Things* (Harmondsworth, Middlesex: Penguin Books)

Georgescu-Roegen, N. [1971] *The Entropy Law and the Economic Process* (Cambridge, Mass.: Harvard Univ. Press)

Gordon, D. [1955] 'Operational propositions in economic theory' *Journal of Political Economy* 63, 150-61

Gordon, D. and A. Hynes [1970] 'On the theory of price dynamics' in E. Phelps (ed.) *Microeconomic Foundations of Employment and Inflation Theory* (New York: Norton) 369-93

Grossman, S. and J. Stiglitz [1976] 'Information and competitive price systems' *American Economic Review, Proceedings* 66, 246-53

Haavelmo, T. [1944] 'The probability approach in econometrics' *Econometrica Supplement* 12, 1-115

Hahn, F. [1973] *On the Notion of Equilibrium in Economics* (Cambridge: Cambridge Univ. Press)

Hanson, N. [1965] *Patterns of Discovery* (Cambridge: Cambridge Univ. Press)

Hattiangadi, J.N. [1978] 'Structure of Problems' *Philosophy of the Social Sciences* 8, 345-65

Hayek, F. [1933/39] 'Price expectations, monetary disturbances and malinvestments' in *Profits, Interest and Investments* (London: Routledge)

Hayek, F. [1937/48] 'Economics and knowledge' *Economica* 4 (NS), 33-54 (reprinted in Hayek [1948])

Hayek, F. [1945/48] 'The uses of knowledge in society' *American Economic Review* 35, 519-30 (reprinted in Hayek [1948])

Hayek, F. [1948] *Individualism and Economic Order* (Chicago: Univ. of Chicago Press)

Hayek, F. [1952] *The Counter Revolution of Science* (London: Allen & Unwin)

Hearnshaw, L.S. [1979] *Cyril Burt: Psychologist* (Ithaca: Cornell Univ. Press)

Hempel, C. [1965] *Aspects of Scientific Explanation* (New York: Free Press)

Hempel, C. [1966] *Foundations of Natural Science* (Englewood Cliffs: Prentice-Hall)

Hicks, J. [1939/46] *Value and Capital* 2nd. ed. (Oxford: Clarendon Press)

Hicks, J. [1937] 'Mr. Keynes and the classics: a suggested interpretation' *Econometrica* 5, 147-59

Hicks, J. [1965] *Capital and Growth* (Oxford: Oxford Univ. Press)

Hicks, J. [1973] 'The Austrian theory of capital and its rebirth in modern economics' in J. Hicks and W. Weber (eds.) *Carl Menger and the Austrian School of Economics* (Oxford: Oxford Univ. Press) 190-206

Hicks, J. [1976] 'Some questions of time *in* economics' in A. Tang, F. Westfield and J. Worley *Evolution, Welfare and Time in Economics* (Toronto: Heath) 135-51

Hicks, J. [1979] *Causality in Economics* (Oxford: Blackwell)

Hicks, J. and R. Allen [1934] 'A reconsideration of the theory of value' *Economica* 1 (NS), 54-76 and 196-219

Hirshleifer, J. and J. Riley [1979] 'The analytics of uncertainty and information: an expositional survey' *Journal of Economic Literature* 17, 1375-421

Hollis, M. and E. Nell [1975] *Rational Economic Man* (Cambridge: Cambridge Univ. Press)

Hughes, R. I. G. [1981] 'Quantum logic' *Scientific American* 245, 202-13

Hume, D. [1739] *Treatise on Human Nature*

Hutchison, T. [1938] *The Significance and Basic Postulates of Economic Theory* (London: Macmillan)

Jarvie, I. [1964] *The Revolution in Anthropology* (London: Routledge & Kegan Paul)

Kaldor, N. [1957] 'A model of economic growth' *Economic Journal* 67, 594-621

Kamin, L. J. [1974] *The Science and Politics of I.Q.* (New York: Wiley)

Keynes, J. [1937] 'The general theory of employment' *Quarterly Journal of Economics* 51, 209-23

Klein, L. [1946] 'Remarks on the theory of aggregation' *Econometrica* 14, 303ff.

Koopmans, T. [1957] *Three Essays on the State of Economic Science* (New York: McGraw-Hill)

Koopmans, T. [1979] 'Economics among the sciences' *American Economic Review* 69, 1-13

Kuhn, T. [1962/70] *The Structure of Scientific Revolutions* 2nd. ed. (Chicago: Chicago Univ. Press)

Kuhn, T. [1971] 'Notes on Lakatos' *Boston Studies in the Philosophy of Science* 8, 135-46

Lachmann, L. [1976] 'From Mises to Shackle: an essay on Austrian economics and the kaleidic society' *Journal of Economic Literature* 14, 54-62

Lakatos, I. [1971] 'History of science and its rational reconstructions' in R. Buck and R. Cohen (eds.) *Boston Studies in the Philosophy of Science* 8 (Dordrecht, Netherlands: Reidel), 91-136

Lancaster, K. [1966] 'A new approach to consumer theory' *Journal of Political Economy* 74, 132-57

Latsis, S. [1972] 'Situational determinism in economics' *British Journal for the Philosophy of Science* 23, 207-45

Latsis, S. [1976] *Methodology and Appraisal in Economics* (Cambridge: Cambridge Univ. Press)

Leibenstein, H. [1979] 'A branch of economics is missing: micro-micro theory' *Journal of Economic Literature* 17, 477-502

Leijonhufvud, A. [1976] 'Schools, 'revolutions' and research programmes in economic theory' in Latsis [1976] 65-108

Leontief, W. [1947] 'Introduction to the theory of the internal structure of functional relationships' *Econometrica* 15, 361ff.

Leontief, W. [1971] 'Theoretical assumptions and nonobserved facts' *American Economic Review* 61, 74-81

Lucas, R. [1980] 'Methods and problems in business cycle theory' *Journal of Money, Credit and Banking* 12, 696-715

Malinvaud, E. [1966] *Statistical Methods of Econometrics* (Chicago: Rand-McNally)

Marshall, A. [1926/64] *Principles of Economics* 8th ed. (London: Macmillan)

Maslow, A. [1954] *Motivation and Personality* (New York: Harper & Row)

Modigliani, F. [1977] 'The monetarist controversy or, should we forsake stabilization policies?' *American Economic Review* 67, 1-19

Muth, J. [1961] 'Rational expectations and the theory of price movements' *Econometrica* 29, 315-35

North, D. [1978] 'Structure and performance: the task of economic history' *Journal of Economic Literature* 16, 963-78

Nerlove, M. [1972] 'Lags in economic behavior' *Econometrica* 40, 221-51

Neumann, J. von [1937/45] 'A model of general equilibrium' *Review of Economic Studies* 13, 1-9

Newman, G. [1976] 'An institutional perspective on information' *International Social Science Journal* 28, 466-92

Newman, G. [1981] *Individualism and the Theory of Short-run Aggregate Economic Coordination*, Ph.D. Thesis, Simon Fraser University

Newton, I. [1704/1952] *Optics* (Chicago: Univ. of Chicago Press)

Okun, A. [1980] 'Rational-expectations-with-misperceptions as a theory of the business cycle' *Journal of Money, Credit and Banking* 12, 817-25

Pareto, V. [1916/35] *The Mind and Society* (New York: Dover)

Pirsig, R. [1974] *Zen and the Art of Motorcycle Maintenance* (New York: Bantam)

Poincaré, H. [1905/52] *Science and Hypothesis* (New York: Dover)

Popper, K. [1934/59] *Logic of Scientific Discovery* (New York: Science Editions)

Popper, K. [1944/61] *Poverty of Historicism* (New York: Harper & Row)

Popper, K. [1945/66] *The Open Society and its Enemies* 5th. ed. (New York: Harper & Row)

Popper, K. [1972] *Objective Knowledge* (Oxford: Oxford Univ. Press)

Quine, W. [1965] *Elementary Logic* rev. ed. (New York: Harper & Row)

Quine, W. [1972] *Methods of Logic* (New York: Holt, Rinehart & Winston)

Robbins, L. [1981] 'Economics and political economy' *American Economic Review, Proceedings* 71, 1-10

Robinson, J. [1933] *The Economics of Imperfect Competition* (London: Macmillan)

Robinson, J. [1967] *Economics: An Awkward Corner* (New York: Pantheon)

Robinson, J. [1974] 'History versus equilibrium' *Thames Papers in Political Economy*

Robinson, J. and J. Eatwell [1973] *An Introduction to Modern Economics* (London: McGraw-Hill)

Rotwein, E. [1959] 'On 'The methodology of postive economics'' *Quarterly Journal of Economics* 73, 554-75

Rotwein, E. [1980] 'Friedman's critics: a critic's reply to Boland' *Journal of Economic Literature* 18, 1553-5

Rowcroft, J. [1979] *The Production Function in the Neo-Classical Theory of the Firm*, Ph.D. Thesis, Simon Fraser University

Russell, B. [1912/59] *The Problems of Philosophy* (Oxford: Oxford Univ. Press)

Russell, B. [1945] *A History of Western Philosophy* (New York: Simon & Schuster)

Russell, B. [1950/60] 'Philosophy and politics' in *Authority and the Individual* (Boston: Beacon Press)

Salop, S. [1976] 'Information and monopolistic competition' *American Economic Review, Proceedings* 66, 240-5

Samuelson, P. [1938] 'A note on the pure theory of consumer behavior' *Economica* 5 (NS), 61-71

Samuelson, P. [1947/65] *Foundations of Economic Analysis* (New York: Atheneum)

Samuelson, P. [1948] 'Consumption theory in terms of revealed preference' *Economica* 15 (NS), 243-53

Samuelson, P. [1950] 'The problem of integrability in utility theory' *Economica* 17 (NS), 355-85

Samuelson, P. [1952] 'Economic theory and mathematics: an appraisal' *American Economic Review* 42, 56-66

Samuelson, P. [1953] 'Consumption theorems in terms of overcompensation rather than indifference comparisons' *Economica* 20 (NS), 1-9

Samuelson, P. [1963/66] 'Modern economic realities and individualism' in J. Stiglitz *The Collected Scientific Papers of Paul Samuelson* (Cambridge, Mass.: MIT Press), 1407-18

Samuelson, P. [1963] 'Problems of methodology: discussion' *American Economic Review, Proceedings* 53, 231-6

Samuelson, P. [1964] 'Theory and realism: a reply' *American Economic Review* 54, 736-9

Samuelson, P. [1965] 'Professor Samuelson on theory and realism: reply' *American Economic Review* 55, 1164-72

Samuelson, P. [1967] 'Monopolistic competition revolution' in R. Kuenne (ed.) *Monopolistic Competition Theory: Studies in Impact* (New York: Wiley)

Samuelson, P. and A. Scott [1975] *Economics* (Toronto: McGraw-Hill)

Sargent, T. [1976] 'A classical macroeconomic model for the United States' *Journal of Political Economy* 84, 207-37

Schumpeter, J. [1909] 'On the concept of social value' *Quarterly Journal of Economics* 23, 213-32

Schumpeter, J. [1928] 'The instability of capitalism' *Economic Journal* 38, 361-86

Schumpeter, J. [1942/50] *Capitalism, Socialism and Democracy* 3rd. ed. (New York: Harper & Row)

Scitovsky, T. [1976] *Joyless Economy* (Oxford: Oxford Univ. Press)

Shackle, G. [1972] *Epistemics and Economics* (Cambridge: Cambridge Univ. Press)

Simon, H. [1963] 'Problems of methodology: discussion' *American Economic Review, Proceedings* 53, 229-31

Simon, H. [1979] 'Rational decision-making in business organizations' *American Economic Review* 69, 493-513

Smale, S. [1976] 'Dynamics in general equilibrium theory' *American Economic Review, Proceedings* 66, 288-94

Smith V. [1969] 'The identification problem and the validity of economic models: a comment' *South African Journal of Economics* 37, 81

Solow, R. [1956] 'A contribution to the theory of economic growth' *Quarterly Journal of Economics* 70, 65-94

Solow, R. [1979] 'Alternative approaches to macroeconomic theory: a partial view' *Canadian Journal of Economics* 12, 339-354

Sraffa, P. [1926] 'The laws of returns under competitive conditions' *Economic Journal* 38, 535-550

Stewart, I. [1979] *Reasoning and Method in Economics* (London: McGraw-Hill)

Stigler, G. [1963] 'Archibald vs. Chicago' *Review of Economic Studies* 30, 63-4

Stigler, G. and G. Becker [1977] 'De gustibus non est disputandum' *American Economic Review* 67, 76-90

Tarascio, V. and B. Caldwell [1979] 'Theory choice in economics: philosophy and practice' *Journal of Economic Issues* 13, 983-1006

Wald, A. [1936/51] 'On some systems of equations of mathematical economics' *Econometrica* 19, 368-403

Watkins, J. [1957] 'Between analytic and empirical' *Philosophy* 32, 112-31

Weisskopf, W. [1979] 'The method is the ideology: from a Newtonian to a Heisenbergian paradigm in economics' *Journal of Economic Issues* 13, 869-84

Weintraub, E. [1977] 'The microfoundations of macroeconomics: a critical survey' *Journal of Economic Literature* 15, 1-23

Weintraub, E. [1979] *Microfoundations* (Cambridge: Cambridge Univ. Press)

Wisdom, J. [1963] 'The refutability of 'irrefutable' laws' *British Journal for the Philosophy of Science* 13, 303-6

Wong, S. [1973] 'The 'F-twist' and the methodology of Paul Samuelson' *American Economic Review* 63, 312-25

Wong, S. [1978] *The Foundations of Paul Samuelson's Revealed Preference Theory* (London: Routledge & Kegan Paul)

Names Index

Subject Index

agreement: and Conventionalism 188-9; dangers of forced 192; methodological 191-2; need for 191-2; and objectives 195-6

aggregation, problem of 90

Arrow's (IM)Possibilities theorem 31

Austrian School of economics: models 105; and Popper 166, 169

authoritarianism: and the hidden agenda of science 190-1, and the philosophy of science 161-2, and the Problem of Induction 175

causality 107-9

choice criteria: and Conventionalism 18-22; limitations of 22-3; validations and confirmations 23-5, 126

choice-problem: and Conventionalism 17-18, 21-3, 147; false problems 193-6, and Inductivism 14; and metaphysics 170; and objectives 195; and problem-dependent methodology 196

comparative statics 5, 156-8

confirmations and disconfirmations: and corroboration 170-1; model-building 121; and positive economics 125-8; and statistical criteria 125-7; vs. truth and falsity 124-5; *see also* choice criteria

Conventionalism: and the 'growth of knowledge' 162-3, 171; vs. Inductivism 18-20; liberal vs. conservative 16-17, 18-20; and popular alternatives 141-2, and Pragmatism 142-3; and Psychologism 42-3; and rational expectations 67-71; retreat to 17-18; and the sequence of models 163-4; short-run vs. long-run versions 20; and theory-choice criteria 22-26, 156, 157-8

conventions, problem of 18, 73-4

Correspondence Principle 136, 184

decision-making: and individualism 37-9; and knowledge 176; and methodology 181-4

dynamics: elements of dynamic models 96-7; vs. explanations of 97; neoclassical models of 98-102, 184-7; and prices 101-2; and real-time individualism 176-87

Empiricism vs. Instrumentalism 149

epistemology: and economic theory 181-3, 184, 185; vs. methodology 166-7; Popper's 171, 176-7, 178, 186

equilibrium and expectations 67-71; vs. imperfect competition 59-61; and incentives 54; and knowledge 67-71; and Psychologism 53-4 *see also* general equilibrium

expectations: and individualism 74-5; and the problem of conventions 73-4

falsifiability: and Conventionalism 19, 22, 172-3; is it necessary? 136-7; and Popper's methodology 164-5, 170; and tautology avoidance 135-6; and testability 22, 23, 136, 137, 168; and verifiability 23, 25

general equilibrium: and aggregation 86-8; and linear models 86-8, 90-1; vs. macroeconomics 80-6

generality: and Conventionalism 22; vs. simplicity 146-8, 156

Hicks-Allen demand theory 8

'hidden agenda': and avant-garde research 49-54, 116; and foundations 8-9; methodology and 155-8; and neoclassical economics 20-1, 28-9, 48-9

history of economic thought: continuity-based 5-6, 7, 161-2; Conventionalist 159-60, 163; the Inductivist tradition 158-9; methodology and 5, 158-64; two views 5-6, 158-61

ideal-type methodology 180

individualism: as an agenda item 39-43; vs. coordination 52-3, 192; and dynamics 178; and explanation 29-33; as an explanatory problem 37-9; vs. holism 28-9, 36; as Inductivism 40-2; institutional 29, 32-3; methodological 28, 28-33; psychologistic 30-2, 61-3; and rational expectations 74-5; as a research program 28-37; reductive 30-2, 48; in the short-run 176-87

induction: the problem of 14-16; the problem with 16-17